The Europeanisation Contract Law

CW00644382

For many years, legal scholars around Europe have debated the possibility of a 'European' law of contract. The most significant contribution to date has been the Principles of European Contract Law. In the meantime, a process of Europeanising contract law has been driven by the legislative activity of the European Union, which has adopted a string of directives touching on various aspects of contract law, mainly consumer law. Many of these directives have dealt with fairly isolated aspects of contract law.

Consequently, the European influence has hitherto been rather fragmented, and lacks overall coherence. However, the EU's contribution to date could also be regarded as a process of putting down markers for more thorough European intervention in the future. Indeed, it seems that such a process is now moving forward with the development of a Common Frame of Reference on European contract law and wholesale review of the existing consumer *acquis*.

The overall aim of this book is to trace the process of Europeanisation of contract law by examining critically the developments to date and their impact on English law, in particular, as well as the implications of the EU's desire to move towards greater coherence. The arguments for and against greater convergence in the field of contract law are also covered.

Christian Twigg-Flesner LLB (Hons) PCHE PhD is a Senior Lecturer in Private Law at the University of Hull. He is also a member of the Acquis Group, working on the Principles of Existing EC Private Law, and on the Consulting Board of the Society of European Contract Law (SECOLA).

The Harmonisation of
Contract Law

The Europeanisation of Contract Law
Current controversies in law

Christian Twigg-Flesner

Routledge·Cavendish
Taylor & Francis Group
LONDON AND NEW YORK

First published 2008
by Routledge-Cavendish
2 Park Square, Milton Park, Abingdon, Oxon, OX14 4RN

Simultaneously published in the USA and Canada
by Routledge-Cavendish
270 Madison Ave, New York, NY10016

*Routledge-Cavendish is an imprint of the Taylor & Francis Group,
an informa business*

© 2008 Christian Twigg-Flesner

Typeset in Times New Roman by
RefineCatch Limited, Bungay, Suffolk
Printed and bound in Great Britain by
TJ International, Padstow, Cornwall

British Library Cataloguing in Publication Data
A catalogue record for this book is available from the British Library

Library of Congress Cataloging-in-Publication Data
Twigg-Flesner, Christian, 1975–
    The Europeanisation of contract law : current controversies in law /
Christian Twigg-Flesner
    p. cm.
    1. Contracts—Europe.   2. Contracts—European Union countries—
Codification   3. Law—European Union countries—International
unification   I. Title.
    KJC1720.T85 2008
    346.2402—dc22   2007048584

ISBN10: 0–415–46592–3 (hbk)
ISBN10: 1–84568–050–2 (pbk)
ISBN10: 0–203–92700–1 (ebk)

ISBN13: 978–0–415–46592–2 (hbk)
ISBN13: 978–1–84568–050–3 (pbk)
ISBN13: 978–0–203–92700–7 (ebk)

This book is dedicated to my parents,
David and Antje Twigg-Flesner

Contents

Table of cases

UK CASES

Table of legislation

Preface

This book deals with the Europeanisation of contract law, that is, the impact of European Union legislation on domestic contract law. It is a fascinating area of study because of the interaction between EU law, contract law and comparative law, but it can also be a frustrating endeavour to attempt to get a firm grip on the subject. The absence of an introductory book, particularly from the perspective of a common lawyer, struck me as a gap in the literature, and I hope that this book manages to fill that gap. My intention has been to provide a way into this subject – accessible, but not simplistic, to enable a reader who is new to the material to gain solid foundations from which to launch into further research and study, although I hope that seasoned scholars may also find a return to basics helpful. I recall Hans Micklitz's observation at a conference a few years ago that it was about time for legal scholars to take a step back and ask 'what exactly are we doing here?' ('Was machen wir hier eigentlich?'). This is my attempt to ponder that question.

My approach in this book is to examine the contribution of EU law from the perspective of English law – it is, essentially, an 'English European law' book. Inevitably, my particular domestic law perspective will have coloured the analysis of both existing law and looming developments, although I have also borrowed from my continental colleagues, particularly with regard to the structure adopted for Chapter 3 (although I am sure my German colleagues will frown at my attempt to utilise a 'systematised' approach to setting out the *acquis communautaire* on contract law).

In preparing this book, I have benefited from discussions with friends and colleagues from around Europe, notably within the Acquis Group. Particular mention should go to Hugh Beale, Geraint Howells, Hans Micklitz, Hans Schulte-Nölke, Reiner Schulze and Thomas Wilhelmsson (not all members of the group, of course).

I am grateful for the support and guidance from friends and colleagues in the Law School at Hull, the Acquis Group and elsewhere. A special thank you goes to Catherine Mitchell (Hull) and Lorna Woods (Essex) for reading and commenting on various draft chapters. Any mistakes are, of course, my own. My thanks are also due to Routledge-Cavendish, particularly Fiona Kinnear, for their interest in this project and their patience in awaiting its completion.

Thanks are also due to Jan and Len Clucas for providing a quiet working environment away from busy university life during the early stages of writing this book. Above all, I would not have managed to complete the book without the support of Bev and Sophie – thank you both for being wonderful.

The law as stated in this book reflects the law in force in December 2007. Minor updates were possible during the production process. The changes which the Treaty of Lisbon will make – assuming that it is ratified – have, where appropriate, been indicated in the footnotes, but the main text is written on the basis of the Treaties as they were in 2007.

1 The concept(s) of Europeanisation

1.1 INTRODUCTION

This book is about the Europeanisation of contract law. This is undoubtedly a controversial topic, which has already given rise to such an amount of scholarly analysis that Wilhelmsson has rightly remarked that writings on this have 'become so voluminous that it seems impossible to follow in all its details'.[1] The primary purpose of the present work, therefore, is to provide an overview of the field to serve as an introduction. It attempts to take stock of developments to date, as well as discuss current activities. More generally, it will also consider the arguments advanced on both sides of the debate about the need and desirability of the process of Europeanisation. It is assumed that the reader will have knowledge of both contract law and some European Union law, but is not familiar with the Europeanisation of contract law itself.

In this opening chapter, the different facets of Europeanisation will be explored. The driving force behind this process is, of course, the European Union (EU),[2] and the following chapters will concentrate on the EU's achievements so far, as well as its future plans. This is therefore predominantly a 'European law' book, concentrating on the EU's impact on contract law. However, to regard the process of

---

1 T Wilhelmsson, 'The ethical pluralism of late modern Europe and codification of European contract law' in J Smits (ed.), *The Need for a European Contract Law* (Groningen: Europa Law Publishing, 2005), p 123.
2 Historically, the law-making powers resided with the European Community, rather than the European Union. However, this distinction will disappear once the Lisbon Treaty 2007 enters into force (probably in January 2009), and this book will therefore refer to the EU throughout.

Europeanisation purely as a matter for the EU would be to ignore the work that has been undertaken by legal scholars across Europe in this sphere. The remainder of this chapter will therefore provide the context within which the EU's activities are taking place.

1.2 CONTRACT LAW

This book deals with the impact of EU law on contract law, that is, the law relating to the formation, performance and discharge of contractual obligations. It may be distinguished from the law of torts, which is concerned with wrongful acts or omissions causing harm. Both are part of the law of obligations and the wider category of private law.

Trying to provide a succinct definition of contract creates problems in itself, because the notion of 'contract' varies from jurisdiction to jurisdiction. Whilst Treitel's basic description of contract as 'an agreement [of the contracting parties] giving rise to obligations which are enforced or recognised by law'[3] goes a long way towards capturing the essence of what a contract is, particular jurisdictions may regard other forms of voluntarily created obligations as forming part of the law of contract. For example, English law does not regard a gift as a form of contractual obligation, unlike French law.[4] For present purposes, it is not necessary to explore this further save to note that the different conceptions of 'contract' in the various Member States create an initial hurdle on the way towards Europeanisation, because there may be disagreement about the precise target area of such activity.

1.3 DEFINING THE PROBLEM

1.3.1 A brief detour into legal history [5]

Although the current debate about Europeanisation is of recent origin, to some it may seem as if history is turning full circle. In the 12th

---

3 GH Treitel, *The Law of Contract*, 11th edn (London: Sweet & Maxwell, 2003).

4 Cf R Sacco, 'Formation of Contracts', in A Hartkamp *et al., Towards a European Civil Code*, 3rd edn, Nijmegen: Ars Aequi, 2004, pp 353–4; B Pozzo, 'Harmonisation of European contract law and the need for creating a common terminology' (2003) 11 *European Review of Private Law* 754–67.

5 Generally, see RC van Caenegem, *European Law in the Past and the Future* (Cambridge: CUP, 2002).

century, continental Europe went through a process of re-developing and adopting Roman law (the *ius civile*), which evolved into the *ius commune*, that is, a 'common law'. In essence, the many different principalities and kingdoms that existed across Europe at the time shared a common law, which served to supplement existing local laws and customs. In addition, the *ius commune* provided a common legal language, and it was deployed in interpreting local laws to achieve a degree of consistency.[6]

The rise of the nation-State in the 19th century, and the creation of larger and stronger states on the continent, also resulted in the 'nationalisation' of the *ius commune*,[7] producing such well-known codifications as the German Civil Code,[8] or the French Code civil.[9] A side-effect of this development was that legal scholarship, which until then was European, concentrated on national law, and legal education, legal training, and professional requirements followed and became more divergent. Foreign judgments, as well as scholarly literature, were disregarded. Whereas previously, Latin had been the common legal language across Europe, it was replaced by the respective domestic languages.

English law was not part of the continental *ius commune*. It does not follow in the Roman tradition, unlike the continental legal systems, although some Roman law principles have found their way into English law, both in the common law and in the principles of equity. Unlike on the continent, there was never a wholesale codification of private law in England. Instead, the law of contract evolved through individual decisions by the courts. The fact that different paths were taken by English law on the one hand and the majority of the other European jurisdictions on the other is frequently referred to as the 'common law–civil law divide'. This divide is still regarded as perhaps the greatest

---

6 H Coing, 'European common law: historical foundations', in M Capelletti (ed), *New Perspectives for a Common Law of Europe* (Florence: European University Institute, 1978).

7 For an account of the various factors which brought about the demise of the *ius commune*, see P Steiner, 'The *ius commune* and its demise' (2004) 25 *Journal of Legal History* 161–7.

8 There may be interesting parallels between the German codification movement of the 19th century and present-day efforts towards a European private law: see AJ Kanning, 'The emergence of a European private law: lessons from 19th century Germany' (2007) 27 *Oxford Journal of Legal Studies* 193–208.

9 PAJ van den Berg, *The Politics of European Codification* (Groningen: European Law Publishing, 2007).

difficulty in the Europeanisation of contract law today.[10] It is, of course, an over-simplification to refer to all the non-English jurisdictions in Europe collectively as 'civil law' systems, because these sub-divide further, into for example those following the Romanistic or the Germanic legal tradition and the Nordic systems, which form a distinct group and do not have a civil code. The common features of these legal traditions permit their broad classification as 'civil law' systems. But even though the common law may appear very different from the civil law systems, Zimmermann has argued persuasively that these differences are less stark than is widely assumed.[11] But whatever common origins there are, the situation that obtains today is that there are more contract law systems in the EU than there are Member States,[12] and several different legal traditions.

1.3.2 The (inadequate?) solution of private international law

This variety of legal systems poses an obvious problem for any contract involving parties from more than one jurisdiction, particularly in the EU which seeks to promote cross-border trade. Whenever there are contractual negotiations between parties based in different jurisdictions, there are two questions to consider (in addition to whatever the substance of their agreement might be): (1) which court would deal with any disputes which might arise (jurisdiction); and (2) which law would govern the resolution of that dispute (applicable law)?

These questions are resolved through the principles of private international law (also known as the conflict of laws).[13] As an early example of Europeanisation, the Member States of the EU agreed separate conventions on jurisdiction (Brussels Convention[14]) and applicable law (Rome Convention[15]). Following the broadening of the EU's competence[16] in

---

10 See Chapter 6, pp 185–7.

11 R Zimmermann, 'Roman law and the harmonisation of private law in Europe', A Hartkamp *et al.*, *Towards a European Civil Code*, 3rd edn, Nijmegen: Ars Aequi, 2004.

12 In Britain, English and Scottish contract law are different, for example.

13 See, eg, D McClean and K Beevers, *Morris – The Conflict of Laws*, 6th edn (London: Sweet & Maxwell, 2005).

14 (Brussels) Convention on jurisdiction and the enforcement of judgments in civil and commercial matters 1968 (1998) OJ C 27/1 (consolidated version).

15 (Rome) Convention on the law applicable to contractual obligations 1980 (1998) OJ C 27/34 (consolidated version).

16 The EU can only act within the areas of competence conferred upon it. This is discussed further in Chapter 2.

this field,[17] the Brussels Convention has been replaced by Regulation 44/2001,[18] and negotiations for a 'Rome I' regulation were completed in December 2007.[19]

It is beyond the scope of this book to examine either measure in any detail. With regard to questions of *jurisdiction*, it suffices to note that the Brussels Regulation, in 'matters relating to contract',[20] allocates jurisdiction to 'the courts for the place of performance of the obligation in question' (Art 5(1)(a)). For consumer contracts (that is, those between a trader[21] and a person acting for a purpose regarded as outside his trade or profession), there are separate provisions which apply primarily[22] where a contract has been concluded in the consumer's domicile, or where the trader directs his activities to that Member State and the contract is within the scope of these activities (Art 15(1)(c)). In deciding where to take legal action, the consumer has the choice between the courts of his domicile or that of the trader (Art 16(1)), but he may only be sued in his domicile (Art 16(2)).

As far as the *applicable law* is concerned, the Rome Convention[23] provides the relevant rules to determine this. It starts from party autonomy; that is, the parties can choose the applicable law[24] by including an express term to that effect in the contract (Art 3(1)). If there is no choice of law clause in the contract, then the law of the country with which the contract is most closely connected is applicable (Art 4(1)). Art 4(2) provides guidance on how to establish the country with the closest connection:

17 At the time of negotiating these, no competence had been conferred on the EU to adopt legislation on aspects of private international law. Since the Treaty of Nice, a new Title IV in the Treaty provides an appropriate legal basis for such legislation.
18 Regulation 44/2001/EU on jurisdiction and the recognition and enforcement of judgments in civil and commercial matters (2001) OJ L 12/1.
19 At the time of writing, the UK had yet to decide whether to opt into the Regulation – under one of its 'opt-outs', it is not automatically bound by measures adopted in this field of law. A 'Rome-II' regulation on the law applicable to non-contractual obligations was agreed in 2007: see Regulation 864/2007 on the law applicable to non-contractual obligations (2007) OJ L 199/40, and the UK has opted into this. There will be a consultation in early 2008.
20 'Contract' has to be given an autonomous meaning for the purposes of the Regulation, and may therefore be understood differently from what it might mean in any particular Member State. On autonomous interpretation, see Chapter 4, p 109.
21 That is, a 'person who pursues commercial or professional activities' (Art 15(1)(c)).
22 For the full scope, see Art 15.
23 McClean and Beevers, *op. cit.*, chapter 13.
24 This has to be the law of a state.

  (i) The country where the party who is to effect the performance which is characteristic of the contract has, at the time of conclusion of the contract, his habitual residence,[25] or, in the case of a body corporate or unincorporate, its central administration.

  (ii) If the contract is entered into in the course of that party's trade or profession, the country where the principal place of business is situated, or the country where another place of business is situated if the contract specifies that performance is to be effected through that place of business.

This freedom of choice is also central to the Rome-I Regulation (Art 3),[26] although interestingly, Recital 16 states that if the Community were to adopt rules of substantive contract law 'in an appropriate instrument', the parties may choose this. This will be significant if one of the Commission's long-term proposals for an 'optional instrument' on contract law becomes reality (see Chapter 5, p 159). Art 4 of the Rome-I Regulation contains more detailed rules on determining the applicable law if the parties have not made an express choice.

Art 5 of the Convention contains specific rules for consumer contracts:

  (2) Notwithstanding the provisions of Article 3, a choice of law made by the parties shall not have the result of depriving the consumer of the protection afforded to him by the mandatory rules of the law of the country in which he has his habitual residence:

    – if in that country the conclusion of the contract was preceded by a specific invitation addressed to him or by advertising, and he had taken in that country all the steps necessary on his part for the conclusion of the contract, or

    – if the other party or his agent received the consumer's order in that country, or

    – if the contract is for the sale of goods and the consumer travelled from that country to another country and there gave his order, provided that the consumer's journey was

25 On the notion of 'habitual residence' and 'domicile', see McClean and Beevers, *op. cit.*, chapter 2.

26 The text as agreed in December 2007 can be found in European Parliament document A6-0450/2007. Some linguistic changes are possible.

arranged by the seller for the purpose of inducing the consumer to buy.

(3) Notwithstanding the provisions of Article 4, a contract to which this Article applies shall, in the absence of choice in accordance with Article 3, be governed by the law of the country in which the consumer has his habitual residence if it is entered into in the circumstances described in paragraph 2 of this Article.

Interestingly, these rules offer no particular protection for those consumers who actively take advantage of the opportunities offered by the internal market. In the conversion of the Convention to a regulation, this will be addressed.[27] As proposed in the Commission's draft Regulation,[28] under Art 6(1) of the Rome-I Regulation, the law of the consumer's habitual residence will be applicable if the professional with whom the consumer is contracting:

(a) pursues his commercial or professional activities in the country where the consumer has his habitual residence, or
(b) by any means, directs such activities to that country or to several countries including that country,

and the contract falls within the scope of these commercial or professional activities. However, with regard to the contracts covered by Art 6(1) of the Regulation, the parties may instead choose the applicable law as per Art 3, although such a choice may not deprive the consumer of the mandatory rules for his protection under the law of his habitual residence (Art 6(2)). Where a contract does not satisfy the requirements of Art 6(1)(a) or (b), the general rules in Arts 3 and 4 of the Regulation apply instead.

Finally, Art 7 of the Convention deals with mandatory rules, that is, rules which cannot be excluded by the terms of a contract. As will be seen in this book, many consumer protection rules have the status of mandatory rules. The upshot of Art 7 is that mandatory rules of a particular jurisdiction which has a close connection with the contract may be given effect where the law of that jurisdiction specifies that those

---

27 Cf *Green Paper on the Conversion of the Rome Convention into a Community Instrument*, COM (2002) 654 final, section 3.2.7.
28 COM (2005) 650 final (draft Art 5).

rules must be applied irrespective of the law otherwise applicable to the contract. Their application is not automatic, but depends on their nature and purpose, as well as the consequences of their application or non-application. This has been changed in Art 9 of the Rome-I Regulation to the extent that what are now called 'overriding mandatory provisions' are to be applied without restriction.

Whilst private international law seeks to deal with the questions of jurisdiction and applicable law, it does not remove all the problems with cross-border contracting. In particular, whilst there may be clarity about the applicable law, the inevitable consequence is that the applicable law will be unfamiliar to at least one of the contracting parties (or rather, their legal advisers), if not both.[29] There will be a cost implication because of the need to seek additional expert legal advice on the unfamiliar jurisdiction. In a commercial setting, this may be less significant, because many rules of contract law are effectively operating as default rules and can be amended by the terms of the contract. However, some provisions are essential in order to recognise the binding force and validity of the contract, and knowledge of these provisions may be essential. Moreover, some provisions of national law are mandatory rules, and cannot be displaced by the terms of the contract. Although less of a problem in commercial contracts, there can still be occasional problems even there. To overcome these limitations, the focus of Europeanisation has shifted to substantive law.

1.4 EUROPEANISATION EXPLORED

For the purposes of this book, the term 'Europeanisation' is used to cover the various activities of the EU which affect contract law. However, this term is also sometimes used in a much wider sense to cover, for example, scholarly activities.[30] It is beyond the scope of this work to deal with all facets of Europeanisation in depth, but a brief overview is given here.

---

29 Parties may choose a 'neutral' law. In many international commercial contracts, English law has been chosen as the applicable law for contracts where neither party had any connection with England.

30 See also R Michaels and N Jansen, 'Private law beyond the state? Europeanization, globalization, privatization' (2006) 54 *American Journal of Comparative Law* 843–90, pp 861–4.

1.4.1 Unification, harmonisation, approximation and convergence

A note on terminology: in the Europeanisation debate, there is often reference to terms such as 'unification', 'harmonisation', 'approximation', or 'convergence'.[31] Unification suggests that the legal systems of two or more jurisdictions cease to be distinct and are replaced by a single legal text.[32] 'Harmonisation' and 'approximation' are synonymous with one another in the European context, and refer to the introduction of common rules on particular aspects in the Member State, although, as will be seen, there is a degree of freedom for each State as to how they give effect to these rules.

Finally, there is the notion of 'convergence', which denotes similarity on particular aspects between different jurisdictions.[33] According to Brownsword, one can determine convergence in different ways by focusing on:[34]

(i) formal doctrine;
(ii) underlying principles;
(iii) the result which formal doctrine indicates in given fact situations;
(iv) the actual result reached in given fact situations;
(v) values and interests affected by particular disputes;
(vi) contracting practice.

The process of Europeanisation seeks to achieve both harmonisation and convergence. It will be seen that the focus at the European level is largely on convergence with regard to formal doctrine and the results such doctrine indicates ((i) and (iii) in Brownsword's classification), rather than any of the other factors. Unsurprisingly, this focus has not gone without criticism.[35]

---

31 For a very useful account, see L Nottage, 'Convergence, divergence and the middle way in unifying or harmonizing private law' (2004) 1 *Annual of German and European Law* 166–245.
32 See further C Baasch-Andersen, 'Defining uniformity in law' (2007) 12 *Uniform Law Review* 5–56.
33 R Brownsword, *Contract Law – Themes for the Twenty-First Century* (Oxford: OUP, 2006), p 173.
34 *Ibid.*, p 174.
35 See Chapter 5, p 165.

1.4.2 Europeanisation by the EU

Europeanisation of contract law is shaped by the adoption by the EU of directives dealing with particular aspects of contract law.[36] By adopting legislation which subsequently has to be given effect to by each of the Member States in their domestic laws, the EU has effectively created various islands, or blots, of European law within national contract law. As will be seen, this is primarily done in order to pursue one of the EU's fundamental objectives: the creation of an internal market free from obstacles to trade.

The activities of the EU are sometimes referred to as 'top-down' harmonisation, that is, as the prescription of particular rules from above. This may be contrasted with 'bottom-up' harmonisation, which describes a progressive development towards greater assimilation, perhaps in substance rather than form, of national laws.

To date, the EU's contribution has largely involved the adoption of discrete pieces of legislation dealing with issues that had been identified as a concern for the smooth operation of the internal market. Here, the focus has predominantly been on aspects of consumer contract law, rather than general contract law (that is, those aspects of contract law not limited to a particular category of contract such as employment or consumer contracts), or even the law specifically relating to business-to-business transactions. The reason for this may be that general contract law is essentially dispositive law; that is, its rules primarily fill any gaps in the bargain between the parties. The contract, as agreed between the parties on the basis of party autonomy, determines the relationship between the parties (although there are some rules of contract law affecting the validity of the contract which are extraneous to the bargain, of course).[37] However, consumer law seeks to protect consumers, who are perceived as a weaker party to any contract and therefore in need of special protection,[38] and rules on consumer contracts are usually mandatory. The existence of different consumer protection standards in the EU Member States (or near-total lack thereof in some countries) can therefore have an impact particularly on businesses seeking to operate throughout the internal market. But although consumer

---

36 On this process, see C Joerges, 'Europeanization as process: thoughts on the Europeanization of private law' (2005) 11 *European Public Law* 63–84.

37 H Beale, 'The "Europeanisation" of contract law', in R Halson, *Exploring the Boundaries of Contract* (Aldershot: Dartmouth, 1996).

38 Eg I Ramsay, *Consumer Law and Policy*, 2nd edn (Oxford: Hart Publishing, 2007), chapter 2.

law is at the centre of the EU's activities, measures have been adopted outside the sphere of consumer law.[39]

The Europeanisation of contract law by the EU is therefore essentially instrumental – its purpose is to improve the functioning of the internal market. As will be seen in Chapter 2, this raises issues about competence, that is, the extent to which legislation may be adopted at the European level. Furthermore, because of the interaction between European and domestic law in this area, national legislatures as well as national courts and the European Court of Justice (ECJ) all have a role to play in the process of Europeanisation. This book is primarily concerned with how these elements have interacted in Europeanising contract law. Before examining the EU's contribution in more depth, it is appropriate to outline other Europeanisation activities, as these have some bearing on the further development of the EU's activities.

1.4.3 Spontaneous Europeanisation

A further instance of Europeanisation is what might be called 'spontaneous Europeanisation'. This is the situation where a national legislator extends the rules or concepts introduced by an EU measure to areas not covered by EU law. The effect of this is that a rule of European origin is applied to circumstances falling outside the ambit of EU regulation. This may be done in order to retain consistency, that is, to avoid creating a situation whereby similar circumstances are treated differently without clear justification. There is a risk that such spontaneous harmonisation may have a negative impact on domestic law, if the effect of extending an EU rule beyond its prescribed scope is to reduce existing levels of regulation, particularly in the context of consumer protection.[40]

1.4.4 Regulatory competition and Europeanisation

The economic concept of 'regulatory competition'[41] refers to the competition between different jurisdictions for the most efficient rule. To the extent that parties are free to choose the law applicable to their

---

39 A more detailed discussion is in Chapter 3.

40 M Loos, 'The influence of European consumer law on general contract law' (2007) 15 *European Review of Private Law* 515–31.

41 See, eg, G Wagner, 'The virtues of diversity in European private law', in J Smits (ed), *The Need for a European Contract Law* (Groningen: Europa Law Publishing, 2005).

contract, they may seek to use a law which they regard as the most efficient. Moreover, if they perceive the law of one jurisdiction as more efficient generally, they might even move their activities to that jurisdiction altogether.[42] In order to retain these activities within their territory, national law might need to change, and might do so by adopting rules from other jurisdictions which appear to be more efficient. This may eventually lead to a degree of convergence between different jurisdictions.

In a similar vein, a court faced with an issue involving ambiguous law, or a gap in the law, might look to other European jurisdictions to consider how they deal with the problem.[43] It may be that this leads to the identification of an approach common to several jurisdictions which the court might, in turn, consider favourably for developing national law.[44] It is, however, essential that the relevant economic and social circumstances are similar, and the various interests affected by the rule have similar concerns, in order for such borrowing to work.[45]

1.4.5 Europeanisation as a scholarly endeavour

A lot of activity on the Europeanisation of contract law has been undertaken by legal scholars, rather than the European institutions. On one level, individual scholars have undertaken research of a comparative kind, often studies on how different jurisdictions within Europe handle particular aspects of contract law. For this purpose, a number of dedicated academic journals have been launched within the last 15 years or so, including the *European Review of Private Law* and the *European Review of Contract Law*. These, together with general European law journals, regularly feature such comparative papers, as well as analyses of the contributions made by the EU to the Europeanisation process.

In addition, there are several well-known research groups focusing on the Europeanisation of contract law in one way or another. Their

---

42 The ability to move between jurisdictions is, of course, one of the opportunities which has been greatly enhanced by the EU.

43 Cf H Collins, 'The voice of the community in private law discourse' (1997) 3 *European Law Journal* 407–21, pp 419–20.

44 For an interesting example of how divergent judges' views on this issue may be, see the respective comments of Lords Millet and Hobhouse in *Shogun Finance Ltd v Hudson* [2003] UKHL 62; [2004] 1 All ER (Comm) 332.

45 R van den Bergh, 'Forced harmonisation of contract law in Europe: not to be continued', in S Grundmann and J Stuyck, *An Academic Green Paper on European Contract Law* (The Hague: Kluwer, 2002), p 264.

objectives and working methods differ, with some exploring the feasibility of even greater uniformity of contract law across the EU, whereas others concentrate on promoting an understanding of different legal systems. As will be seen in Chapter 5, their work is now feeding into developments at the European level, and a short overview of the most significant groups is given here.[46]

1.4.5.1 Commission on European Contract Law – Lando Commission

The so-called Lando Commission (named after its chairman, Professor Ole Lando) was founded in 1982, although its history dates back to discussions that were had following the initial proposal for a Convention on the applicable law (which later became Rome Convention).[47] At that time, some scholars felt that what was needed was a uniform private law, rather than a uniform conflict of laws system. The Lando Commission was a private initiative of (self-selecting) legal scholars, taken from all the EU Member States at the time. Its objective was to undertake a comparative analysis of the laws of all the Member States with the intention of developing fundamental rules, or principles, of European contract law. It may be observed that the term 'principles' may be a misnomer, as the work undertaken resulted in the creation of model rules of contract law. Their work became the *Principles of European Contract Law* (PECL), which are widely known.[48] They were published in three parts,[49] with the final part completed in 2001. PECL only deal with general contract law, and there are no provisions on specific categories of contracts, such as consumer or employment contracts; nor do the PECL deal with matters other than contract law.

The Lando Commission pursued a dual objective: first, it sought to identify, through comparative research, what was common to the various jurisdictions already, and to restate this in the form of coherent principles (adopting the US 'restatement' approach). Second, it considered which rule might be best for a 'common European' approach.

---

46 For a detailed account (in German), see K Riedl, *Vereinheitlichung des Privatrechts in Europa* (Baden-Baden: Nomos, 2004).
47 O Lando, 'Preface', in O Lando and H Beale, *Principles of European Contract Law Parts I and II* (The Hague: Kluwer Law International, 2000).
48 KP Berger, 'The principles of European contract law and the concept of the "creeping codification" of law' (1999) 7 *European Review of Private Law* 21–34.
49 Lando and Beale, *op. cit.*; O Lando, E Clive, A Prüm and R Zimmermann, *Principles of European Contract Law Part III* (The Hague: Kluwer Law International, 2003).

The Commission therefore did not seek to defend particular national rules, nor identify merely the lowest common denominator; instead, it attempted to come up with the most suitable rule for the European context.

For each topic, there are model rules, followed by comments which explain what the rules mean and how they should be interpreted. There are then simple illustrations of how each rule might be applied in practice. This is followed by detailed national notes, which explain how the law of each of the Member States relates to the principle stated.

With regard to the purposes which the finished product might serve, a number of possible uses were mentioned.[50] First, PECL could be the basis of further EU legislation. Second, parties to a contract could incorporate the PECL as terms of their contract, and could thereby effectively disapply much of the national law that would otherwise be applicable to the contractual relationship. Third, PECL could be a guide to interpreting the law, in particular by offering solutions for filling gaps in the national law. In that sense, the PECL could also provide inspiration for national legislatures in considering improvements to domestic contract law. It will not come as a surprise that, in the Lando Commission's view, PECL might ultimately be a precursor to a European Contract Code.

The Lando Commission completed its work in 2001. Many of its members have gone on to join the Study Group on a European Civil Code, which was also given the authority to develop the PECL further, as necessary.

1.4.5.2 *Study Group on a European Civil Code*

The SGECC was founded in 1998, inspired by two resolutions by the European Parliament which called for the development of a draft European Civil Code.[51] In many ways, it is the successor to the Lando Commission, most obviously because it is not only using PECL as a springboard for its work, but also because it has assumed the task of reviewing the PECL. The working methods also resemble those of the Lando Commission. Its purpose is to extend the PECL work to other aspects of private law, both by considering a wider range of topics and

---

50 Lando and Beale, *op. cit.*, pp xxiii–xxiv.
51 Resolution A2-157/89 on Action to bring into line the Private Law of the Member States (1989) OJ C158/400; Resolution A3-329/94 on the Harmonisation of certain sectors of the Private Law of the Member States (1994) OJ C 205/518.

by taking into account the laws of the many countries that have joined the EU since the PECL were first drafted. As part of this process, any changes that need to be made to the PECL to reflect the principles developed in related areas of private law are dealt with, and the work of the SGECC will eventually result in a revised version of the PECL.

The SGECC's work is now more than a purely scholarly endeavour: it is one of the two principal drafting groups responsible for creating the 'Common Principles of European Private Law', that is, the draft Common Frame of Reference. This aspect of the SGECC's activities will be considered in more detail in Chapter 5.

1.4.5.3 Acquis Group

The EU has already adopted a considerable body of legislation in the field of contract law, but has done so largely in a piecemeal fashion. The Acquis Group has set itself the objective of analysing the existing *acquis communautaire*, that is, the body of rules found in EU secondary legislation and judgments of the European Court of Justice, in order to identify which, if any, principles of general application may be derived from the hotchpotch of individual directives. The work of the Acquis Group is particularly significant in the ongoing debate about greater EU intervention in the field of contract law, and will be considered in more depth in Chapter 5.

1.4.5.4 Accademia dei Giusprivatisti Europei (Pavia)

The Pavia Group was founded by Professor Gandolfi in Pavia in 1990, also with the purpose of creating uniform rules of private law. Its primary purpose has been to create a contract code for all the EU Member States. Motivated by a perceived need for European codification based on the shortcomings of the existing approach (notably the directives adopted by then), particularly its randomness, the Pavia Group wanted to present a more consistent and coherent approach. Whilst Ole Lando was merely hopeful that the PECL might be the first step towards a European code, Gandolfi and his colleagues pursue this aim more directly. Although the purpose of the Pavia Group is to create a code that could become a model for all the European jurisdictions, their methodology is a rather different one from that adopted by the Lando Commission. There are essentially two sources used by the Group: the main inspiration are the sections of Italian civil code dealing with contract law, which, in the view of the Group, is a good synthesis of the French and German approaches and thereby already presents a degree of harmonisation of contract law. However, the obvious gap here is a link to the common law jurisdictions, especially England. Here, the Pavia Group was able to find a 'trump card' in the form of the so-called 'McGregor contract code', a draft codification of English contract law prepared in the early 1970s, initially at the request of the Law Commission, although it later abandoned any moves towards the codification of contract law. The draft code had not been published at the time, but was made available to the public for the first time as a result of the work by the Pavia Group.[52] The essence of the Pavia Group's code therefore is a synthesis of the Italian code and the McGregor code, although other jurisdictions were also considered in drafting the detailed sections of the code. Initial work was completed in 1998 and the draft code was published in French (which was the Group's working language).

1.4.5.5 Common Core Project (Trento)

A different scholarly approach has been adopted by the Common Core Project (commonly referred to as the Trento project), which was founded in 1994 by Professors Bussani and Mattei, then based in Trento (Italy).[53] Its objective is not the harmonisation or unification of private law across Europe; rather, it seeks to identify whether there is a core common to the various European jurisdictions in particular areas of private law. Its goal is to promote understanding of the various legal systems, and to create a 'map' of current European private law.

Its methodology is also very different. It follows the 'functional' approach to comparative law, focusing on substance rather than terminology; indeed, legal ideas need to be divorced from the various national terminologies for this process to work.[54] For each topic, questionnaires are devised based around hypothetical fact scenarios. The various national correspondents are then asked to analyse how their national law would 'solve' each scenario. One of the interesting features of this project is that it does not limit its focus to a specific area of law where the solution to a particular problem requires the use of

52 H McGregor, *Contract Code Drawn up on Behalf of the English Law Commission* (Milan: Giuffre Editore, 1993).
53 M Bussani and U Mattei (eds), *The Common Core of European Private Law* (The Hague: Kluwer Law International, 2003); M Bussani and U Mattei (eds), *Opening Up European Law* (Munich: Sellier, 2007).
54 Cf N Kasirer, 'The common core of European private law in boxes and bundles' (2002) 10 *European Review of Private Law* 417–37.

provisions from another area of law.[55] Published volumes on contract law deal with the enforceability of promises,[56] good faith,[57] and mistake.[58]

1.4.6 Europeanisation and legal education

Away from any immediate attempts towards harmonisation, or at least systematisation of the substantive law, Europeanisation also occurs with regard to legal education.[59] On the whole, legal education is still predominantly a domestic affair, despite the various European integration efforts and exchange schemes such as *Erasmus* and *Socrates*. Law students spend the vast majority of their studies on areas of domestic law, perhaps with the exception of some coverage of the fundamental aspects of EU law, and rarely study law in a comparative context. Basedow notes that law students 'are marked by a nationalism which is unknown in other sectors of higher education'.[60] He is critical of the fact that law curricula across Europe focus on national law only, particularly during the first two or so years of study. This is then often contrasted with EU law, which is fragmented and appears to disrupt the order of the national legal system. Basedow pleads for the introduction of more European-focused teaching in areas such as contract law, in order to gain a better appreciation of the relevance of European law to domestic law and not to be perturbed by the impact of European law on the domestic legal system.

One possible route towards the Europeanisation of contract law is therefore a change in the way law is taught at universities. An inspiration is the approach adopted in the United States of America. There is a considerable degree of diversity in the private law systems of the individual states. However, this diversity is handled well in the manner in which law is taught in the USA. Indeed, Kötz observes that diversity

---

55 Brownsword, *op. cit.*, pp 175–6, comments that some of the Trento work seems to focus rather too much on formal doctrine and insufficiently on underlying principles or values.

56 J Gordley (ed), *The Enforceability of Promises in European Contract Law* (Cambridge: Cambridge University Press, 2001).

57 R Zimmermann and S Whittaker (eds), *Good Faith in European Contract Law* (Cambridge: Cambridge University Press, 2000).

58 R Sefton-Green (ed), *Mistake, Fraud and Duties to Inform in European Contract Law* (Cambridge: Cambridge University Press, 2005).

59 Of course, many of the other scholarly initiatives can have an educational purpose, too. For example, PECL could be used in the context of a 'comparative contract law' course.

60 J Basedow, 'The case for a European Contract Act', in *Green Paper*, p 153.

is a lesser problem for a federal system such as the USA 'if the lawyers working in that system have been trained on the basis of the same legal material, speak the same legal language, share a common learning experience, and have therefore no trouble talking with each other in their professional capacity'.[61] US legal education therefore examines what is common to the jurisdictions. Legal education could be enhanced by adopting a similar approach in Europe: rather than restricting law teaching to national law, perhaps interspersed with a bit of comparative law, the focus could be on what is common to the jurisdictions within Europe instead. The objective of such an educational approach would be to increase familiarity with other jurisdictions, including the terminology used elsewhere.[62] There might be difficulties with such an approach: in England and Wales, for example, the Law Society and Bar Council impose clear requirements on University law schools about the content of degree programmes which concentrate on domestic law rules and principles.[63] Moreover, knowledge of one's 'own' law is essential, and introducing comparative elements too early could result in students not knowing enough about their national laws to evaluate what is common to the European jurisdictions, and where there is diversity.

1.4.6.1 Ius Commune *casebook project*

Nevertheless, efforts are being made to promote a more European approach to legal education. One of the many academic initiatives in this field, the *Ius Commune* casebooks, are designed to contribute to this development.[64] The objective of these casebooks is to compile important court decisions and legislation, together with appropriate commentary, explanations and comparative overviews, on particular areas of law. Again, the primary purpose is not harmonisation, but rather the

---

61 H Kötz, 'A common private law for Europe: perspectives for the reform of European legal education', in B de Witte and C Forder (eds), *The Common Law of Europe and the Future of Legal Education* (Maastricht: Metro, 1992), p 34.

62 An interesting example is H Kötz and A Flessner, *European Contract Law* (Oxford: Clarendon Press, 1997), which is a comparative textbook on key aspects of contract law.

63 *Joint Statement Issued by the Law Society and the General Council of the Bar on the Completion of the Initial or Academic Stage of Training by Obtaining an Undergraduate Degree* (2002), available at http://www.lawsociety.org.uk/documents/downloads/ becomingacademicjointstate.pdf (last accessed 5 March 2007).

64 Generally, P Larouche, 'Ius Commune casebooks for the common law of Europe: presentation, progress, rationale' (2000) 1 *European Review of Private Law* 101–9.

discovery of similarities and divergences in the private laws of the EU Member States. Its findings may be useful for lawyers and legal scholars in understanding how different legal systems approach particular problems, as well as serving as an educational tool for legal education. It does not take an all-encompassing approach, with the main focus tending to be on French, German and English law, because they are perceived as the 'main representatives' of the legal traditions within Europe. This project is the paradigm of the 'bottom-up' approach to Europeanisation. Volumes already published deal with tort,[65] contract,[66] unjust enrichment[67] and non-discrimination. Forthcoming volumes deal with property law[68] and consumer law.[69]

1.5 STRUCTURE OF THE BOOK

The preceding short overview of the different facets of Europeanisation shows that it is a rich area for study. The remaining chapters of this book focus on Europeanisation by the EU. In the following chapter, the framework within which this process occurs is examined, concentrating on the EU's competence, as well as its tools, for Europeanisation. The role of the European Court of Justice is also considered. Chapter 3 then seeks to provide an overview of the EU's legislative activity to date. In Chapter 4, the role of national law is examined, focusing on the obligation to implement legislation as well as the role of national courts in interpreting and applying Europeanised rules. Chapter 5 then turns to the proposals made for further Europeanisation, which may potentially result in much wider action being taken at the European level. By way of conclusion, the final chapter outlines the debate about the need, or otherwise, for a European Contract Code.

---

65 W van Gerven, J Lever, P Larouche, C von Bar, G Viney (eds), *Cases, Materials and Text on National, Supranational and International Tort Law – Scope of Protection* (Oxford: Hart Publishing, 1998).

66 H Beale, H Kötz, A Hartkamp, D Tallon (eds), *Cases, Materials and Text on Contract Law* (Oxford: Hart Publishing, 2002).

67 J Beatson and EJH Schrage (eds), *Cases, Materials and Text on Unjustified Enrichment* (Oxford: Hart Publishing, 2003).

68 S Van Erp (ed), *Cases, Materials and Text on National, Supranational and International Property Law* (Oxford: Hart Publishing, 2008).

69 H Micklitz, J Stuyck and E Terryn (eds), *Cases, Materials and Text on Consumer Law* (forthcoming).

2 Framework of Europeanisation

2.1 INTRODUCTION

This and the following two chapters will concentrate on the process of 'top-down' Europeanisation of contract law, that is, the various harmonisation measures adopted at the European level which have had to be implemented into national law (also known as 'positive harmonisation'). However, in addition, EU law may also strike out those contract law rules which might affect the free movement of goods or services, which are part of the four fundamental freedoms enshrined in the EU Treaties[1] ('negative harmonisation'). This chapter first examines the extent to which national contract law rules might infringe the prohibition against rules which affect the free movement of goods. It will then concentrate on the framework at the European level within which Europeanisation takes place by examining the competence of the European legislator to act in the field of contract law, the legal instruments used, and finally the particular contributions made by the European Court of Justice.

2.2 NATIONAL CONTRACT RULES AND FREE MOVEMENT

The first issue to consider is whether national contract law rules could be in conflict with the provisions on the free movement of goods. If that is the case, then a degree of Europeanisation could be achieved by challenging rules which contravene the relevant Treaty provisions.

---

1 Note that, once the Lisbon Treaty 2007 becomes effective, the EC Treaty will be renamed the Treaty on the Functioning of the European Union (TFEU).

Art 28 prohibits quantitative restrictions, and all measures having an equivalent effect, on the import of goods into a Member State (Art 29 deals with similar restrictions on exports).[2] As such, this provision has a *deregulatory effect*, that is, it can be used to strike down national measures which have the effect of hindering trade. It is well known that Art 28 has a very broad reach, applying to '[a]ll trading rules enacted by Member States which are capable of hindering, directly or indirectly, actually or potentially, intra-Community trade . . .'.[3] Many trading rules, however, are not restricted to imports and apply generally, although they may affect imports more severely than domestic goods. The *Dassonville* formula is not restricted to overtly discriminatory rules and can equally cover national rules which apply to both imports and domestically produced goods ('indistinctly applicable measures'). In the famous *Cassis de Dijon* case,[4] the ECJ confirmed that Art 28 applied also to indistinctly applicable measures, which would be contrary to the prohibition if they satisfied the *Dassonville* criteria. However, the Court acknowledged that not all such domestic measures would be struck down and that some restrictions on the marketing of products had to be accepted

> [. . .] insofar as those provisions may be recognised as being necessary in order to satisfy mandatory requirements relating in particular to the effectiveness of fiscal supervision, the protection of public health, the fairness of commercial transactions and the defence of the consumer.[5]

Art 28 was therefore given a very wide scope, and it was not until 1993 that the ECJ took steps to restrict its reach in the judgment in *Keck and Mithouard*.[6] It held, in the context of a preliminary reference to consider the compatibility of a prohibition on resale below cost, that 'certain selling arrangements' were no longer caught by the *Dassonville* formula, provided that these affected domestic and imported goods in the same manner, in law and in fact. Only rules which relate to 'requirements to be met' by goods were still subject to Art 28.

---

2 Art 28 will become Art 34 TFEU, and Art 29 will become Art 35 TFEU.
3 Case 8/74 *Procureur de Roi v Dassonville* [1974] ECR 837.
4 Case 120/78 *Rewe v Bundesmonopolverwaltung für Branntwein (Cassis de Dijon)* [1979] ECR 649.
5 *Ibid.*, para 8.
6 Case C-267/91 *Keck and Mithouard* [1993] ECR I-6097.

However, it remains difficult to assess domestic contract law rules in the context of Art 28. Several questions arise: are matters of substantive contract law caught by Art 28 at all? Differences in the substantive contract laws of the Member States can adversely affect the operation of the internal market and thereby the free movement of goods and services by increasing the reluctance of businesses and consumers to buy abroad out of concern over variations in national laws. But it remains uncertain whether such rules can be challenged under Art 28. Even if Art 28 is engaged, would rules of contract law in be regarded as 'requirements to be met', and therefore subject to Art 28, or as 'selling arrangements', or something else altogether? In fact, can one even try to undertake a classification of private law rules on the basis of this distinction? The position is not at all clear, and the case law of the ECJ provides limited assistance.

In C-339/89 *Alsthom Atlantique v Compagnie de construction méchanique Sulzer SA*,[7] the ECJ had to consider the compatibility with Art 29 of a provision in the French civil code imposing strict liability on the supplier of goods for any latent defects.[8] The facts involved a dispute about the quality of ship engines fitted in two cruise liners which had been supplied to a Dutch company. Alsthom sued Sulzer, the engine manufacturer, before the French courts. Under Art 1643 of the French *code civil*, a seller is liable for hidden defects even if he was not aware of them, unless he expressly excluded this liability in the contract. According to French case law, this Article creates an irrebuttable presumption that the seller is aware of any defects in the goods, and that this presumption can only be excluded in a contract with another professional operating in the same line of business (see para 5). Sulzer argued that this case law meant that French law differed from that in any other Member State, and that this had the effect of obstructing the free movement of goods. The Court held that it did not constitute an unlawful restriction. This was because it was not directed at exports, but applied to all contracts to which French law applied. Moreover, the parties to an international sales contract are free to choose the law applicable to their contract and thereby avoid the application of the French rule altogether (para 15).

---

7 [1991] ECR I-107.
8 Note that case law under Art 29 has established that for a national provision to fall foul of Art 29, it must be discriminatory, and a rule of reason approach is not available. See L Woods, *Free Movement of Goods and Services* (Aldershot: Ashgate, 2004), chapter 6.

In C-93/92 *CMC Motorradcenter GmbH v Pelin Baskiciogullari*,[9] CMC sold Yamaha motorcycles to customers in Germany which had been obtained through parallel imports. Whilst the guarantee given with the motorcycle could be invoked against any authorised Yamaha dealer, German authorised dealers generally refused to do so. Under German law (*culpa in contrahendo*), CMC should have disclosed this information to a customer (Mrs B), but did not do so. CMC argued that this rule was contrary to Art 28. The ECJ held that *culpa in contrahendo* applied to all contractual relationships governed by German law, and that it was not designed to regulate trade (para 10). Furthermore, the obligation to provide information did not create the risk of obstructing trade; rather, it was the practice of the German dealers that caused concern (para 11). The Court concluded that the impact of the rules was 'too uncertain and too indirect' to be regarded as hindering trade between Member States.

Neither case is unequivocal in ruling out the applicability of Arts 28 and 29 to domestic contract law rules. *CMC* seems to take the view that it will generally be very difficult to demonstrate any effect on inter-State trade, which would mean that national provisions of contract law could generally not be challenged under Arts 28 and 29. Furthermore, *Alsthom* makes the point that the adverse effect of certain rules could be avoided through an appropriate choice of law clause. That may be true as a matter of legal principle, but in practice, it may often be very difficult for one contracting party to agree with the other on the appropriate law to govern that contract. Moreover, this analysis only works to the extent that the national rules are regarded as non-mandatory. Those rules of domestic law which *are* mandatory cannot be evaded by choosing the law of another jurisdiction.[10] It remains to be seen if such rules (many of which are found in consumer law) *would* be caught by Art 28. Of course, if that were the case, the consequence would be that the rule challenged would be struck down. That would leave a gap in domestic law, and something would have to take its place – but the ECJ has neither the power to substitute legislation that is compliant with Art 28, nor to offer guidance to the Member State concerned on amending domestic law to remove the infringement. The better view is that it would generally be possible to justify these rules, particularly in the consumer

---

9 [1993] ECR I-5009.
10 Distinguishing between mandatory and non-mandatory rules is more difficult in practice than the basic division suggests: see M Hesselink, 'Non-mandatory rules in European contract law' (2005) 1 *European Review of Contract Law* 44–86.

contract law field, on the basis of the *Cassis de Dijon* 'mandatory requirements'.[11] Indeed, it has been suggested that all private law rules (not just contract law) could be treated as 'mandatory requirements' to avoid the consequences of finding that they might breach Art 28.[12]

2.3 EUROPEANISATION AND COMPETENCE

The Europeanisation of contract law has largely proceeded on the basis of legislation which seeks to harmonise aspects of domestic law. However, the harmonisation of domestic laws in any particular area is not an objective pursued by the EU as an end in itself – there is no general aim to unify all the laws of the Member States. Rather, harmonisation is used in order to pursue the specific objectives of the Community. These are set out in Art 3 of the Treaty.[13] This does not mention EU action in the field of contract law, or private law generally. Consequently, any legislation in this field will have to tie in with one (or more) of the EU's stated objectives. Relevant objectives include the creation of the internal market (Art 3(1)(c)), an undistorted system of competition (Art 3(1)(g)), the approximation of Member States' laws *to the extent required for the operation of the common market* (Art 3(1)(h)),[14] and a contribution to the strengthening of consumer protection (Art 3(1)(t)).

The question that arises, therefore, is which role contract law can play in contributing to the attainment of these objectives. The creation of an internal market entails that businesses – and consumers – do not limit their activities to their Member State, but make full use of the opportunities offered by the market through cross-border contracting. However, as was noted in the previous chapter, each Member State has its own national law of contract. Although there are obvious substantive parallels among all these national contract laws, there are also aspects which will be more specific to one or a small number of jurisdictions.[15] Consequently, such differences might make it more difficult for

---

11 H Muir-Watt, 'The conflict of laws as a regulatory tool', in F Cafaggi, *The Institutional Framework of European Private Law* (Oxford: OUP, 2006), p 129.

12 B Heiderhoff, *Gemeinschaftsprivatrecht* (Munich: Sellier ELP, 2005), pp 25–6.

13 After the Lisbon Treaty becomes effective, the objectives now stated in Art 3 will be found in Arts 3–6 TFEU.

14 Emphasis added.

15 Eg, the different approaches to pre-contractual disclosure – see R Sefton-Green (ed), *Mistake, Fraud and Duties to Inform* (Cambridge: Cambridge University Press, 2004).

both businesses and consumers to engage in cross-border transactions, which, in turn, could be seen as hindering the pursuit of one, if not several, of the core objectives of the European Treaty.

However, this does not mean that the EU has an unfettered ability to adopt legislation on contract. In fact, the EU does not have unlimited powers to adopt legislation in any particular field – its powers, or competence, are limited by the confines of the Treaty. This is enshrined in Art 5 of the Treaty,[16] which imposes several limitations on the powers of the EU. First of all, it emphasises that it can only act within the limits of the powers conferred on it by the Treaty and the objectives it pursues. This is generally known as 'conferred competence'. In respect of some areas, the EU will have a wide power to act – its competence is broad (and occasionally exclusive), but there are many areas where the EU's competence is limited. In most of its areas of activity, the Member States and the EU share the competence to adopt legislation. Where the EU does not have exclusive competence,[17] it may only take action

> if and insofar as the objectives of the proposed action cannot be sufficiently achieved by the Member States and can therefore, by reason of the scale or effects of the proposed action, be better achieved by the Community.[18]

This is the 'subsidiarity' principle. It embodies two criteria: (1) the Community must be better placed to act than the Member States individually, that is, supranational action is needed to deal with a particular issue; and (2) the scale or effects of whatever has been proposed make the Community the better actor. In order to clarify the scope of this test further, a protocol was annexed to the Treaty of Amsterdam 1997. This contains three criteria which attempt to facilitate the application of the two criteria in Art 5 itself: first, the issue in question must have a transnational (or cross-border) aspect which could not satisfactorily be regulated by other Member States; action by the Member States alone would conflict with Treaty requirements;[19] and Community action

---

16 After the Lisbon Treaty becomes effective, a re-drafted Art 5 of the Treaty on European Union will replace the current Art 5 of the EC Treaty.

17 Although it is far from clear in which areas the Community has exclusive competence: see J Steiner, L Woods and C Twigg-Flesner, *EU Law*, 9th edn (Oxford: Oxford University Press, 2006), p 50.

18 Art 5, second sentence.

19 Eg, by creating new barriers to free movement, or new obstacles to the operation of the internal market.

would produce clear benefits by reason of its scale or effects. Although the principle has been invoked in cases involving a challenge to the legality of EU legislation, it has not yet been deployed to strike down such a measure.[20]

Finally, the EU's powers are further restricted by the principle of proportionality. According to Art 5(3), '[a]ny action by the Community shall not go beyond what is necessary to achieve the objective of [the] Treaty'. This seems to require that the EU is clear about the objectives a particular measure seeks to pursue and how its substance can help to attain this goal.

These, then, are the basic conditions for the exercise of the EU's power to adopt any kind of legislation. Consequently, it is necessary to identify whether any competence has been conferred on the EU to legislate in the field of contract law. To do so, it is necessary to consider those provisions in the Treaty which could form the basis for the adoption of legislation in this area.

2.3.1 Legal bases for adopting contract law measures

This section will turn to the obvious candidates for an appropriate legal basis for Europeanisation measures in the field of contract law. Of course, with a significant number of directives already adopted, there are legal bases already in use (notably Art 95), but these have their limitations and other provisions may be considered as alternatives in the future (see Chapter 5).[21]

2.3.1.1 Article 95

Most of the measures adopted in the field of contract law are based on Art 95 (ex 100a) of the Treaty.[22] This Article was introduced by the Single European Act 1986 (SEA) with a view to speeding up the creation of the single market. Prior to the SEA, harmonisation measures had to be adopted on the basis of Art 94 (ex 100).[23] Art 94 provides the

---

20 The ECJ has usually handed down a decision based on other grounds, such as the use of the wrong legal basis.
21 Generally, J Ziller, 'The legitimacy of codification of contract law in view of the allocation of competences between the European Union and its Member States', in M Hesselink (ed), *The Politics of a European Civil Code* (The Hague: Kluwer, 2006).
22 This will become Art 114 TFEU once the Treaty of Lisbon becomes effective.
23 Article 94 will become Art 115 TFEU; the order of the old Arts 94 and 95 has been reversed by the Treaty of Lisbon.

adoption of harmonising directives which directly affect the establishment or functioning of the common market. It requires unanimity
within the Council, and only involves the Parliament by way of consultation. Prior to the introduction of Art 95, this was the main legal basis
used for the adoption of legislation in the field of contract law. Art 95
introduced a more efficient procedure, allowing for harmonisation measures to be adopted by qualified majority voting. Furthermore, the
co-decision procedure,[24] giving Parliament greater involvement and
the power to block the adoption of legislation, is followed. Art 95(1)
provides:

> By way of derogation from Article 94 and save where otherwise
> provided in this Treaty, the following provisions shall apply for the
> achievement of the objectives set out in Article 14. The Council
> shall, acting in accordance with the procedure referred to in Article
> 251 and after consulting the Economic and Social Committee,
> adopt the measures for the approximation of the provisions laid
> down by law, regulation or administrative action in Member States
> which have as their object the establishment and functioning of the
> internal market.[25]

Art 95 can form the basis for measures which have the object of establishing the internal market, as well as measures which relate to its
functioning. Art 95 is used to reduce or remove altogether competitive
disadvantages which are the result of higher costs of having to comply
with rules which are stricter in some Member States than in others.

Art 95 has formed the basis of most consumer protection directives,
as well as directives in many other areas. For many years, it was
assumed that Art 95 had a wide scope, allowing for the adoption of
broad legislation which may have had only a tenuous link to the internal
market objective. This assumption was proved incorrect in *Germany v
Parliament and Council* (case C-376/98),[26] resulting in annulment of
Directive 98/43/EC on Tobacco Advertising and Sponsorship. In that
case, the Directive prohibited outright advertising of and sponsorship
by tobacco, including on products such as parasols and ashtrays. The
ECJ held that Art 95 was an inappropriate legal basis for the Directive

---

24 See below, p 35.
25 Once the Treaty of Lisbon becomes effective, Art 114 TFEU (replacing Art 95) will no
longer contain the words 'by way of derogation from Article 94'; instead, new Art 115
TFEU (replacing Art 94) will become a provision derogating from Art 114 TFEU.
26 C-376/98 *Germany v Parliament and Council* [2000] ECR I-8419.

because it not only failed to improve competition but, in effect, sought to eliminate it altogether. The main significance of the case is that the Court took the opportunity to clarify the scope of Art 95. Advocate-General Fennelly urged caution in using Art 95 as a legal basis:

> ... the pursuit of equal conditions of competition does not give *carte blanche* to the Community legislator to harmonise any national rules that meet the eye ... it would risk transferring general Member State regulatory competence to the Community if recourse to Article 100a [now 95] ... were not subject to some *test of the reality of the link between such measures and internal market objectives.*[27]

If the effect on the competitive conditions was 'merely incidental',[28] Art 95 would not be the correct legal basis. The ECJ itself took a very similar line. It first noted that Art 95 could form the basis only for measures which are intended to improve the conditions for the establishment and functioning of the internal market. Crucially, this did not mean that it gave a general power to the EU to regulate the internal market.[29] To hold otherwise would bring about a conflict with Art 5 of the Treaty, which provides that the Community/Union must act within its powers.[30] The Court went on to say:

> A measure adopted on the basis of Article 100a [now 95] of the Treaty must *genuinely* have as its object the improvement of the conditions for the establishment and functioning of the internal market.[31]

In many cases, Art 95 formed the legal basis for measures which did not merely seek to remove existing divergences, but also harmonised aspects where there was a potential for the emergence of *future* obstacles to trade which could be caused by the diffuse development of the national legal systems. Art 95 could legitimately be used for such a purpose if 'the emergence of such obstacles [is] likely and the measure in question [is] designed to prevent them',[32] but a 'mere finding of disparities

---

27 Opinion, para 89.
28 *Ibid.*, para 91.
29 Para 83.
30 See above.
31 Para 84. Emphasis added.
32 Para 86.

between national rules and of the abstract risk of obstacles to the exercise of fundamental freedoms or of distortions of competition'[33] could not justify the adoption of a measure on the basis of Art 95. The distortions sought to be eliminated must be 'appreciable' so as to avoid giving 'practically unlimited' powers to the EU.[34]

There is therefore a burden on the European legislator to identify obstacles to the functioning of the internal market before adopting harmonising legislation on the basis of Art 95. It is necessary to establish first of all that disparate national laws actually constitute a barrier to free movement or distort competition, and then that EU action contributes to the establishment and functioning of the internal market but goes no further. This may require a detailed analysis of the competitive conditions prevailing in a particular sector in order to establish whether an identified obstacle to free movement or competition is appreciable so as to justify action.

It may be thought that the limited – if any – applicability of Art 28 to contract law rules,[35] even in the consumer law field, might rule out any kind of action on the basis of Art 95. After all, if a particular provision does not constitute an obstacle to the free movement of goods, how could its existence be a distortion of the competitive conditions for the internal market? Although, in the absence of ECJ case law addressing this issue, this question remains unresolved,[36] the uses to which Art 95 has been put suggests that its scope is wider, and that harmonisation is possible even though a national rule is not caught by Art 28.[37]

2.3.1.2 Consumer contract law and the internal market

The difficulties of finding sufficient competence in the Treaty for adopting legislation in the field of contract law is illustrated by focusing on consumer contract law. When plans were first made for a legislative programme in the field of consumer law, the lack of a clear legal basis for this purpose made it necessary to find an existing provision on which consumer law could 'piggy-back'. The obvious candidate was

---

33 Para 84.
34 Para 107.
35 See the discussion in the previous section.
36 S Weatherill, 'European private law and the constitutional dimension' in F Cafaggi, *The Institutional Framework of European Private Law* (Oxford: OUP, 2006).
37 G Davies, 'Can selling arrangements be harmonised?' (2005) 30 *European Law Review* 371–85.

Art 94,[38] dealing with the 'establishment or functioning of the internal market', and it became the basis for the adoption of consumer protection directives in the mid-1980s.[39] Only after the Maastricht Treaty of 1992 was consumer policy given a specific legal basis in the Treaty with the addition of Arts 3(s) and 129a (now Arts 3(1)(t) and 153 respectively).[40] However, a brief look at the legal basis of the various measures on consumer contract law shows that the relevant legal basis was first Art 94, and then Art 95. The adoption of directives in the consumer protection field has therefore become inextricably linked with the establishment and functioning of the internal market. This has had an inevitable impact on the scope of the legislation adopted, as it is not primarily concerned with the creation of a coherent body of consumer protection, but rather with harmonising those areas of domestic consumer law where the existing variations were such as to affect the operation of the internal market.

Initially, the use of Art 94 was simply justified on the basis that '. . . legislation differs from one Member State to another [and] any disparity between such legislation may directly affect the functioning of the common market'.[41] This bold assertion that the mere fact that laws are different between Member States was sufficient to harmonise would clearly not withstand scrutiny after *Tobacco Advertising*. However, it appears that the weakness of this assertion was recognised relatively quickly, and a more sophisticated argument evolved. First, a gloss was added in later directives, according to which the variation in national laws in the areas covered had the effect of distorting competition, which justified action on the basis of Art 95.[42]

However, evidence in support of these assertions remained slender, and a variation on this then began to emerge: the idea that consumer confidence in the internal market suffered because of variations in consumer protection. Thus, Directive 90/314/EEC on Package Travel was justified *inter alia* on the basis that 'disparities in rules protecting

---

38 After the Treaty of Amsterdam entered into force, the EU Treaty was renumbered.
39 Notably Directive 84/450/EEC concerning misleading and comparative advertising [1984] OJ L 250/17; Directive 85/374/EEC concerning liability for defective products [1985] OJ L 210/29, and Directive 85/577/EEC on contracts negotiated away from business premises ('door-step selling') [1985] OJ L 372/85.
40 J Stuyck, 'European consumer law after the Treaty of Amsterdam: Consumer policy in or beyond the internal market' (2000) 37 *Common Market Law Review* 367–400.
41 See the recitals to Directive 85/577/EEC on doorstep selling.
42 See, eg, recital 2 of Directive 93/13/EEC on Unfair contract terms or recital 1 of Directive 94/47/EU on Timeshare.

consumers in different Member States are a disincentive to consumers in one Member State from buying packages in another Member State . . .'.[43] This 'consumer confidence' argument has become the dominant justification for action in the consumer field. The gist of it is that consumer confidence is adversely affected by variations in domestic consumer laws, and that harmonisation is required to boost consumer confidence. On that basis, harmonising consumer laws will encourage consumers to shop in another Member State, safe in the knowledge that businesses elsewhere in the EU have to comply with the same rules as apply in their home Member State. Whether this is really borne out in practice remains to be seen. Scholars have certainly been sceptical about this.[44] For example, Goode has famously expressed his reservations thus:

> This conjures up a vision of a woman from, say, Ruritania, who visits Rome and there, in the Via Condotti, sees a fabulous dress, a dress to die for. She is about to buy it but then caution prevails: I must not buy this dress because I am not familiar with Italian law. Clearly a very sophisticated consumer, and one who by inference *is* familiar with Ruritanian law.[45]

Nevertheless, the consumer confidence argument continues to be advanced in support of legislation adopted on the basis of Art 95. Most recently, Recital 4 to Directive 2005/29/EC on unfair commercial practices[46] states:

> These disparities cause uncertainty as to which national rules apply to unfair commercial practices harming consumers' economic interests and create many barriers affecting business and consumers . . . Such barriers also make consumers uncertain of their rights and undermine their confidence in the internal market.

---

43 Recital 7 of Directive 90/314/EEC.
44 For a critical analysis of this justification, see T Wilhelmsson, 'The abuse of the "confident consumer" as a justification for EC consumer law' (2004) 27 *Journal of Consumer Policy* 317–37.
45 R Goode, 'Contract and commercial law: the logic and limits of harmonisation', in FW Grosheide and E Hondius, *International Contract Law* (Antwerp: Intersentia, 2004).
46 This directive is not concerned with consumer *contract* law (see Art 3(2) of the directive), although there are overlaps with the contract law directives.

Just as there may be doubts about the strength of the 'consumer confidence' argument,[47] so one can take issue with the wider suggestion that variations in law are real barriers to trade. In most instances, variations in national law do not make cross-border transactions impossible; rather, they become more costly because of the need to compile information about the law in another Member State. It may also make it more difficult for companies to operate across the EU using one set of contract terms and one marketing strategy, but that in itself does not make trade impossible.[48]

2.3.1.3 Consumer protection: Article 153

As mentioned, Art 153 has been introduced into the Treaty specifically on consumer protection.[49] Art 153(1) sets out the general objective:

> [i]n order to promote the interests of consumers and to ensure a high level of consumer protection, the Community shall contribute to protecting the health, safety and economic interests of consumers, as well as to promoting their right to information, education and to organise themselves in order to safeguard their interests.

Art 153(2) requires that consumer protection requirements must be taken into account in the context of other Community policies and activities.[50] Consumer protection therefore should assume greater prominence in the context of EU activity generally. However, as an independent legal basis, Art 153 is of limited use. Thus, Art 153(3)(a) links the pursuit of consumer protection firmly to the internal market competence in Art 95, providing additional legislative competence only for 'measures which support, supplement and monitor the policy pursued by the Member States' (Art 153(3)(b)). Such measures must be adopted using the co-decision procedure in Art 251 and, crucially, will leave Member States the option of 'maintaining or introducing more stringent

---

47 Although for a more positive view, see S Weatherill, 'Reflections on the EU's competence to develop a European contract law' [2005] *European Review of Private Law* 405–18.

48 H Schulte-Nölke, 'EU law on the formation of contract – from the Common Frame of Reference to the "blue button" ' (2007) *European Review of Contract Law* 332–49.

49 Art 153(1) and (3)–(5) will become Art 169 TFEU once the Lisbon Treaty comes into force, but no substantive changes are made to the scope of this provision.

50 This will become Art 12 TFEU.

protective measures' (Art 153(5)) which must be compatible with the Treaty. To date, only one (non-contract law) directive has been adopted on the specific legal basis in Art 153(3)(b).[51] This provision has therefore largely been ignored for consumer law directives that have been adopted since this legal basis became available.[52]

2.3.2 A limited competence for Europeanisation?

The threshold for using the most popular basis to date, Art 95, has been raised in the wake of *Tobacco Advertising*, although there has not yet been a challenge to a contract law directive on this basis. However, it may make it more difficult to adopt further measures in the future. In the consumer law field, the scope of Art 153 remains unexplored and no proposals for a contract-law measure has been put forward on this basis. The confines of the Treaty provisions granting competence to Europeanise contract law by a 'top-down' approach renders this process essentially instrumental to the overarching objective pursued by the EU: the functioning of the internal market. These limitations need to be borne in mind when discussing the substance of the measures adopted thus far.[53]

2.4 EUROPEANISATION BY DIRECTIVES

The process of Europeanisation by the EU has largely been carried out through the adoption of directives harmonising particular aspects of the domestic laws of the Member States.[54] The Treaty itself does not use the language of harmonisation but, instead, refers to 'approximation' of the laws of the Member States. Harmonisation is not the same as 'unification',[55] dealing with selected aspects of a particular area of law,

---

51 Directive 98/6/EC on Price Indications.
52 Also, the *Green Paper on the Review of the Consumer Acquis* does not mention the possibility of utilising Art 153(3)(b) as an alternative for action. Cf C Twigg-Flesner, 'No sense of purpose or direction?' (2007) 3 *European Review of Contract Law* 198–213.
53 Alternative legal bases are explored in Chapter 5.
54 Generally, see PC Müller-Graff, 'EU directives as a means of private law unification', in A Hartkamp *et al.*, *Towards a European Civil Code*, 3rd edn (Nijmegen: Ars Aequi, 2004).
55 Unification is much more extensive than harmonisation. Unification would involve the complete replacement of domestic laws with a new set of laws adopted at the European (or some other international association) level.

although the extent to which there may be differences in the domestic laws of the Member States after the implementation of a harmonising measure depends on the type of harmonisation pursued by it.

2.4.1 Legislative procedure

Measures adopted on the basis of Art 95 follow the co-decision procedure in Art 251.[56] Both the European Parliament and the Council of Ministers (representing national governments) must agree to a measure for it to be adopted. All proposals are made by the Commission (Art 251(2)). Parliament gives the proposal a first reading and may suggest amendments. The Council then considers whether to adopt the proposal (including any amendments made by Parliament). If it wishes to make amendments, it adopts a Common Position. This is returned to Parliament, together with the Commission's evaluation of the Common Position. Parliament will then give the amended proposal a second reading, and may approve or reject the Common Position.[57] Alternatively, it may make further amendments to the Common Position. The Commission is then required to give its opinion on the Parliament's amendments, before the Council reconsiders the proposal. The amended Common Position may be adopted by the Council by qualified majority voting, except with regard to those amendments on which the Commission has given a negative opinion; for the latter, unanimity is required. If the Council does not adopt the amended common position, a Conciliation Committee comprising Parliament and Council representatives is convened to develop a compromise text. If that fails, or if Parliament and/or Council do not approve the compromise text, the act is not adopted.

The co-decision procedure is the most democratic of the various legislative procedures available at the European level and seeks to ensure that both the elected representatives and the national governments can influence a European act before it becomes law. However, the Commission has considerable control over the process and can influence the substance of proposals, albeit at the risk of losing a proposal altogether.

---

56 This will become the 'ordinary legislative procedure' in Art 294 TFEU once the Lisbon Treaty comes into force. Although this will generally retain the current format, Art 294 TFEU has been revised, and the different stages of this legislative procedure will be set out more clearly.
57 Approval results in adoption of the act; rejection will bring the procedure to an end and the act will not be adopted.

2.4.2 Implementing directives – general obligations

According to Art 249, a directive is '. . . binding, as to the result to be achieved, upon each Member State to which it is addressed, but shall leave to the national authorities the choice of form and methods'.[58] Member States are then obliged to implement a directive into their domestic laws. A directive only specifies a *result* to be obtained, requiring Member States' laws to be amended to ensure that the outcome required by a directive can be reached under the relevant domestic measures. Member States have the freedom to choose the appropriate 'form and methods' to achieve this, and a 'copy-out' approach by which the text of a directive is given effect in domestic law in unamended form is not required. There may be good reasons for not doing so: first, there may be a clash in the terminology used by a directive and established domestic rules, and adopting a different wording in the implementing legislation might avoid this. Second, the rules contained in a directive may be difficult to fit into existing domestic legislation, unless they are expressed differently and in a language more suitable for the domestic context. In the context of contract law, this will often be due to the fact that a directive will only address a small number of matters, leaving important related aspects unaddressed. Third, there may already be domestic legislation which achieves the result required by a directive, obviating the need for further legislative action.[59]

The ECJ has confirmed that the use of terminology which differs from a directive, but which does not produce a substantive departure is permissible.[60] In addition, the Court has held that

> the transposition of a directive into domestic law does not necessarily require that its provisions be incorporated formally and verbatim in express, specific legislation,[61]

although this is subject to the overriding requirement that domestic legislation must

> . . . guarantee the full application of the directive in a sufficiently clear and precise manner so that, where the directive is intended to

---

58 This will become Art 288 TFEU.
59 See, eg, case 29/84 *Commission v Germany* [1985] ECR 1661.
60 Case 363/85 *Commission v Italy* [1987] ECR 1733.
61 Eg case C-59/89 *Commission v Germany* [1991] ECR I-2607, para 18.

create rights for individuals, the persons concerned can ascertain the full extent of their rights . . .[62]

Thus, the results-based obligation under Art 249 does not require the adoption of a dedicated domestic measure, nor is it necessary to adopt the terminology used in a directive. The 'general legal context' could be sufficient, provided that the directive is applied in a sufficiently clear and precise manner.[63] However, where national law departs from the wording and structure of a directive, the burden on the Member State to demonstrate compliance with EU law in such circumstances is a high one.[64]

The additional requirement that individuals are able to ascertain the full extent of their rights could, however, necessitate the adoption of legislation even where the case law of a Member State has already developed such as to achieve the result required by a directive. The ECJ has accepted that case law which applies and interprets domestic legislation is relevant in assessing compliance with EU law,[65] but where such case law is not unanimous or sufficiently well established to ensure an interpretation in conformity with EU law, a Member State may be found in breach of its obligation to give full effect to a directive.[66]

Moreover, exclusive reliance on case law is unlikely to be sufficient. In *Commission v Netherlands*,[67] the Commission claimed that the Dutch implementation of the Unfair Contract Terms Directive[68] was inadequate, and the Dutch government had responded that the relevant provisions of Dutch law were capable of case law interpretation in accordance with the Directive. The ECJ sided with the Commission and held that

. . . even where the settled case law of a Member State interprets the provisions of national law in a manner deemed to satisfy the requirements of a directive, that cannot achieve the clarity and precision needed to meet the requirement of legal certainty [which] is particularly true in the field of consumer protection.[69]

---

62 *Ibid.*
63 Case C-58/02 *Commission v Spain* [2004] ECR I-621.
64 Eg case C-70/03 *Commission v Spain* [2004] ECR I-7999.
65 See, in particular, C-300/95 *Commission v UK* [1997] ECR I-2649.
66 Case C-372/99 *Commission v Italy* [2002] ECR I-819.
67 Case C-144/99, [2001] ECR I-3541.
68 Directive 93/13/EEC.
69 Case C-144/99, para 21.

From the UK's perspective, where the doctrine of precedent (*stare decisis*) ensures that case law has a particularly strong standing, this decision is worrying because it appears to indicate that the existence of case law, even where settled and reaching the same result as a directive, might not be sufficiently clear and certain to ensure compliance with EU law.[70] Consequently, legislation would be required to enshrine the relevant rules of law in statute. However, this does not mean that only verbatim reproduction of the Directive in domestic law would suffice, and more suitable terminology can still be used.[71] Nevertheless, whilst the full implications of this judgment remain uncertain, it does point in the direction of codifying even well-established domestic case law in order to meet the demands of legal certainty.

The obligations of the Member States will often extend beyond ensuring that domestic provisions are in place which correspond with rules from a directive. Harmonising directives often only deal with selected aspects of the area of law concerned, and there will consequently be gaps which will need to be filled by domestic legislation. Sometimes, such gaps will be acknowledged explicitly in the text of a directive, and require that national legislation is adopted to fill the gap, but not postulate a particular approach. Thus, many directives may specify that an individual, such as a consumer, is to be given a specific right, but it will be left to domestic law to come up with an appropriate sanction for circumstances where that right has been interfered with. In other instances, the implementation of a directive will require that domestic rules which are not directly within the scope of the directive, but deal with related matters, are amended so as not to undermine the effectiveness of the harmonising measure.

Using directives for harmonisation, rather than directly applicable regulations, has the advantage that each Member State can choose the most appropriate means of achieving the required result. Moreover, whilst the same substantive rule will be applicable in every jurisdiction, it will take effect as a provision of domestic law. However, the selective coverage of aspects of contract law can also be problematic, particularly for codified legal systems, because of the difficulties caused by having to amalgamate a European rule with existing national law. Moreover, the

---

70 See also A Johnston and H Unberath, 'Law at, to or from the centre?', in F Cafaggi, *The Institutional Framework of European Private Law* (Oxford: OUP, 2006), esp pp 178–85.

71 H Beale, 'Unfair terms in contracts: proposals for reform in the UK' (2004) 27 *Journal of Consumer Policy* 289–316, pp 302–3.

effectiveness of Europeanisation by directive depends heavily on how seriously each Member State takes its obligation to implement the directive into national law. Unfortunately, instances of incorrect implementation, or even non-implementation, are not uncommon.

2.4.3 Consequence of non-implementation: state liability

If a Member State has failed to implement a directive properly, action may be taken in accordance with Art 226, discussed further below. Also, national courts need to consider if they can interpret and apply national law in such a way as to achieve the outcome required by the directive.[72] However, if this is not possible, or if a Member State has failed to implement a directive altogether, there is the possibility for an individual affected by this to bring a claim against the Member State itself under the principle of state liability. The *Francovich* and *Brasserie du Pêcheur* line of cases[73] has established that a Member State may be liable to an individual in circumstances where a rule of EU law has been infringed and

(a) the rule of law infringed by the Member State concerned was intended to confer rights on individuals;
(b) the breach by the Member State is sufficiently serious;
(c) there is a direct causal link between the breach of the obligation on the Member State and the damage sustained by the parties.

Its application in the context of (consumer) contract law is demonstrated by the case of *Rechberger*.[74] This case involved Directive 90/314/EEC on Package Travel. Art 7 of the Directive requires, in very broad terms, that the organiser of a package holiday is required to provide 'sufficient evidence of security for the refund of money paid over and for the repatriation of the consumer in the event of insolvency'.[75] Austria, which joined the EU in January 1995, had implemented the Directive, but applied the domestic provisions dealing with financial protection only for contracts with a departure date after 1 May 1995. A newspaper had arranged with an organiser for an offer of package holidays at a very low price for its subscribers. The offer was taken up by more people

---

72 This is known as the doctrine of 'indirect effect', which will be considered in more detail in Chapter 5 when dealing with the role of the national courts.
73 Cases C-6 and 9/90, *Francovich v Italy* [1991] ECR I-5357; cases C-46 and 48/93 *Brasserie du Pêcheur SA v Germany* and *Factortame v UK* [1996] ECR I-1029.
74 C-140/97 *Rechberger and Greindl v Republic of Austria* [1999] ECR I-3499.
75 This provision is considered again further below.

than expected, causing financial difficulties for the organiser and eventually the organiser's bankruptcy. Some customers were covered by the guarantee scheme which Austria had adopted to comply with Art 7 of the Directive, but the sums paid were insufficient to cover all the money paid by the customers; others were not protected at all because their departure date fell between January and May 1995. As part of their action before the Austrian courts, the claimants argued that Austria was liable under the state liability doctrine. The ECJ held that Austria was in breach by not applying the legislation implementing Art 7 from 1 January 1995, and additionally for not implementing Art 7 fully to ensure that consumers could recover their prepayments, and that this breach was sufficiently serious. Consequently, as the national court had already indicated that the other criteria for state liability were satisfied, Austria was liable and had to pay compensation.

However, although a claim in state liability is a possibility, it seems unlikely that this will happen regularly. The conditions under which a Member State is liable are not easily satisfied, and often, the damage sustained by an individual may not make it worthwhile to pursue such a claim.[76] Nevertheless, the possibility of such action needs to be borne in mind, as in those areas of contract law which have been subject to Europeanisation, an individual will have an alternative remedy in circumstances where domestic law fails to reflect fully the requirements of EU law.

2.4.4 Minimum and maximum harmonisation

As will be seen in the next chapter, there are two different types of harmonisation: 'maximum' and 'minimum' harmonisation. Although the implications of both types are most obviously considered from the perspective of national law (see Chapter 4), a basic explanation of these two concepts is given here, before discussing the substance of the various contract law directives.

2.4.4.1 Maximum harmonisation

A maximum (or 'full') harmonisation measure specifies a level of regulation from which the Member States cannot deviate. It is not possible

---

76 It is conceivable that there may be actions in the consumer contract field if steps towards improving the enforcement of consumer law result in the possibility of collective action, that is, legal action on behalf of many individual consumers. See Commission, *EU Consumer Policy Strategy 2007–2013* (COM (2007) 99 final), p 11.

to derogate from this to create a higher level of protection, even where such a higher level would appear to be justified for the protection of particular interests, such as consumers.[77] The effect of a maximum harmonisation measure is generally to pre-empt the Member States' competence to act in the area it covers.[78] However, matters in related areas but falling outside the scope of the harmonising measure are not pre-empted, and Member States continue to have a power to legislate. Establishing the extent of Member States' freedom to act therefore requires a careful analysis of the scope of a total harmonisation measure to establish the boundaries of the occupied field and therefore the extent to which Member State competence has been pre-empted. In essence, this is a question of construction, or interpretation, of the Community measure concerned.[79]

Moreover, Member States may continue to have a limited power of action within the occupied field, if the harmonising measure itself permits derogation from the Community standard in specific areas. This is frequently done by granting Member States an option whether to adopt a particular rule.[80] However, it is important to appreciate that any permission to derogate from a maximum harmonisation measure is restricted to the specific circumstances set out in that measure, and it will not be permissible to depart from the standard adopted in such a measure in any other respect.[81]

2.4.4.2 Minimum harmonisation

A minimum harmonisation measure will adopt a base-line standard of regulation which all the Member States must attain in their domestic laws. It is not permissible to fall below the minimum standard. However, in contrast to maximum harmonisation, Member States retain

---

77 See, eg, C-52/00 *Commission v France* [2002] ECR I-3827.

78 See Case 60/86 *Commission v UK (Dim-Dip Lights)* [1988] ECR 3921 and Case 16/83 *Prantl* [1984] ECR 1299 for early judgments on this issue.

79 See S Weatherill, 'Pre-emption, harmonisation and the distribution of competence to regulate the internal market', in C Barnard and J Scott, *The Law of the Single European Market – Unpacking the Premises* (Oxford: Hart Publishing, 2002), p 52.

80 Furthermore, the legal basis upon which a measure was adopted may allow for derogation in certain circumstances: for example, it is possible to deviate from a harmonisation measure adopted on the basis of Art 95 in accordance with Arts 95(4) and 95(5) respectively.

81 C-52/00 *Commission v France* [2002] ECR I-3827, para 16. See also C-183/00 *Sanchez v Medicina Asturiana SA* [2002] ECR I-3901. Both cases involved Directive 85/374/EEC on Product Liability.

the power to exceed the minimum level and to adopt a higher standard
of regulation, subject to the overarching requirement that this must
still be compatible with the EU Treaty. Minimum harmonisation therefore does not eliminate altogether divergent national rules, but instead
reduces the substantive differences between these by such an extent that
the functioning of the internal market is no longer seriously affected.
In practice, however, minimum harmonisation only narrows Member
State freedom to regulate. Sometimes, the level of regulation adopted in
a minimum harmonisation measure is high and the actual freedom left
for Member States to adopt higher standards is very limited. Often (and
particularly in the context of consumer law), there is considerable scope
for divergence between the Member States above the minimum level,
which may raise questions about the effectiveness of a particular harmonisation measure: minimum harmonisation does not eliminate the
diversity in the laws and regulations between the Member States, but
merely serves to reduce its breadth. Differences do remain, and may
continue to pose a barrier to the functioning of the single market. Of
course, this raises the question whether a Member State can require,
for example, a business from another State to comply with higher levels
of protection, if that business already complies with the minimum
required by the directive.[82] The bulk of the directives on consumer protection were adopted as minimum harmonisation directives, but in view
of the continuing variation in the domestic consumer laws and the
perceived obstruction to the smooth operation of the internal market
this may cause, there is now a trend towards maximum harmonisation
(or 'targeted full harmonisation'). This issue is considered in more
depth in Chapter 5.

2.4.5 Directives and Europeanisation

The process of Europeanisation largely involves the approximation, or
harmonisation, of national law, rather than the creation of a European
layer of contract law, through the adoption of directives which need to
be implemented into domestic law. An obvious problem is that the
success of the entire process depends on the degree of compliance by
the Member States. Their obligation is first and foremost to ensure that
national law fully reflects the requirements of the relevant directives.
However, as will be seen in the following chapter, directives do not

---

82 Cf S Grundmann, 'European contract law(s) of what colour?' (2005) 1 *European
Review of Contract Law* 184–210, pp 191–2.

provide a complete 'code', but depend for their effectiveness on related areas of national law, as well as appropriate action by the Member States. Chapter 4 will consider how the UK, in particular, has responded to this challenge.

2.5 THE ROLE OF THE EUROPEAN COURT OF JUSTICE

Before turning to the substance of the Europeanisation programme, it is necessary to consider the role of one key actor in the Europeanisation of contract law: the European Court of Justice.[83] In addition to the Community legislature, it can also affect the development of European contract law. It was already seen that it has developed the scope of Arts 28 and 29 on the free movement of goods, and fleshed out the obligations of the Member State with regard to the implementation of directives into domestic law. The ECJ will become involved in the sphere of contract law primarily in two situations: either when asked by a domestic court to give a preliminary ruling on the interpretation of an EU measure under Art 234, or in the context of enforcement proceedings taken by the European Commission against a Member State under Art 226.

2.5.1 Preliminary rulings: Article 234

Art 234 empowers the ECJ to give preliminary rulings[84] *inter alia* on the interpretation of European legislation[85] at the request of a 'national court or tribunal'.[86] National courts generally have a discretion to request such a ruling from the ECJ if an answer to a question regarding the interpretation of EU law is necessary to dispose of a case before that court (Art 234(2)). But if the national court is one 'against whose decision there is no judicial remedy under national law' (Art 234(3)), a

---

83 For a more general discussion, see W van Gerven, 'The ECJ case law as a means of unification of private law?', in A Hartkamp *et al., Towards a European Civil Code*, 3rd edn, Nijmegen: Ars Aequi, 2004.

84 Generally, J Steiner, L Woods and C Twigg-Flesner, *op. cit.*, chapter 9.

85 Art 234 will become Art 267 TFEU.

86 Somewhat controversially, this does not include an arbitration panel except where arbitration is compulsory. So in C-125/04 *Denuit v Transorient-Mosaique Voyages & Cultures SA* [2005] ECR I-923, an arbitration panel set up to resolve disputes *inter alia* in respect of package holidays was not a 'court or tribunal' because the parties were not obliged to refer their dispute to arbitration (para 16).

preliminary ruling must be sought. However, there is no obligation to request a ruling if a previous decision by the ECJ has already dealt with the same question of interpretation,[87] or if the question of EU law is irrelevant. Furthermore, if the 'correct application of the law is so obvious as to leave no scope for reasonable doubt',[88] there is also no need for a reference.[89] In other words, if the national court is of the view that the matter is 'reasonably clear and free from doubt',[90] a reference is unnecessary. It will be seen in Chapter 4 that the English courts have frequently taken this view in deciding not to make a reference, sometimes on fairly tenuous grounds.

The preliminary rulings procedure is available only to resolve questions of EU law, which includes the interpretation or application by domestic courts of national law implementing EU legislation. In the field of contract law, the relevant EU directives tend to deal with certain aspects of the law only, and Member States have some freedom to broaden the scope of their national law beyond that of the corresponding directive (for example, by applying legislation to areas not included within the scope of a directive). In such circumstances, the ECJ has been prepared to give an interpretation of the relevant EU measure, even though the case before the national court fell outside the scope of that measure.[91]

Crucially, where a reference is made, the ECJ has no power to resolve the dispute before the national court; it can merely give guidance on how the relevant provisions of EU law should be interpreted. This is done in the context of the facts about the case provided by the national court when it requests a preliminary ruling, and the ECJ may give some indication how EU law might be applied to those facts.[92] Ultimately, it is for the national court to come to a decision regarding the application of the relevant provisions in light of the ECJ's guidance to the dispute before it.

---

87 Case 28-30/62 *Da Costa en Schake NV v Nederlandse Belastingsadministratie* [1963] ECR 31 and case 283/81 *CILFIT SrL v Ministerio della Sanita* [1982] ECR 3415.

88 Case 283/81 *CILFIT, op. cit.*

89 The latter point is often referred to as *acte clair*.

90 Per Lord Denning in *HP Bulmer Ltd v J Bollinger SA* [1974] CH 401.

91 C-28/95 *Leur-Bloem v Inspecteur der Belastingdienst* [1997] ECR I-4161.

92 On occasion, this has been unequivocal, leaving national courts with little room for departing from the ECJ's view (eg C-206/01 *Arsenal Football Club v Reid* [2002] ECR I-10273), although it may be that the facts are more complicated than stated in the request for the preliminary ruling, giving the national court some leeway in coming to a different conclusion. See also C-392/93 *R v HM Treasury ex parte British Telecommunications plc* [1996] ECR I-1631, where the ECJ effectively resolved the dispute.

With regard to the Europeanisation of contract law, it is through the preliminary reference procedure, in particular, that the ECJ has shaped important aspects of this process. Its rulings in this field have generally helped to clarify the scope of the various directives in this area, although occasionally, its judgments have raised more questions than were answered.[93] However, whilst the ECJ's role in this context should only be concerned with the interpretation of legislation, it has sometimes taken a rather liberal view of its jurisdiction, which, on occasion, appears to have broadened the scope of EU legislation unexpectedly. The Court's case law is considered further in Chapter 3, but a number of examples here can illustrate how the ECJ's judgments impact on Europeanisation.

For example, as seen, the Package Travel Directive (90/314/EEC) requires that the organiser and/or retailer of a package holiday has to provide sufficient evidence of the arrangements they have made for securing the refund of payments made by the consumer as well as the cost of repatriation, in the event of their insolvency (Art 7). Although this has been expressed in slightly odd terms, referring only to the evidence of such arrangements, it seems that there should be an underlying obligation on the retailer/organiser to make suitable arrangements of this kind. In *Dillenkofer*,[94] questions arose over Germany's implementation of this provision. In particular, it was not at all clear from its wording whether Art 7 was intended to grant individual consumers a specific right guaranteeing the refund of payments they had already made. The ECJ first established that the result to be achieved by this provision was an obligation on the organiser of a package holiday to make suitable arrangements to protect consumers' prepayments and to ensure their repatriation in the event of insolvency.[95] The Court went on to say:

> The purpose of Article 7 is accordingly to protect consumers, who thus have the right to be reimbursed or repatriated in the event of the insolvency of the organiser from whom they purchased the package travel. Any other interpretation would be illogical, since the purpose of the security which organisers must offer under

---

93 See, eg, the body of case law that has built up under the Doorstep Selling Directive. See Chapter 3, pp 72–3.
94 Case C-178/94 *Dillenkofer and others v Federal Republic of Germany* [1996] ECR I-4845.
95 Para 34.

Article 7 of the Directive is to enable consumers to obtain a refund of money paid over or to be repatriated.[96]

The argument by the German and UK Governments that Art 7 was effectively only an obligation to provide information was rejected on the basis that an obligation to provide evidence 'necessarily implies that those having that obligation must actually take out such security';[97] otherwise, the obligation to provide evidence would be 'pointless'.[98]

On the one hand, the ECJ's ruling on the meaning of Art 7 is to be welcomed for ensuring that the consumer protection objective pursued by this Directive is given its full effect. On the other hand, the wording of Art 7 appears to have restricted the obligation on the organiser to one of information to the consumer, and a more plausible reading of that provision would have been to say that the obligation exists *where such arrangements had been made by the organiser*. If the organiser had not put into place any arrangements, he would not be able to provide any evidence to that effect, and the consumer may, on the basis of that information, have chosen not to book that particular holiday, or to run the risk of the organiser becoming insolvent. So an alternative interpretation that could have been reached by the ECJ is that there is an obligation to provide evidence of arrangements 'where these have been made'. Indeed, had there been an intention of the legislator to make it mandatory for an organiser to put such protection into place, the directive could have been expected to have been much more precise on this point.

One can see, therefore, that the ECJ does, on occasion, take a rather expansive view of what interpretation of legislation might entail, and there is a strong argument that in *Dillenkofer*, the ECJ exceeded its remit and effectively engaged in making the law, rather than merely interpreting it.

Dillenkofer is not the only instance where the ECJ's interpretation is getting perilously close to law-making. In the context of (consumer) contract law, the *Leitner* decision[99] has become the standard example for an instance of expansive interpretation. This was another case under the Package Travel Directive, this time involving Art 5, which imposes liability on the organiser and/or retailer of a package holiday where there has been an improper performance of the contract. The

---

96 Para 36.
97 Para 41.
98 *Ibid.*
99 C-168/00 *Simone Leitner v TUI Deutschland* [2002] ECR I-2631.

claimant in that case was a child who became ill with salmonella after eating contaminated food whilst on holiday. This affected much of the holiday, and on returning home, the claimant brought an action for damages to cover both the personal injury suffered, and the non-material damage caused by the loss of enjoyment. The Directive does not explicitly refer to non-material loss, and Member States varied as to whether they allowed recovery for such loss. The ECJ observed that this variation could constitute a distortion of competition, and as the objective of the Directive was to reduce such distortions in the market for package holidays, a consistent line on the meaning of 'damage' had to be adopted.[100] The Court then observed that

> . . . the fact that the fourth subparagraph of Article 5(2) provides that Member States may, in the matter of damage other than personal injury, allow compensation to be limited under the contract provided that such limitation is not unreasonable, means that the Directive implicitly recognises the existence of a right to compensation for damage other than personal injury, including non-material damage.[101]

The Court has, in part, taken the harmonising objective of the Directive as a basis for the expansive interpretation of 'damage' for the purposes of the Package Travel Directive. The reasoning is not entirely convincing – from a rule which, in effect, prohibits a limitation of damage in the case of personal injury, the court derives a need to give that term a broad interpretation.[102]

However, despite such apparently expansive views of its jurisdiction under Art 234, the ECJ has adopted a more cautious attitude when asked directly to deal with the application of legislation to the facts of a given case. In C-237/02 *Freiburger Kommunalbauten GmbH Baugesellschaft & Co KG v Hofstetter*,[103] the ECJ was asked whether a particular term satisfied the fairness test in Directive 93/13/EEC on unfair terms in consumer contracts. The Court declined to do so, noting that

> in the context of its jurisdiction under Article 234 to interpret Community law, the Court may interpret general criteria used by

---

100 Para 21.
101 Para 23.
102 Cf the introduction to the comparative casenote at [2003] 11 *European Review of Private Law* 91–102, p 93.
103 [2004] ECR-I 3403.

the Community legislature in order to define the concept of unfair terms. However, it should not rule on the application of these general criteria to a particular term, which must be considered in the light of the particular circumstances of the case in question.[104]

This is entirely in accordance with the Court's jurisdiction under Art 234. However, it has raised questions among commentators about the risks posed to the aim of harmonisation by divergences in how national courts apply a particular provision.[105] A general and flexible provision, such as the unfairness test in the Unfair Contract Terms Directive,[106] leaves a great deal of discretion to national courts, and there is concern that this may result in opposing views on the application of such a provision to a particular case. However, this seems to overstate the problem: there is invariably a risk with any legal rule that requires a court to use its discretion in applying that rule to the circumstances of a particular case in that two courts, even in the same Member State, may come to conflicting views.[107] Giving the ECJ a more prominent position in applying the law to individual cases would significantly alter the nature of EU law, and elevate the Court to a supreme court for all the Member States. Whilst those striving for greater uniformity might welcome such an approach, it would be such a fundamental shift in the relationship between national jurisdictions and the EU that it should not be considered seriously at this point in time.

2.5.2 Enforcement action: Article 226

A further opportunity to provide an interpretation of provisions of EU law may arise in the context of enforcement proceedings under Art 226.[108] This empowers the Commission to take action against a Member State which has not complied with its obligations under EU law. One such instance is a failure by a Member State fully to implement a directive – sometimes by not doing so at all, or, as is also often the case, by implementing it incorrectly. The Commission will first persuade the Member State concerned to bring its national law into line, but if its attempts are unsuccessful, it can ask the Court to declare that

---

104 Para 22.
105 P Rott, 'What is the role of the ECJ in private law?' [2005] 1 *Hanse Law Review* 6.
106 Discussed in Chapter 3, at 3.6.1.
107 S Weatherill, 'Can there be a common interpretation of European private law?' (2002) 31 *Georgia Journal of International and Comparative Law* 139–66, pp 163–4.
108 This will become Art 258 TFEU.

the Member State concerned has failed to fulfil its obligations under EU law.

Where a case comes before the ECJ, the Court will have an opportunity to give its views on how the relevant provision of EU law should be interpreted in order to establish whether the Member State concerned is in breach of its obligations. For example, if a Member State relies on legislation that existed before a Directive was adopted, the ECJ has to consider what the EU measure means before comparing this to the corresponding national law.[109]

However, as such rulings are handed down without the factual context of a specific dispute, unlike judgments under Art 234, the interpretation of a specific provision of EU law is usually of a more general nature. In addition, the Commission has tended to focus on how the provisions from a directive have been transposed into domestic law, without necessarily considering more closely whether the objective pursued by a directive has been fully attained. Its focus is largely on textual correspondence. The ECJ has similarly not looked much beyond finding correspondence, or preferably equivalence, between the text of a directive and the text of the implementing legislation. However, a lack of congruence in form does not inevitably mean that the result in applying the domestic rules by the national courts will fail to achieve that prescribed by the directive. This is particularly so where legal terminology is used which has not been defined in a directive and where there are differences in the national understanding of such terminology.[110]

If the ECJ finds that a Member State is in breach, changes have to be made to national law to bring this into line with EU law. A continuing failure to do so may result in further proceedings before the court under Art 228,[111] and the ECJ may then impose a financial penalty on the Member State.[112]

2.5.3 Conclusions: the role of the ECJ

The ECJ clearly has a central role to play in the Europeanisation of contract law, and, through its judgments on the interpretation of the

109 Eg, C-144/99 *Commission v Netherlands* [2001] ECR I-3541 (unfair contract terms).
110 See A Gambaro, 'The Plan d'action of the European Commission – a comment' [2003] *European Review of Private Law* 768–81.
111 This will become Art 260 TFEU.
112 Outside the field of contract law, but still within the private law field, see C-52/00 *Commission v France* [2002] ECR I-3827 (Art 226 proceedings), followed by C-177/04 *Commission v France* [2006] ECR I-2461 (Art 228 proceedings), dealing with France's failure correctly to implement Directive 85/374/EEC on Product Liability.

directives in the field of contract law, it clarifies the impact of EU legislation in this sphere. However, the ECJ has, on occasion, pushed the
boundaries of its powers to interpret legislation to its limits (and, as
some may argue, beyond), and has thereby engaged in law-making.
Nevertheless, the ECJ's essential role as the body charged with the
interpretation, rather than application, of EU law allows it to make
important contributions to the Europeanisation of contract law.

2.6 CONCLUSION

This chapter has sought to provide an overview of the framework
within which the process of Europeanisation takes place. The EU's
competence in this field is not unfettered, although quite where the
limits are remains to be explored. Despite these constraints, the impact
of EU law can be felt in many areas of contract law. The following
chapter will turn to examine the contribution made by the various EU
measures in this field.

3 Europeanisation: the story so far

3.1 INTRODUCTION

This chapter examines the *acquis communautaire* on contract law.[1] Rather than discussing all the features of each measure in turn, a broad distinction has been made between different aspects of contract: the pre-contractual phase; contract formation and validity; the substance of the contract; performance; and remedies.[2] In respect of each of these, it is possible to identify relevant EU law, although it will soon become clear that the current pattern of Europeanisation of contract law can be characterised as rather patchy.

The *acquis* can be divided further into consumer and non-consumer *acquis*. The allocation to either field is arbitrary, because many 'non-consumer' measures contain provisions for consumers. The division follows the responsibilities of DG SANCO, the directorate-general in charge of consumer protection, and DG MARKT, the internal market directorate – but quite where the dividing line between the two falls is not clear. This, too, is a feature of the Europeanisation of contract law – the apparent lack of co-ordination within the Commission and the resulting impact on legislation proposed and adopted.

Whilst the consumer directives have had the most obvious impact on contract law, the process of Europeanisation is not of exclusive concern to consumer law; there have been a number of important measures outside that field.

---

1 See also, for example, S Grundmann, 'The structure of European contract law' (2001) 4 *European Review of Private Law* 505–28.
2 This is a slightly different distinction from the one adopted by H Schulte-Nölke, 'EU law on the formation of contract – from the Common Frame of Reference to the "blue button" ' (2007) *European Review of Contract Law* 332–49, p 334.

This chapter will therefore give an overview of Europeanisation as it has happened thus far. The focus in this chapter is on the contract law elements of the various directives, and other matters also regulated in these measures are not discussed at all, or only mentioned in passing.

3.2 AREAS NOT COVERED

Defining what constitutes the contract law *acquis* is an inexact science, and one may disagree as to which areas of law should be included.[3] For present purposes, several areas are excluded outright. These include the various public contracts, that is, public procurement and services of general interest.[4]

There is also no discussion of competition law. Arts 81 (on anti-competitive agreements) and 82 (abuse of market dominance) of the Treaty[5] can both affect the substance of contracts, particularly those between commercial parties ('undertakings') by prohibiting certain terms which could be regarded as having an anti-competitive effect. In addition to these Articles, there are a number of regulations, so-called block exemptions,[6] which can also affect the substance of contracts by prohibiting the use of certain terms. However, a detailed consideration remains beyond the scope of this book.[7]

An emerging area which may eventually add significantly to the landscape of European contract law is the field of travel law,[8] most famous for Regulation 261/2004 on denied boarding and overbooking,[9] a significant addition to the arsenal of consumer protection instruments, albeit a controversial one.[10] More recently, a regulation on rail passengers'

---

3   For a wide reading, see H Micklitz, 'The concept of competitive contract law' (2005) 23 *Penn State International Law Review* 549–85.

4   On the latter, see P Rott, 'A new social contract law for public services?' (2005) 1 *European Review of Contract Law* 323–45.

5   These will become Arts 101 and 102 TFEU respectively once the Lisbon Treaty comes into force.

6   Eg, Regulation 2790/1999 on vertical restraints (1999) OJ L 326/21.

7   Eg, G Monti, 'The revision of the consumer *acquis* from a competition law perspective' (2007) 3 *European Review of Contract Law* 295–314.

8   J Karsten, 'Passengers, consumers and travellers: the rise of passenger rights in EU transport law and its repercussions for community consumer law and policy' (2007) 30 *Journal of Consumer Policy* 117–36.

9   (2004) OJ L 46/1.

10 E Varney and M Varney, 'Grounded? Air passenger rights in the European Union', in C Twigg-Flesner, D Parry, G Howells and A Nordhausen, *The Yearbook of Consumer Law 2008* (Aldershot: Ashgate, 2007).

rights and obligations was adopted,[11] which is likely to have a similar impact.

Another field which may have a significant impact on contract law is non-discrimination. Although directives in this field are largely concerned with employment law,[12] two directives are of broader application: Directive 2000/43/EC on equal treatment between persons irrespective of racial or ethnic origin,[13] and Directive 2004/113/EC on equal treatment between men and women in the access to and supply of goods and services.[14] Both directives have an effect on contract law; indeed, non-discrimination is perhaps one of the EU's noteworthy contributions to contract law, but for reasons of space, this is not discussed further.[15]

Finally, one particular consumer law directive is also not discussed in depth: Directive 2005/29/EC on Unfair Commercial Practices (UCPD).[16] The UCPD introduces a prohibition of all unfair commercial practices in consumer transactions. Around 30 practices, listed in Annex I to the UCPD, are prohibited outright, but all commercial practices can be assessed against a general clause (Art 5(2)). The general clause is supplemented by Art 6 (prohibiting misleading actions, including false information, or deceptive information relating to various matters listed); Art 7 (misleading omissions) and Art 8 (aggressive commercial practices involving harassment, coercion or undue influence). According to Art 3(2), this Directive is 'without prejudice to contract law and, in particular, to the rules on the validity, formation or effect of a contract'. Crucially, this does not mean that national (or EU) contract law rules may not be influenced by the UCPD, but merely that there is no obligation under the Directive to make changes to contract

---

11 Regulation 1317/2007 on rail passengers' rights and obligations (2007) OJ L 315/14.
12 Directive 2000/78/EC on a General Framework for Equal Treatment in Employment and Occupation (2000) OJ L 303/16 and Directive 2006/54/EC on Equal Treatment of Men and Women in Matters of Employment and Occupation (2006) OJ L 204/23.
13 (2000) OJ L 180/22.
14 (2004) OJ L 373/37.
15 See further J Neuner, 'Protection against discrimination in European contract law' (2006) 2 *European Review of Contract Law* 35–50; for a critical view, M Storme, 'Freedom of contract: mandatory and non-mandatory rules in European contract law' (2007) 15 *European Review of Private Law* 233–50.
16 (2005) OJ L 149/22. See J Stuyck, E Terryn and T van Dyck, 'Confidence through fairness? The new directive on unfair business-to-consumer commercial practices in the internal market' (2006) 43 *Common Market Law Review* 107–52; G Howells, H-W Micklitz and T Wilhelmsson, *European Fair Trading Law – The Unfair Commercial Practices Directive* (Aldershot: Ashgate, 2006).

law. However, the UCPD might still have an indirect effect on contract law, for example by influencing the manner in which some of the contract law directives are interpreted.[17] Also, in view of the proximity of some of the UCPD's concepts to doctrines of national contract law, there may be a progressive adjustment of contract law to follow the pattern of the UCPD.[18] Nevertheless, as its immediate impact on contract law is too uncertain, it is not discussed more fully here.

3.3 OVERVIEW: KEY DIRECTIVES

3.3.1 The consumer *acquis*

Before turning to the substantive provisions, it will be useful to set out the directives in the field of consumer contract law which have been adopted to date.[19] In essence, there are two types of directive, on the one hand those dealing with particular marketing or selling methods, and then those focusing on specific types of contract. From the short overview, it can be seen that many of the directives falling into the first category contain many exclusions from their scope, some of which have given rise to litigation. These exclusions are not consistent across the directives.

These directives were adopted over a 20-year period, and it is easy to tell how their drafting has evolved, not only in terms of detail but also in response to developments in marketing practices and, of course, the rise of electronic commerce. The early directives all adopted a minimum harmonisation approach; that is, Member States were free to introduce or maintain provisions in the field covered by a directive which granted consumers a higher level of protection. More recent directives have moved away from this approach towards full or maximum harmonisation. Indeed, the European Commission has stated that its preferred approach in the consumer law field will be full harmonisation wherever

---

17 S Whittaker, 'The relationship of the Unfair Commercial Practices Directive to European and national contract laws', in S Weatherill and U Bernitz, *The Regulation of Unfair Commercial Practices under EC Directive 2005/29* (Oxford: Hart, 2007).

18 C Twigg-Flesner, D Parry, G Howells and A Nordhausen, *An Analysis of the Application and Scope of the Unfair Commercial Practices Directive* (London: DTI, 2005), pp 49–61 (available at www.berr.gov.uk/files/file32095.pdf (last accessed 9 November 2007)).

19 On EU consumer law generally, see S Weatherhill, *EU Consumer Law and Policy*, 2nd edn, Cheltenham: Edward Elgar, 2006.

possible.[20] It has commenced a process of reviewing the existing *acquis* with a view to improving the current directives and moving towards full harmonisation in areas where there has previously only been minimum harmonisation. As part of this process, a research study was commissioned to examine how eight consumer law directives were implemented into the domestic laws of all the EU Member States. This revealed that there were noticeable variations in the national laws even after harmonisation, not helped by the fact that there were also many shortcomings in transposing these directives.[21] The findings of this study informed the preparation of a *Green Paper on the Review of the Consumer Acquis*, discussed further in Chapter 5.

One of the perennial difficulties with the various directives has been the degree of inconsistency in the definition of key concepts (such as 'consumer' and 'seller', or 'trader')[22] and terminology (such as 'durable medium'). Whilst clearly problematic, the issue of definitions and terminology is not addressed separately in this chapter.

3.3.1.1 Doorstep Selling (85/577/EEC)[23]

Among the first contract law directives was the 'Doorstep Selling' Directive,[24] which is a minimum harmonisation measure (Art 8).[25] It applies to contracts concluded between a consumer and a trader (or anyone acting on behalf of or in the name of the trader[26]) for the

---

20 *EU Consumer Policy Strategy 2007–2013* (COM (2007) 99 final), p 7.
21 See H Schulte-Nölke, C Twigg-Flesner and M Ebers, *Consumer Law Compendium – Comparative Analysis* (Munich: Sellier, 2008).
22 See *Consumer Compendium*, parts 4A and 4B.
23 The directive is a very basic measure, ostensibly designed to contribute to the operation of the common market. However, in light of the threshold established in the *Tobacco Advertising* jurisprudence, the argument put forward in the recitals that the laws on doorstep selling varied between the Member States and that approximation was therefore required, is, at best, unconvincing: S Weatherill, *op. cit., EU Consumer Law and Policy*, describes it as 'extraordinarily terse' (p 94). See also 'On the way to a European contract code?' (editorial comments) (2002) 39 *Common Market Law Review* 219–55, p 222.
24 Council Directive 85/577/EEC to Protect the Consumer in Respect of Contracts Negotiated away from Business Premises (1985) OJ L 372/85.
25 Total bans on doorstep selling may therefore be justified, unless they conflict with the Treaty: Case 382/87 *Buet v Ministère Public* [1989] ECR 1235.
26 It has been held that where a third party is acting on behalf of the trader, the trader need not know that the particular contract was concluded in circumstances to which the Directive applies: C-229/04 *Crailsheimer Volksbank v Conrads and others* [2005] ECR I-9273.

supply of goods or services,[27] which are concluded either during an excursion organised by a trader away from his business premises, or where the trader has visited the consumer's home (or that of another consumer), or the consumer's place of work, and that visit has not been requested expressly by the consumer (Art 1(1)). Furthermore, if the consumer did invite the trader, but the contract is for goods or services in respect of which the consumer had no knowledge, or could not reasonably have had the knowledge, that the trader also supplied these, the Directive also applies (Art 1(2)). However, a number of contracts are excluded from its scope, including those which relate to the construction, sale or rental of immovable property, as well as contracts for other rights relating to immovable property[28] – although contracts for the repair of such property are included (Art 3(2)(a)).[29] Insurance contracts (Art 3(2)(d)), contracts for securities (Art 3(2)(e)), and those for the supply of foodstuffs, beverages and other goods for current consumption which are supplied by regular roundsmen (Art 3(2)(b)), are also excluded. Contracts concluded on the basis of a catalogue which the consumer can read without the trader being present, in respect of which there is to be continuity of contact between trader and consumer, and which provides information about the right to cancel within seven days, are also not covered by the Directive (Art 3(2)(c)). Finally, Member States are given the option to apply the rules from the Directive only to contracts for which the consumer would have to pay at least €60.

27 It has been held that the latter term includes a contract guaranteeing the repayments under a credit contract, but also that the Directive does not cover contracts of guarantee entered into by a consumer where the corresponding credit is between a bank and a business: C-45/96 *Bayerische Hypotheken- und Wechselbank AG v Dietzinger* [1998] ECR I-1199. Cf N Bamforth, 'The limits of European Union consumer contract law' (1999) 24 *European Law Review* 410–18.

28 But a contract which includes a timeshare agreement may be within the scope of the Directive if the contract also covers the provision of services of a higher value than the timeshare right: C-423/97 *Travel Vac SL v Sanchis* [1999] ECR I-2195.

29 Loans secured on an immovable property are essentially credit agreements, and the creation of the security over immovable property is insufficient for the exclusion to apply: C-481/99 *Heininger v Bayerische Hypo- und Vereinsbank AG* [2001] ECR I-9945.

3.3.1.2 Distance Selling (97/7/EC)

The Directive on Distance Selling[30] also concerns a selling method, but additionally contains provisions on contract performance.[31] It is also a minimum harmonisation directive (Art 14). It applies to contracts which are concluded exclusively by means of distance communication (Art 2(1)), that is, means which are used without the simultaneous presence of the supplier and consumer to conclude a contract (Art 2(4)). However, once again, not all contracts are covered, and there is a list of exclusions.[32] Key exclusions are contracts for the construction and sale of immovable property; those relating to other rights in immovable property, with the exception of rentals; and contracts concluded at an auction (Art 3(1)). The rules on the provision of information (Arts 4–5), the right of withdrawal (Art 6), and the obligation to perform within 30 days (Art 7(1)) do not apply to contracts for the supply of foodstuffs, beverages or other goods intended for immediate consumption supplied to the consumer's home or workplace by regular roundsmen; nor do these apply to contracts for accommodation, transport,[33] catering or leisure services where a specific date or period for performance is fixed at the time of concluding the contract (Art 3(2)).

3.3.1.3 Distance Marketing of Financial Services (2002/65/EC)

When the Distance Selling Directive was adopted, the provision of financial services was excluded from its scope, and the Distance Marketing of Financial Services Directive was adopted in September 2002 to fill this gap.[34] This Directive, unlike many other consumer directives, is a maximum harmonisation directive. To a large extent, it mirrors the framework of the Distance Selling Directive, and there are many

---

30 Directive 97/7/EC of the European Parliament and of the Council on the protection of consumers in respect of distance contracts (1997) OJ L 144/19.

31 Other provisions deal with exempting a consumer from having to pay for unsolicited goods or services (inertia selling; Art 9; note that inertia selling was prohibited under Directive 2005/29/EC on Unfair Commercial Practices, para 29 of Annex I) and restrictions on the use of automated calling systems and fax machines without having obtained prior consent from a consumer (Art 10).

32 See Art 3 for the full list.

33 Which has controversially been held to extend to contracts for hiring a car: C-336/03 *easyCar (UK) Ltd v Office of Fair Trading* [2005] ECR I-1947.

34 Directive 2002/65 of the European Parliament and Council concerning the distance marketing of consumer financial services (2002) OJ L 271/16.

corresponding provisions (for example, on inertia selling (Art 9) and restrictions on automated calling systems (Art 10)). Indeed, the definitions of the essential concepts, such as 'distance contract' and 'means of distance communication', are aligned. The Directive only applies to financial services sold at a distance, although the definition of such services is broad, covering 'any service of a banking, credit, insurance, personal pension, investment or payment nature' (Art 2(b)).

3.3.1.4 Unfair Contract Terms (93/13/EEC)

Unlike the directives mentioned so far, the Unfair Contract Terms Directive[35] directly affects the substance of all contracts concluded between a consumer and a seller or supplier (Art 1(1)).[36] It renders ineffective all non-negotiated terms which fail to meet its standard of fairness. This Directive is discussed more fully below.

3.3.1.5 Package Travel (90/314/EEC)

A directive dealing with a particular type of contract is the Package Travel Directive.[37] This is also a minimum harmonisation measure (Art 8). The definition of 'consumer' for the purposes of this Directive is unusually broad, covering not only the person who buys the package, but also other beneficiaries under the package and any person to whom the original purchaser transfers the package (Art 2(4)). This extends the level of protection beyond the immediate parties to any package travel contract, and is therefore an exception to the principle of privity of contract.

A package is a pre-arranged combination of at least two of accommodation, transport, and other tourist services not ancillary to transport and accommodation, offered or sold at an inclusive price, covering a period of at least 24 hours or including overnight accommodation (Art 2(1)). Whether an arrangement is a package is determined when the contract is made; consequently, a package put together at the

---

35 Directive 93/13/EEC on unfair terms in consumer contracts (1993) OJ L 95/29.
36 According to Recital 10, contracts of employment, contracts relating to succession rights, contracts relating to rights under family law, and contracts relating to the incorporation and organisation of companies, and partnership agreements, are excluded from the scope of the Directive.
37 Directive 90/314/EEC on package travel, package holidays and package tours (1990) OJ L 158/90.

request of a consumer is also covered.[38] Invoicing the various components separately will not take the arrangement outside the scope of the Directive. Although largely concerned with providing pre-contractual information, it also contains several provisions on performance.

3.3.1.6 Timeshare (94/47/EC)

The Timeshare Directive[39] also deals with a specific type of contract. It applies to contracts 'relating directly or indirectly to the purchase of the right to use one more immovable properties on a timeshare basis' (Art 1) concluded for at least three years, under which a right to use immovable property for a specified period of the year of at least one week's duration is provided in return for payment of a global price (Art 2). For the purposes of this Directive, 'immovable property' includes both entire buildings and parts of a building used as accommodation (Art 2). This Directive is also of a minimum harmonisation character (Art 11), and it is made clear at the outset that the Directive only deals with information and its communication, and the right of withdrawal (Art 1). A proposal for a revised directive was presented in June 2007.[40]

3.3.1.7 Sale of Consumer Goods and Associated Guarantees (99/44/EC)

The directive which has undoubtedly had the greatest impact on contract law[41] to date is the Consumer Sales Directive.[42] It contains rules on the conformity of goods sold to consumers with the contract of sale, and remedies which a consumer can exercise against a seller if goods do not conform. There is also a provision dealing with consumer guarantees. It applies to contracts for the sale of consumer goods ('any tangible movable item' with the exception of (i) goods sold by execution

---

38 C-400/00 *Club Tour, Viagens e Turismo SA v Alberto Carlos Goncalves Garrido* [2002] ECR I-4051.
39 Directive 94/47/EC of the European Parliament and Council on the protection of purchasers in respect of certain aspects of contracts relating to the purchase of the right to use immovable properties on a timeshare basis (1994) OJ L 280/94.
40 COM (2007) 303 final.
41 D Staudenmeyer, 'The Directive on the Sale of Consumer Goods and Associated Guarantees – a milestone in the European consumer and private law' (2000) 4 *European Review of Private Law* 547–64.
42 Directive 99/44/EC on certain aspects of the sale of consumer goods and associated guarantees (1999) OJ L 171/12.

or otherwise by authority of law and (ii) water and gas when not 'put up for sale' in a limited volume or quantity, and (iii) electricity (Art 1(2)(b)). Although there is no complete definition of sale, Art 1(4) states that sales include 'contracts for the supply of consumer goods to be manufactured or produced', and Art 2(5) extends the Directive's provisions to contracts for the supply and installation of goods 'if installation forms part of the contract of sale . . . and the goods were installed by the seller or under his responsibility'.[43] Member States may exclude second-hand goods sold at public auction where consumers have the opportunity of attending the sale in person from the scope of the definition of 'consumer goods' (Art 1(3)).

3.3.1.8 Consumer credit

A Directive on aspects of consumer credit was first adopted in 1987,[44] but market developments and a desire to deepen the level of regulation has resulted in the proposal for a new directive. The Common Position for a new Consumer Credit Directive was adopted in late 2007,[45] but at the time of writing, the Directive had yet to be adopted.[46] The revised Directive will deal with pre-contractual and contractual information, the annual percentage rate of interest, a right of withdrawal, and provisions on the early repayment of credit. Most provisions are intended to be of a full harmonisation standard (in contrast to the current Directive, which is only of a minimum character). It applies to a wide range of credit agreements for amounts between €200 and €100,000 (Art 2(2)(c)), which are agreements 'whereby a creditor grants or promises to grant to a consumer a credit in the form of a deferred payment, a loan, or other similar financial accommodation' (Art 3(c)), although it excludes 'budget-plan'-style arrangements often used for paying for utility services such as gas or electricity. However, a range of credit agreements are excluded from the scope of the Directive, including mortgages (Art 2(2)(a)), those relating to property interests in land (Art 2(2)(b)), hire-purchase agreements (Art 2(2)(d)), overdrafts to be repaid within one month (Art 2(2)(e)), credit on which no interest is

---

43 See D Oughton and C Willett, 'Liability for incorrect installation and other services associated with consumer goods', in G Howells, A Nordhausen, D Parry and C Twigg-Flesner, *Yearbook of Consumer Law 2007* (Ashgate: Aldershot, 2007).

44 Directive 87/102/EEC on the approximation of the laws, regulations and administrative provisions of the Member States concerning consumer credit (1987) OJ L 42/48.

45 (2007) OJ C 270E/1.

46 All references in this book are to the common position.

charged (Art 2(2)(f)), credit granted by an employer (Art 2(2)(g)), deferred repayments (Art 2(2)(j)) and pawn-broking (Art 2(2)(k)), and several less common arrangements.

3.3.2 Beyond the consumer *acquis*

Although the consumer *acquis* is clearly the area where there has been the most activity, EU law has occasionally gone beyond this field to deal with non-consumer contracts. The most significant measures are set out below. As already mentioned, some also contain consumer rules.

3.3.2.1 Commercial Agency (86/653/EEC)

One of the earliest directives in the field of contract law is the Directive on Commercial Agents.[47] A commercial agent is a 'self-employed intermediary who has continuing authority to negotiate the sale or the purchase of goods on behalf of another person . . . called the "principal" or to negotiate and conclude such transactions on behalf of and in the name of that principal' (Art 1(2)).[48] The Directive deals with the respective rights and obligations of principal and agent; the agent's remuneration, and aspects relating to the conclusion and termination of the agency contract. Its provisions are mandatory and cannot be evaded through the choice of a non-Member State law where the commercial agent operates in an EU Member State.[49]

3.3.2.2 Electronic Commerce (2000/31/EC)

The so-called e-Commerce Directive[50] is primarily concerned with the free movement of 'information society service providers', and deals with matters such as their establishment, the use of commercial communications, contracts concluded by electronic means, and the liability of intermediary service providers. This measure also contains

47 Directive 86/653/EEC on the co-ordination of the laws of the Member States relating to self-employed commercial agents (1986) OJ L382/86.
48 This includes authority to conclude a single contract which is extended, if the agent had continuing authority to negotiate extensions: C-3/04 *Poseidon Chartering v Zeeschip* [2006] ECR I-2505.
49 C-381/98 *Ingmar GB Ltd v Eaton Leonard Technologies Inc* [2000] ECR I-9305.
50 Directive 2000/31/EC of the European Parliament and Council on certain legal aspects of information society services, in particular electronic commerce, in the Internal Market (2000) OJ L 178/1.

several provisions of relevance to the process of contract formation by electronic means.

3.3.2.3   Late Payment of Commercial Debts (2000/35/EC)

A matter of some concern in commercial transactions has been delay in payment, particularly for small and medium-sized enterprises (SMEs). This Directive[51] therefore puts into place rules that deal with late payment, that is, payment which has not been made within the 'contractual or statutory period of payment' (Art 2(2)), in the context of commercial transactions ('transactions between undertakings, or between undertakings and public authorities, which lead to the delivery of goods or the provision of services for remuneration' (Art 2(1))).

3.3.2.4   Insurance Mediation (2002/92/EC)

Largely concerned with setting out basic rules for the taking-up and pursuit of insurance and reinsurance mediation (Art 1), this Directive[52] also contains some pre-contractual information obligations.

3.3.2.5   Life Assurance (2002/83/EC)

The Directive on Life Assurance[53] largely focuses on harmonising the regulatory conditions regarding life assurance businesses. Chapter 4 of Title 3 of the Directive (Arts 32–36) contains provisions specifically on contract law.[54]

3.3.2.6   Services (2006/123/EC)

Controversial whilst it made its way through the legislative process, the Services Directive[55] is primarily concerned with the freedom of

---

51 Directive 2000/35/EC on combating late payment in commercial transactions (2000) OJ L 200/35. It has been suggested that this Directive, adopted on the basis of Art 95, is concerned with industrial policy rather than the internal market, and it also seems that it would not meet the threshold for the use of Art 95 in the post-*Tobacco Advertising* climate: 'On the way to a European contract code?' (editorial comments) (2002) 39 *Common Market Law Review* 219–55, p 222.

52 Directive 2002/92/EC on Insurance Mediation (2002) OJ L 9/3.

53 Directive 2002/83/EC concerning Life Assurance (2002) OJ L 345/27.

54 Art 32 deals with the law applicable to the insurance contracts, and Art 34 with a prohibition on prior approval of policy conditions and scales; neither is relevant for present purposes.

55 Directive 2006/123/EC on Services in the Internal Market (2006) OJ L 376/36.

establishment of service providers and the free movement of services. A short section on the 'Quality of Services' has some impact on contract law in that it requires that certain information is given before a contract is concluded.

3.3.2.7 Payment Services (2007/64/EC)

This Directive,[56] which replaces an earlier Directive on cross-border credit transfers,[57] applies to both consumer and non-consumer contracts. If one contracting party is a consumer, then many of the rules, such as those imposing information duties, are mandatory; in a B2B context, they are only default rules. The Directive applies to a broad range of payment services (such as payments into and withdrawals from accounts and fund transfers, as well as the use of credit cards (Art 4 and Annex), although certain transactions are excluded (for example, payment in cash, charitable collections, cash-back, cash machines (ATM), and others (Art 3 contains a detailed list of exclusions). The Directive is rather technical in how it deals with the regulation of payment services, dealing first (Arts 5–29) with the general requirements imposed on payment service providers (defined in Art 1), and then with various aspects regarding the payment service itself. Many of these rules deal with the contractual rights between a payer (that is, the person who asks for a payment to be made) and the payment service provider. These relate to both the provision of information at various stages of the transaction as well as the performance of a payment transaction. To a large extent, these rules are adopting a full harmonisation standard, and they do not permit Member States to derogate (although the contracting parties may agree more favourable terms and conditions to payment service users than those required by law (Art 86(3))).

3.4 THE PRE-CONTRACTUAL PHASE

A hallmark of many European contract law measures is that they contain detailed rules affecting the period leading up to the conclusion of a contract, particularly through the imposition of pre-contractual information duties (PCIDs). This is the case with both consumer- and

---

56 Directive 2007/64/EC on Payment Services in the Internal Market (2007) OJ L 319/1.
57 Directive 97/5/EC of the European Parliament and Council on Cross-border Credit Transfers [1997] OJ L 43/25.

non-consumer-specific measures. There are various directives which contain PCIDs. Some of these merely state the items of information that must be provided, to which others add rules on the form in which this is given, and others still expressly refer to the language to be used. The field of PCIDs is one where there has been considerable EU activity.

3.4.1 Content of information

In the *Doorstep Selling* Directive, the only item of pre-contractual information that needs to be given relates to the right of withdrawal.[58] The *Distance Selling* Directive contains more detailed obligations on pre-contractual information. Thus, the supplier has to provide the consumer with certain items of information before a contract is concluded (Art 4): (a) the supplier's identity, and, where prepayments are required, his address; (b) main characteristics of the goods or services; (c) price, including all taxes; (d) delivery costs, where appropriate; (e) arrangements for payment, delivery or performance; (f) where it is available,[59] the existence of the right of withdrawal; (g) the cost of using the means of distance communication if it varies from the basic rate; (h) period during which the offer/price remain valid; and (i) the minimum duration of the contract, where the goods or services are to be supplied permanently or recurrently. In the case of telephone communications, there is an additional obligation on the supplier to make clear his identity and the commercial purpose of the call (Art 4(3)).

Similarly, the Directive on the *Distance Selling of Financial Services* contains an obligation to provide very detailed items of pre-contractual information, grouped under the following broad headings: supplier (five items), financial service (seven items, including the main characteristics of the financial service, and various items relating to cost), contract (seven items, including details of the right of withdrawal and the minimum duration of a contract to be performed permanently or recurrently), and redress (Art 3(1)). Moreover, although the Directive is otherwise a maximum harmonisation measure, there is scope for derogation in respect of pre-contractual information obligations in two circumstances: (i) existing Community rules on financial services imposing additional pre-contractual information obligations continue to apply; and (ii) until there is further harmonisation, Member States may

---

58 See below.
59 There are restrictions on the right of withdrawal imposed by Art 6(3); see below.

maintain or introduce more stringent provisions, provided that these are compatible with EU law (Art 4).[60]

Several directives on particular types of contracts also contain detailed PCIDs. In the *Package Travel* Directive, a distinction is made between the general marketing of a package holiday, and the information to be provided specifically in the run-up to the conclusion of a contract. With regard to the former, a brochure about a package holiday must contain a wide range of information about the package, and this information is binding on the organiser[61] or retailer[62] of the package,[63] unless either changes have been communicated to the consumer before a contract has been concluded, or changes are agreed subsequently by the parties to the contract (Art 3(2), final part). Before a contract is concluded, a consumer must be provided with written information about passport and visa requirements, as well as health formalities (Art 4(1)(a)). Travel and contact details, as well as information about insurance to cover the cost of cancellation or repatriation, must be provided in writing before the consumer departs (Art 4(1)(b)).

Similarly, the *Timeshare* Directive distinguishes between obligations at the marketing stage and in the immediate pre-contractual phase. A person who requests information about property available on a timeshare basis has to be given a document which includes, as a minimum, 'brief and accurate information' in respect of a number of items listed in the Annex to the Directive, as well as a general description of the properties and how further information may be obtained (Art 3(1)). Any advertising must mention the availability of this information (Art 3(3)). The information provided in this document forms part of the contract. The parties may agree changes to this information, but other than that, the only changes that are permitted are those which result from circumstances beyond the vendor's control (Art 3(2)). The contract itself has to be in writing, and it must include at least the items of information specified in the Annex to the Directive (Art 4, first indent).

---

60 The PCIDs in the Distance Selling of Financial Services Directive overlap with those in other directives, notably the Consumer Credit and Payment Services Directives. Both contain provisions addressing this overlap to avoid the duplication of information duties.

61 A person who organises packages and offers them for sale, whether directly or through a retailer: Art 2(2).

62 A person who sells or offers for sale a package which has been put together by an organiser: Art 2(3).

63 This is an instance where public statements can become contractually enforceable.

The *Consumer Credit* Directive also has separate information obligations applicable to the general marketing stage and pre-contractual stage respectively. When credit is advertised together with an interest rate, a representative example to illustrate the full costs of the agreement has to be included. This example must contain the applicable borrowing rate and applicable charges, the total amount borrowed, the annual percentage rate (APR), duration, any advance payments, number of instalments and total amount payable (Art 4).[64] As the new Consumer Credit Directive is a full harmonisation measure with regard to many of its provisions, it will introduce a standardised 'European Consumer Credit Information' (ECCI) form (a template for which is provided in Annex II to the Directive). Art 5 specifies 19 items of information that must be included on this form, which includes basic information about the credit provider and details of the proposed credit agreement, including the APR, total amount borrowed and repayable, details of repayments, penalties for failing to maintain regular payments and information about early repayment. However, where the agreement relates to an overdraft that has to be repaid within three months or on demand (Art 2(3)), is between members of a credit union (Art 2(5)) or is a rescheduling of an existing debt (Art 2(6)), only 14 items of information must be provided, and the ECCI form is optional.

The pattern of imposing PCIDs is also found in those directives falling outside the narrow consumer *acquis*. Thus, the *Electronic Commerce* Directive contains specific PCIDs for contracts concluded by electronic means, except for those concluded exclusively by electronic mail or equivalent individual communications (Art 10(4)). It is possible for non-consumers to agree to waive these particular requirements, but the information has to be provided to consumers in all cases. The specific information to be given includes: (a) the different technical steps that need to be followed in order to conclude the contract; (b) whether the contract will be filed by the service provider, and whether it will be accessible; (c) how input errors can be identified and corrected before an order is placed; and (d) the languages in which the contract may be concluded (Art 10(1)). With regard to item (c), 'appropriate, effective and accessible technical means' must be provided to enable the identification and correction of input errors before an order is placed (Art 11(2)). In addition, information about relevant codes of conduct must be given (Art 10(2)). A further requirement is that, where the terms of the contract and general conditions are made

---

64   References are to the text of the common position.

available, this must be done in a way that will allow the recipient to store and reproduce them (Art 10(3)).

According to the *Insurance Mediation* Directive, before an insurance contract is concluded (or amended/renewed), a customer has to be given information on (i) the name and identity of the intermediary; (ii) registry details; (iii) voting rights of more than 10% in an insurance undertaking; (iv) voting rights of more than 10% in the insurance intermediary held by an insurance undertaking; (v) complaints procedures; (vi) whether advice is given on behalf of one or several insurance undertakings, or based on fair analysis of available insurance contracts (Art 12(1) and (2)). Furthermore, before a specific insurance contract is concluded, the intermediary has to specify (based on the information given by the customer) the demands and needs of the customer and the reasons for the advice given to the customer in respect of a particular insurance product (Art 12(3)).

Similarly, Art 36 of the *Life Assurance* Directive requires that a (prospective) policy holder is given detailed information about both the assurance undertaking and the 'commitment' (that is, the substance of the insurance policy), including the right of withdrawal and applicable law, before a contract is concluded. Annex III to the Directive sets out the specific items of information.

The *Services* Directive also adds to the field of pre-contractual information duties, particularly with regard to the quality of services.[65] The key provision is Art 22, which specifies that 11 items of information must be given, broadly relating to the main characteristics of the service; price and related costs; the identity of the service provider; contract terms, especially choice of law and jurisdiction clauses; any applicable redress procedures; and – in respect of service providers required to have professional indemnity insurance in accordance with Art 23 of the Directive – details of that insurance. Additionally, the recipient of a service may request information on the professional rules applicable to the regulated professions; multidisciplinary activities and partnerships and measures taken to avoid conflicts of interest; and any relevant codes of conduct, including dispute resolution mechanisms available under a code or through membership of a trade association (Art 22).

---

65 There are, at present, no EU rules on the obligations of service providers and remedies for recipients of services. A proposal for a Directive on Service Liability (COM(1990) 482 final) was abandoned. The European Parliament has called for action in this field: see the resolution of 27 September 2007 on the obligations of cross-border service providers (T6-0421/2007).

Finally, a complex set of provisions on PCIDs is found in the *Payment Services* Directive, with different duties depending on whether a particular payment transaction is a single transaction or within the context of a framework contract (that is, a contract which 'governs the future execution of individual and successive payment transactions and which may contain the obligation and conditions for setting up a payment account' (Art 4(12)), such as a current account). For either type of transaction, there are information duties before a transaction is entered into, once a payment order has been received by a bank, and finally once a payment transaction has been executed.

With regard to a single transaction, the information to be provided before an order is placed covers the information/unique identifier which the payer has to provide, the maximum execution time, the charges payable and (where applicable), the applicable exchange rate (Art 37).

In the context of a framework contract, there is information that has to be provided before such a contract is concluded, as well as when a transaction is ordered in the context of this contract. There is a detailed catalogue of items of information to be given in Art 42, grouped under seven broad headings: (i) payment service provider; (ii) use of payment service; (iii) charges, interest and exchange rates; (iv) communication; (v) safeguards and corrective measures; (vi) changes and termination; and (vii) redress. For each individual payment transaction, information has to be provided about the maximum execution time and the charges payable (Art 46).

In addition, the recipient of the payment is required to provide information to the payer where certain payment instruments (such as credit or debit cards) are used; this information must cover any additional charges raised by the payee, or any reductions offered (Art 50(1)). Furthermore, if the payment service provider imposes a charge for using a particular payment instrument, this information has to be given before the payment transaction is initiated (Art 50(2)).

3.4.2 Form, language and related requirements

In addition to the various items of information to be provided, most of these directives also specify the form in which this should be given. Some directives additionally contain rules as to which language should be used. There are significant variations between the directives, and the following can only give an impression of the divergence, but is not exhaustive.

3.4.2.1 Form and style

Older directives contain rather basic form requirements. Thus, under the *Doorstep Selling* Directive, a consumer must receive written notice of the right of withdrawal by the time of concluding the contract (Art 4).[66] The *Package Travel* Directive specifies that the consumer has to be given a copy of the contract in writing, but adds to this as an alternative 'another form which is comprehensible and accessible to the consumer'.

Since then, the common requirement found in most directives is that information should be provided 'on paper or on another durable medium'.[67] This is found, *inter alia*, in the Directives on *Consumer Credit* (Arts 5(1) and 6(1)); *Insurance Meditation* (Art 13(1)), *Distance Marketing of Financial Services* (Art 5(1)) and *Payment Services* (Art 36(1)).

In the case of *Insurance Mediation*, the customer may request to receive the information orally; it may also be given orally where immediate cover is required (Art 13(2)). According to the *Distance Marketing of Financial Services* Directive, a consumer must be informed in good time before the consumer is bound by a distance contract (Art 5(1)), or immediately after conclusion of the contract if the contract is concluded by a means of distance communication which does not make it possible to provide the required information on paper or another durable medium (Art 5(2)).

As for style, the various directives also have different requirements. In *Package Travel*, any descriptive matter regarding the package has to be free from misleading information (Art 3(1)). For *Insurance Mediation* it has to be given in a clear and accurate manner, comprehensible to the customer (Art 13(1)). The *Payment Services* Directive stipulates that information is provided in easily understandable words and in a clear and comprehensible form (Art 36(1)).

The *Distance Selling* Directive requires that the information is given in a clear and comprehensible manner, and it has to be appropriate to the means of distance communication used (Art 4(2)). Due regard is to be had to the principles of 'good faith in commercial transactions' and

---

66 Note that, according to Arts 1(3) and (4), the Directive also applies to contracts where the consumer has made an offer which was subsequently accepted by the trader. In such circumstances, the information about the right of cancellation must be given when the consumer makes his offer.

67 Not all the directives contain an appropriate definition, and this phrase is often cited as an instance of insufficient clarity in EU legislation: see House of Lords, *European Contract Law – the Way Forward?* (HL Paper 95, 2005), para 40.

those relating to the protection of those unable to give their consent under relevant domestic laws, 'such as minors' (Art 4(2)).

According to the *Services* Directive, information has to be communicated in a clear and unambiguous manner, and in good time before a contract is concluded, or, where there is no written contract, before the service is provided (Art 22(4)). The information required by Art 22 has to be easily accessible, including by electronic means, to the recipient where the service is provided or the contract concluded, and must also appear in any documentation providing a description of the service provided (Art 22(2)).

3.4.2.2 Language

Some directives contain rules on the language to be used. The *Timeshare* Directive requires that both the information document and the contract itself should be in writing and drafted in the language of the Member State where the purchaser is a resident, or the language of which the purchaser is a national. The purchaser has the choice in this case (Art 4, second indent).

Similarly, the *Insurance Mediation* Directive states that information must be given in one of the official languages of the Member State of commitment, or one agreed by the parties (Art 13(1)). In the *Life Assurance* Directive, the Annex adds a language requirement, according to which the information has to be given in an official language of the Member State of commitment, or in another language requested by the policy holder, if permitted by national law (or where the policy holder can choose the applicable law).

The *Payment Services Directive* also requires the official language of the Member State where the payment service is offered or in the language agreed between the parties (cf Arts 36(1) and 41(1) respectively).

3.4.2.3 Other provisions

The *Payment Services* Directive contains two rules not previously found in this form in the *acquis*. Art 32 makes it clear that no charge may be imposed for providing information in respect of a payment service that is required by the Directive. In addition, Art 33 permits Member States to provide that the burden of proof to show that the information has in fact been provided falls on the payment service provider. These provisions apply to all three stages at which information has been provided.

3.4.3 Comment

It will be clear from the preceding overview that the imposition of PCIDs is a feature common to many directives which affect contract law. Their popularity may, at least in part, be explained on the basis that the provision of better information is less interventionist than the introduction of substantive rules, and therefore easier to justify at the European level. One of the main concerns with the *acquis* in its present state is the lack of a consistent approach in creating new PCIDs. Moreover, there seems to be little consideration of whether the information that is provided will assist the recipient in making a more informed decision.[68] Also, the variations regarding form and style between the directives are a cause of unnecessary confusion.

3.5 CONTRACT FORMATION AND VALIDITY

In addition to the pre-contractual stage, there is some legislation surrounding the process of contract formation. Although there are no specific rules dealing with the formation of contracts as such, several directives have introduced a right of withdrawal for consumers, allowing them to withdraw from a contract without penalty for a short time after formation.[69]

Beyond the right of withdrawal, there are several directives requiring that information about the contract is provided once it has been formed. One can also identify provisions which could affect the validity of a contract.

3.5.1 Right of withdrawal

The *Doorstep Selling* Directive paved the way for the popularity of rights of withdrawal. With regard to those contracts falling within the scope of this Directive, Art 5 provides that a consumer has a right to withdraw from a contract[70] for a period of not less than seven

---

68 G Howells, 'The potential and limits of consumer empowerment by information' (2005) 32 *Journal of Law and Society* 349–70.

69 Sometimes referred to as a right of cancellation, but for the sake of consistency, the term 'withdrawal' is used throughout in this chapter.

70 Although the rationale for the right of withdrawal in this context is that the consumer may feel pressured into signing a contract, the availability of this right does not require evidence of such pressure: C-423/97 *Travel Vac SL v Sanchis* [1999] ECR I-2195.

days,[71] starting from the point when the consumer is given information about this right to cancel the contract.[72] The withdrawal period commences once the information on the right has been received in accordance with Art 4. If this is not given, the withdrawal period can, in effect, be indeterminate; consequently, national law may not impose a restriction of, for example, one year from the date of concluding the contract for exercising the right of withdrawal.[73] Where a consumer seeks to exercise his right of withdrawal, it will be sufficient that he gives notice before the period has expired (Art 5(1)). Once notice has been given, the consumer is released from all the obligations under the contract (Art 5(2)). No charge may be made to the consumer for withdrawing from a contract in this context.[74]

National law also has to lay down the consequences of exercising the right of withdrawal, and there is a degree of discretion. In the context of a loan agreement, it was held that an obligation to repay a loan in full and immediately, together with interest at the market rate, would not be incompatible with the directive.[75] Somewhat cryptically, the ECJ has modified this position in circumstances where the consumer was not informed about the existence of the right of withdrawal. Whilst this does not change the obligation, in principle, to repay the loan with interest once the consumer does withdraw, there is an obligation on the Member States to ensure that consumers who were exposed to a risk because they were not informed about their right of withdrawal can avoid 'bearing the consequences of the materialisation of those risks'.[76] The cases concerned involved a loan agreement used to finance the acquisition of a property with a view to letting this, but the rental returns that had been promised failed to materialise. It seems that the ECJ takes the view that a consumer should not have to suffer any more

---

71 This seems to mean 'calendar days', if Art 2(b) of Regulation 1182/71 determining the rules applicable to periods, dates and time limits (1971) OJ L124/1 is applied in this context.

72 See above for the requirement to give this information.

73 C-481/99 *Heininger v Bayerische Hypo- und Vereinsbank AG* [2001] ECR I-9945. In a case pending at the time of writing, the ECJ has been asked whether it is permissible for national law to provide that the period ends one month after both parties have performed fully their obligations under the contract: see C-412/06 *Annelore Hamilton v Volksbank Filder eG*.

74 C-423/97 *Travel Vac SL v Sanchis* [1999] ECR I-2195. See E Ioriatti, 'Annotation' (2001) *European Review of Private Law* 441–48.

75 C-350/03 *Schulte v Deutsche Bausparkasse Badenia AG* [2005] ECR I-9215.

76 C-350/03 *Schulte*; C-229/04 *Crailsheimer Volksbank v Conrads and others* [2005] ECR I-9273.

than he would have done had he withdrawn from the contract after having been informed correctly about the right of withdrawal, although questions about the precise implications of this ruling remain.[77]

Unlike later directives containing a right of withdrawal, the Doorstep Selling Directive makes no provision for so-called linked contracts, that is, contracts such as a separate credit agreement used to provide the finance for the purchase of goods. However, the ECJ has upheld a national rule whereby a consumer's withdrawal from a loan agreement had no effect on the supply contract.[78] In the particular case, the matter was complicated by the fact that the main contract concerned an interest in immovable property, which falls outside the Directive altogether. Both contracts were part of a larger investment scheme, but the ECJ rejected an argument that these contracts should be treated as an economic unit.[79]

A further instance of a right of withdrawal arises where a contract falls within the *Distance Selling* Directive. Here, a consumer can withdraw from the contract, without giving any reasons, for a period of at least seven *working* days.[80] However, subject to agreement between the parties to the contrary, there are several contracts in respect of which there is no right of withdrawal. These include contracts for services where performance has begun with the consumer's agreement before the withdrawal period has expired; contracts for personalised or customised goods, or those which by their nature either cannot be returned or deteriorate rapidly; for audio or video recordings, or computer software, once the packaging has been unsealed by the consumer; for the supply of newspapers, periodicals and magazines, and for gaming and lottery services (Art 6(3)).

The right of withdrawal is linked to the provision of information at the time of contract formation. To complement the provision of information before the contract is concluded, the Distance Selling Directive also requires that certain items of information are confirmed subsequently. In particular, the information mentioned in Art 4 (a)–(f) needs to be provided to the consumer in writing, or in another durable medium, in good time during the performance of the contract, and, in

---

77 See P Rott, 'Linked contracts and doorstep selling' in G Howells, A Nordhausen, D Parry and C Twigg-Flesner, *Yearbook of Consumer Law 2007* (Ashgate: Aldershot, 2007).
78 C-350/03 *Schulte v Deutsche Bausparkasse Badenia AG* [2005] ECR I-9215.
79 Para 78.
80 Periods expressed in working days exclude public holidays and weekend days: Art 3, Regulation 1182/71.

the case of goods, at the latest by the time of delivery, unless the information was already provided in this form before the conclusion of the contract (Art 5(1)). Furthermore, the consumer must be given information about the procedure for exercising the right of withdrawal, a geographical address to which any complaints may be addressed, information about any available guarantees and after-sales services, and the conditions for cancelling the contract where it is either of unspecified duration, or lasting for more than one year (Art 5(1)).

Assuming that the obligation to provide written information under Art 5 has been complied with, the seven-day withdrawal period starts, in the case of goods, on the day the consumer receives them, and in the case of services, either at the time of concluding the contract, or once the information required under Art 5 has been provided (Art 6(1), first part). If the supplier has not complied with Art 5, the period during which the right of withdrawal may be exercised extends to three months, starting from the day of receipt in the case of goods, or the day of concluding the contract in the case of services; if, however, the information required by Art 5 is given during this three-month period, the seven-working-day period will commence at that point (Art 6(1), second part).

Once the consumer has exercised his right of withdrawal, he must be refunded all sums paid to the supplier as soon as possible and at the latest within 30 days, although the consumer may be charged for the direct cost of returning the goods (Arts 6(1) and (2)). Where the consumer's purchase of the goods or service is financed wholly or in part by a credit arrangement, either with the supplier, or with a third party on the basis of the agreement between supplier and consumer, the credit agreement will also be cancelled without penalty when the consumer exercises his right of withdrawal (Art 6(4)). It is for the Member States to come up with the detailed rules for dealing with the cancellation of the credit agreement.

The *Distance Selling of Financial Services* Directive also provides for a right of withdrawal, which is fixed at 14 calendar days. By way of exception, in the case of contracts falling within the Life Insurance Directive,[81] and personal pension operations, the withdrawal period is 30 calendar days (Art 6(1)). The withdrawal period starts either from the day of concluding the contract (although for life insurance contracts, it starts from the day the consumer is informed that the contract has been concluded), or from the day the consumer receives the written

---

81 Directive 2002/83/EC (2002) OJ L 345/1.

terms and conditions and other information if this is after the date of conclusion of the contract (Art 6(1), second part). However, a right of withdrawal is not available in respect of financial services where the price depends on fluctuations in the financial markets which are outside the supplier's control; travel or baggage insurance policies of less than one month's duration; and contracts which have been fully performed before the consumer seeks to exercise his right of withdrawal (Art 6(2)).

In addition, Member States have been given the option not to make available a right of withdrawal in respect of contracts for credit for the purpose of acquiring or retaining property rights in land or building, including for the purpose of renovating or improving a building; or credit secured either by a mortgage on immovable property or another right in immovable property (Arts 6(3)(a) and (b)). (Paragraph (c) also excludes declarations by consumers using the services of an official.)

As with other instances where a right of withdrawal has been made available, a consumer is entitled to exercise this without penalty, and he does not have to give any reasons for exercising it (Art 6(1)). A consumer seeking to withdraw has to follow the 'practical instructions' which were given to him before the contract was concluded, 'by means which can be proved in accordance with national law'(Art 6(6)). It should be noted that these provisions do not apply in respect of credit agreements connected with a distance contract to which the Distance Selling Directive, or the Timeshare Directive, applies (Art 6(7)).

The consumer is entitled to a refund of all prepayments, although he can be required to pay for a service that has already been provided, but this is subject to the requirements that the consumer must have been informed about the amount payable before the contract was concluded, and, where performance of the contract commenced before the expiry of the withdrawal period, that the consumer consented to the start of performance (Art 7). Similarly, the consumer is required to return any sums or property received from the supplier. Both consumer and supplier have to comply with their obligations in this regard within 30 calendar days.

In the context of specific contracts, the *Timeshare* Directive makes available a right of withdrawal to a purchaser of a timeshare right. Provided that the contract includes all the required information, the purchaser has the right to withdraw from the contract without having to give a reason within 10 calendar days of both parties' signing the contract (Art 5, first indent).[82] If the last day of the withdrawal period is

---

82 The proposed replacement would extend this to 14 days: Art 5(1), COM (2007) 303 final.

a public holiday, the period is extended to the first working day thereafter (Art 5, first indent). If the information is not provided, then
the period during which the right of withdrawal may be exercised
is extended to three months, and if the information is provided during
these three months, the 10-day withdrawal period commences at that
point. If the information has not been provided after the three months
have elapsed, then a final 10-day period during which the right of
withdrawal may be exercised commences (Art 5, second and third
indents).

The right of withdrawal is exercised by notifying the person listed
for this purpose in the contract in accordance with whatever procedure
has been put into place in the relevant domestic legislation (Art 5(2)).
The expenses that may be imposed on the purchaser are limited to
those incurred as a result of concluding and withdrawing from the
contract, but these expenses must be mentioned expressly in the contract (Art 5(3)). They are only payable if the information required
under the Directive was provided as required. Furthermore, any linked
credit agreements are also cancelled automatically (Art 7). In a variation from other directives, there is a prohibition on the purchaser
making any advance payments before the end of the withdrawal period
(Art 6).

In the *Consumer Credit* Directive, there is also first an obligation to
provide the contract document on paper or another durable medium
(Art 10(1)). This must provide specified details in a clear and concise
manner (Art 10(2)). Art 10(3) lists 21 items of information which must
be included in the credit agreement.

A consumer has the right to withdraw from a credit agreement within
14 calendar days, starting either from the date the agreement was concluded or the day when the consumer has received a written copy of the
agreement as required by Art 10 if this is later (Art 14(1)).[83] The consumer has to notify the creditor in accordance with the information
given in the credit agreement, and national law may specify what is
required to prove that notification has been given. If the notification is
on paper or on another durable medium available and accessible to the
creditor, it is sufficient that it is despatched before the end of the withdrawal period (Art 14(2)(a)). The capital and any interest accrued
between the date the credit was received and subsequently repaid has to

---

83 Note that Art 14(4) provides that where the consumer has the right to withdraw under
this Directive, other withdrawal rights that may be available under doorstep- or
distance-selling legislation do not apply.

be paid back to the creditor without delay, and within 30 calendar days from dispatching the withdrawal notification (Art 14(2)(b)). No other costs may be imposed on the consumer, except where the creditor had to pay non-returnable charges to a public administrative body (Art 14(2)(b)).

In circumstances where a consumer has obtained goods or services with the assistance of a credit agreement, and the supply contract has exercised a right of withdrawal under applicable Community law,[84] the credit agreement is also cancelled (Art 15(1) – a 'linked credit' agreement).

Outside the core consumer *acquis*, the only directive with a right of withdrawal is the *Life Assurance* Directive. A policy holder who concludes an individual life-assurance contract has a right of withdrawal (Art 35), although Member States are given the discretion to determine the duration of the withdrawal period (which may be no less than 14 days and no more than 30 days from the date the policy holder was informed about the conclusion of the contract). Once the policy holder has given notice of the withdrawal, he is released from all future obligations under the contract. Beyond this, the conditions for withdrawing and the legal consequences are determined by the national law applicable to the contract.

3.5.2 Comment

The right of withdrawal is the paradigm of inconsistent EU legislation, with each measure taking a slightly different approach. For example, the duration of the withdrawal period ranges from seven to 30 days, and is sometimes expressed in days or calendar days, and at other times in working days. Member States are usually free to set a longer period than required under the various directives. Furthermore, there is no consistent procedure that should be followed by a consumer seeking to withdraw from a contract. Also, in some instances, some charges may be imposed on a consumer who withdraws, but not in others. This may be explained as a consequence of the different rationale for granting a right of withdrawal: in *Doorstep Selling*, the pressure-selling aspect justifies a cost-free withdrawal, whereas creating the opportunity to consider alternatives in the context of *Distance Selling* does make the imposition of some costs acceptable. Finally,

---

84 That is, domestic legislation which implements a directive providing for a withdrawal right, such as legislation on doorstep or distance selling.

the consequences of withdrawing from a contract are not regulated consistently.[85]

3.5.3 Post-formation information duties

It has already been mentioned that the directives on *Distance Selling*, *Timeshare* and *Package Travel* link the commencement of the withdrawal period with the provision of information after contract formation. The provision of information on formation is also a feature of the *Payment Services* Directive, which requires that specific items of information are given[86] once a payment order has been made, again distinguishing between single transactions and those made in the context of a framework contract. In respect of a single transaction, the information to be provided covers a reference number for the transaction, the amount of the payment, any charges, the applicable exchange rate and the date the payment order was received (Art 27). Similar information has to be provided in respect of individual transactions made in the context of a framework contract, although in this case, the information may be provided periodically at least once a month, for example, on a bank statement (Art 36).

3.5.4 Formation by electronic means

In the *Electronic Commerce* Directive, there is an obligation on the Member States to ensure that contracts can be concluded by electronic means, and that any relevant legal requirements regarding the process of contract formation applicable under domestic legislation do not impede the formation of contracts by electronic means (Art 9(1)).[87] The validity and legal effectiveness of contracts should not be affected by the fact that they were concluded by electronic means. It can be noted here that this particular provision simply sets out a result, and does not seek to prescribe how the Member States should adjust their

---

85 See further P Rott, 'Harmonising different rights of withdrawal' (2006) 7 *German Law Journal* 1109–46.

86 The related provisions on cost, form and burden of proof were noted above at 3.4.2.

87 A companion measure to the e-commerce Directive, Directive 99/93 of the European Parliament and Council on a Community framework for electronic signatures [1999] OJ L 13/12 (electronic signatures), was adopted to ensure that electronic signatures applied to documents held in electronic form are treated as the equivalent of a handwritten signature on a paper document (Art 5), but it has become largely redundant in light of technological developments.

domestic laws to ensure that contracts can be concluded electronically. Importantly, there are no concrete rules dealing with the point at which a contract concluded by electronic means comes into existence.[88] Several types of contracts are excluded from this requirement, however: contracts creating or transferring rights in real estate (except for rental rights); those which, by law, require the involvement of the courts, public authorities or professions exercising public authority; non-commercial contracts 'of suretyship and on collateral securities'; and those governed by family and succession law (Art 9(2)).

Although not directly on the formation of contracts, the Directive does state that if an order is placed, the receipt of the order has to be acknowledged without undue delay by electronic means (Art 11(1), first indent). Furthermore, an order and an acknowledgement of receipt are deemed to have been received when the respective recipients are able to access them.

3.5.5 Validity

The *Commercial Agency* Directive has a rule on the validity of the contract based on compliance with form.[89] Each party is entitled to receive a signed written document setting out the terms of the agency agreement, and Member States can make the validity of an agency agreement subject to the requirement that it is evidenced in writing (Art 13). This optional requirement is the only specific restriction on the validity of a commercial agency contract that may be imposed by national law. It is therefore not possible for national law to make the entry of the commercial agent in a domestic register a condition of the validity of the contract,[90] although national law may impose other sanctions for a failure to register a commercial agent, provided that these do not undermine other provisions in the Directive.[91] This, however, does not affect general requirements for validity applicable to all contracts.

---

88 This may be contrasted with an earlier draft of the Directive, which did include a provision on the formation of contracts.

89 Note that the unfairness of a term (see below) is sometimes treated as a question of validity; in this chapter, the policing of unfair terms is treated as an issue affecting the substance of a contract.

90 C-215/97 *Bellone v Yokohama SpA* [1998] ECR I-2191; C-456/98 *Centrosteel SrL v Adipol GmbH* [2000] ECR I-6007.

91 C-485/01 *Caprini v Conservatore Camera di Commercio, Industria, Artigianato e Agricoltura* [2002] ECR I-2371.

3.6 THE SUBSTANCE OF THE CONTRACT

This section considers rules which have a direct impact on the substance of a contract. It will be seen that there are far fewer EU measures in this regard, leaving considerable freedom to the contracting parties, as well as domestic law, to determine the substance of their respective rights and obligations. One notable, and significant, exception is the *Unfair Contract Terms* Directive,[92] which can be deployed to police most terms in a broad range of consumer contracts.

3.6.1 Unfair Terms in Consumer Contracts

3.6.1.1 Scope

The *Unfair Contract Terms* Directive renders inapplicable all those terms in a consumer contract which are unfair. However, not all terms can be reviewed: those which are 'individually negotiated' fall outside the scope of the Directive (Art 3); as do those 'which reflect mandatory statutory or regulatory provisions, or provisions of international conventions to which the Member States or the Community are party' (Art 1(2)). The restriction to non-negotiated terms is primarily justified on the basis that at the time the Directive was adopted, 'national laws allow[ed] only partial harmonisation to be envisaged'. The main concern is, therefore, the control of standard form contracts, used for the vast majority of consumer transactions. Control over individually negotiated terms has been left to the Member States, with some extending their national laws to such terms.[93]

It is for the seller or supplier to prove that a term was individually negotiated, rather than for the consumer to prove that it was not (Art 3(2), final sentence). A term will clearly not be individually negotiated where the contract is a 'pre-formulated standard contract' (Art 3(2), second sentence). Moreover, a term should not be regarded as individually negotiated if (a) it has been 'drafted in advance' and (b) the consumer has not been able to influence the substance of the term (Art 3(2)). Furthermore, the fact that 'one specific term' or 'certain aspects of a term' have been individually negotiated does not preclude the application of the unfairness test to the remaining terms of

---

92 See, eg, P Nebbia, *Unfair Contract Terms in European Law* (Oxford: Hart, 2007).

93 In the recent *Green Paper on the Review of the Consumer Acquis*, the Commission consulted on whether the Directive's scope should be extended to include individually negotiated terms.

the contract, if the overall appearance of the contract is that it is a standard form contract.

The assessment of fairness does not relate to the 'main subject matter' or the 'adequacy of the price and remuneration' (Art 4), subject to the proviso that these terms must be in plain intelligible language (Art 4(2)).[94] This means that the main subject matter of the contract cannot be reviewed, nor can the adequacy of the price as compared to the goods or services supplied.[95]

3.6.1.2 The unfairness test

According to Art 3(1), a term will be unfair if 'contrary to the requirement of good faith, it causes a significant imbalance in the parties' rights and obligations under the contract to the detriment of the consumer'. The notion of good faith is central to the Directive, but it is not clear whether 'good faith' and 'significant imbalance' are cumulative, or merely alternative means of expressing the same substantive test – that is, a term which creates a significant imbalance to the detriment of the consumer is contrary to the requirement of good faith, and therefore unfair under the Directive.

Indeed, the meaning of 'good faith' is somewhat uncertain.[96] Unlike English law, most national laws are familiar with the concept, but EU law requires that good faith is interpreted autonomously.[97] However, the Directive offers only limited guidance, and the ECJ has yet to be given the opportunity to interpret this concept.[98] For example, there could be

---

94 It has been suggested that the unfairness test would apply if those terms were not in plain and intelligible language (cf Tizzano A-G in C-144/99 *Commission v Netherlands* [2001] ECR I-3541, para 27), although the consequences of finding that such a term is unfair remain unclear. See also COM (2000) 248 final, p 15.

95 The application of this to contracts of insurance has caused particular difficulties: according to Recital 19, 'the terms which clearly define or circumscribe the insured risk and the insurer's liability' are not assessed as to their fairness because they are factored into the premium, but do particular exclusions from the scope of an insurance policy define the subject matter, or are they simply a restriction of the insurer's liability and therefore subject to review?

96 R Brownsword, G Howells and T Wilhelmsson, 'Between market and welfare: some reflections on Article 3 of the EC Directive on Unfair Terms in Consumer Contracts', in C Willett (ed), *Aspects of Fairness in Contract* (London: Blackstone Press, 1996), p 31, suggest several possible interpretations of the fairness test in Art 3.

97 See Chapter 4, p 137.

98 In C-237/02 *Freiburger Kommunalbauten v Hofstetter* [2004] ECR I-3403, it only noted that the Directive defined the factors which render a contractual term unfair, without expanding on this.

greater clarity on whether there is both a procedural and a substantive aspect to this test, although there is an assumption that there is.[99] In its procedural meaning, it would generally be concerned with a lack of choice and unfair surprise.[100] This would mean that good faith requires the disclosure of all terms, and particular attention being drawn to terms which are onerous on a consumer. It might also mean that there should be the possibility for a consumer to negotiate some of the terms rather than being presented with the standard contract on a take-it-or-leave-it basis in all circumstances.[101]

The substantive element of the test would focus on whether a particular term is inherently unfair, be it by excluding or limiting certain rights of the consumer, or by putting him at a disadvantage if compared to the position of the seller/supplier.

The Directive offers support for both a procedural and a substantive meaning of good faith. Some guidance is given in Recital 19, which specifies that in making an assessment of good faith,

> particular regard shall be had to the strength of the bargaining position of the parties; whether the consumer had an inducement to agree to the term and whether the goods or services were sold or supplied to the special order of the consumer.

This points towards good faith having a procedural aspect – bargaining strength is a matter which will have little bearing on the substantive impact of the relevant term, but is a factor if the term was imposed on the consumer, or if the consumer was induced to accept it.

There are indicators in the Directive that good faith has a substantive aspect, too. Thus, Recital 19 also states that the requirement of good faith may be satisfied by a seller or supplier by dealing fairly and equitably with the other party whose legitimate interests he has to take into account. It has been suggested that this reflects an element of co-operation, disapproving of the unilateral pursuit by the seller or supplier of its own interest and instead favouring a degree of co-operation, by taking into account the legitimate interests of the consumer.[102]

In order to facilitate the application of the unfairness test, the

---

99 See, eg, H Beale, 'Legislative control of fairness: the Directive on Unfair Terms in Consumer Contracts', in J Beatson and D Friedman (eds), *Good Faith and Fault in Contract Law* (Oxford: Clarendon Press, 1995).
100 *Ibid.*, p 245.
101 Brownsword, Howells and Wilhelmsson, *op. cit.*, p 40.
102 G Howells and T Wilhelmsson, *EC Consumer Law* (Aldershot: Ashgate, 1997), p 99.

Directive includes an Annex of an 'indicative and non-exhaustive list of the terms which may be regarded as unfair' (Art 3(3)). This is often referred to as a 'grey' list, because it does not prohibit certain terms outright, but rather suggests that there is a strong likelihood that terms which resemble those in the Annex are unfair (Recital 17). Nevertheless, terms which feature in the list should, at the very least, be treated with some suspicion. The ECJ has noted that a term included in the list may not necessarily be unfair, just as the absence of a term from the list did not mean that it was fair.[103]

The Annex also provides further guidance on the scope of the unfairness test. Generally speaking, all the terms in the Annex, with one exception, are concerned with a substantive imbalance, dealing with exclusions of legal rights or imposing an undue burden on a consumer without a similar burden being assumed by the seller or supplier. Only one term appears to refer to procedural matters: indicative term (i) has the object or effect of 'irrevocably binding a consumer to terms with which he had no real opportunity of becoming acquainted before the conclusion of the contract'. This suggests that insufficient disclosure, or unfair surprise, may render a term unfair, which lends some support to the suggestion that certain procedural matters could have an impact on the assessment of a term's unfairness.

In any event, the bulk of the terms in the indicative list is clearly concerned with substantive unfairness. In many cases, it is possible to identify a 'significant imbalance' in these indicative terms in that the seller/supplier will be entitled to do something without the consumer having a corresponding entitlement. Others, however, are less obviously concerned with an imbalance in the respective obligations of seller/ supplier and consumer. Thus, indicative term (e) is concerned with a requirement imposed on a consumer to pay a disproportionately high sum in compensation if he fails to fulfil his contractual obligations, term (h) relates to automatic extensions to fixed-term contracts and term (p) refers to assignment by the seller/supplier of its contractual rights to a third party without the consumer's consent.

This problem was highlighted by the Economic and Social Committee[104] when responding to the European Commission's report[105] on the implementation of the Directive. The ESC noted, in particular, that

---

103 C-478/99 *Commission v Sweden* [2002] ECR I-4147, para 20.
104 Opinion of the Economic and Social Committee on the 'Report from the Commission on the implementation of Council Directive 93/13/EEC of 5 April 1993 on unfair terms in consumer contracts' (2001) OJ C 116/117 ('the ESC opinion').
105 COM (2000) 248 final.

there are different interpretations of Art 3(1), that different language versions are 'diametrically opposed'[106] and that 'the principle of good faith and how it relates to the notion of contractual imbalance also need to be clarified at Community level . . .'.[107] The ESC goes so far as to question whether it is 'appropriate to continue to use this concept as a supplementary criterion for determining whether a term is unfair'.[108] However, no changes have been made to date.[109]

In applying the test to a particular term, the Directive requires that a number of factors are taken into account. Thus, it is necessary to consider the nature of the goods or services for which the contract was concluded. More significantly, reference should be made, at the time of conclusion of the contract, to all the circumstances attending the conclusion of the contract. Finally, regard should be had to all the other terms of the contract, or of another contract on which the term under consideration is dependent (Art 4(1)). Because of these factors, the assessment of the unfairness of a particular term is a matter for the national courts, and the ECJ will not respond to a request for a preliminary reference regarding the unfairness of a particular term. In C-237/02 *Freiburger Kommunalbauten GmbH Baugesellschaft & Co KG v Hofstetter*,[110] the ECJ was asked by the German Bundesgerichtshof whether a clause in the claimant's standard terms and conditions was unfair. The Court refused to answer that question, noting instead that the ECJ 'may interpret general criteria used by the Community legislature in order to define the concept of unfair terms. However, it should not rule on the application of these general criteria to a particular term . . .'[111] So although the ECJ would be prepared to interpret the concept of good faith generally, it will not comment on how the unfairness test would deal with a specific term.[112]

---

106 Para 4.2.1 of the ESC opinion.
107 Para 4.2 of the ESC opinion.
108 Para 4.2.3 of the ESC opinion.
109 The *Green Paper on the Review of the Consumer Acquis* did not contain any specific proposals in this regard.
110 [2004] ECR-I 3403.
111 Para 22.
112 This approach is often contrasted with the approach in C-240-244/98 *Oceano Grupo Editorial SA v Rocio Quintero and others* [2000] ECR I-4941, where the ECJ said that a jurisdiction clause was unfair, before holding that a domestic court can decide of its own motion whether a term is unfair when deciding on the admissibility of a claim. In this situation, however, the domestic court had not asked the ECJ to consider the unfairness of the term in question, and the ECJ ultimately left the decision on the unfairness of the particular term to the domestic court.

3.6.1.3 *Consequences of unfairness*

Art 6(1) requires Member States to provide that unfair terms 'shall, as provided for under their national law, not be binding on the consumer ...'. Thus, a term which has been found to be unfair will not be enforceable against a consumer. The immediate consequence is that the particular term is effectively struck from the contract. This may not necessarily be fatal to the contract as a whole, and the remainder of the contract will continue to bind both parties provided that the removal of the unfair term does not make the contract incapable of 'continuing in existence without the unfair terms' (Art 6(1)).

The Directive does not offer any further guidance on how it can be determined whether the contract can continue in force without the relevant term(s), and this is therefore a matter to be decided by the domestic courts using their own established principles. However, it is not possible for a court to rewrite the term in order to remove the unfairness.[113] A court would have to consider how crucial the term in question is to the contract as a whole, and whether the removal of the term would require a contractual performance significantly different from that which would have been within the parties' expectations, before concluding whether the contract could be maintained.

3.6.1.4 *Plain and intelligible language*

In addition to the unfairness test, the Directive further requires that where 'all or certain terms' are provided to the consumer in writing, they must be drafted in plain, intelligible language (Art 5).[114] Similar provisions are used in other directives, particularly where certain information is to be made available to a consumer in connection with a particular transaction.[115] It is surprising, however, that the consequences of presenting a particular term in something other than plain, intelligible language are rather limited. Thus, all that is provided in Art 5 is a rule

---

113 Cf G Howells and T Wilhelmsson, *EC Consumer Law* (Aldershot: Ashgate, 1997), p 111, commenting on the practice of the Finnish courts. Note also the English decision in *Bankers Insurance Company Ltd v South and Gardner* [2003] EWHC 380 (QB), 7 March 2003, where the court regarded a term as unfair only in a limited set of circumstances.

114 It has been argued that this might extend to the language type, that is, an official language, although the position is unclear: S Whittaker, 'The language or languages of consumer contracts' (2007) 8 *Cambridge Yearbook of European Legal Studies* 229–57.

115 See, eg, Art 6 of Directive 99/44/EC.

of interpretation that where there is some ambiguity in the meaning of a particular term, the interpretation that is most favourable to the consumer should prevail (*in dubio contra stipulatorem*). However, in contrast to the consequences of a term being found unfair under Art 3, a term which fails to satisfy the 'plain and intelligible language' requirement will not be ineffective.[116]

An interesting question is which standard should be applied in determining whether a term is presented in sufficiently plain and intelligible language. It seems likely that an objective standard should be adopted, and the question to be asked is whether a consumer faced with the term in question would regard it as having been drafted in plain and intelligible language. The objective standard in this context is likely to be the 'average consumer' benchmark developed by the European Court of Justice, although it is arguable that a lower standard should be used, such as that of the 'naïve and inexperienced consumer'.[117]

3.6.2 Consumer guarantees

Another directive with a limited impact on the substance of contracts is the *Consumer Sales* Directive, particularly the provision dealing with guarantees. A guarantee is usually given by a manufacturer, and promises that goods are free from defects in workmanship and materials.[118] For the purposes of the Directive, a guarantee is 'any undertaking by a seller or producer to the consumer, given without extra charge, to reimburse the price paid or to replace, repair or handle consumer goods in any way if they do not meet the specifications set out in the guarantee statement or in the relevant advertising' (Art 1(2)(e)). This emphasises that not only guarantee documents included with the goods are relevant, but also that statements in advertising may be taken into account in determining the scope of a guarantee; indeed, guarantees may be based entirely on undertakings given in general advertising. Guarantees are legally binding on the offeror of the guarantee, but this is subject to the conditions mentioned in the guarantee document and the associated advertising (Art 6(1)). The guarantee must make it clear that the

---

116 Note the Commission's invitation to comment on whether a sanction should be introduced for terms which are not in plain and intelligible language: COM (2000) 248 final, p 18.
117 H Collins, 'Good faith in European contract law' (1994) 14 *Oxford Journal of Legal Studies* 229, p 248.
118 C Twigg-Flesner, *Consumer Product Guarantees* (Aldershot: Ashgate, 2003).

consumer's legal rights in respect of the sale of consumer goods are not affected by it (Art 6(2), first indent). Further, the guarantee must provide, in plain intelligible language, 'the contents of the guarantee and the essential particulars necessary for making claims under the guarantee, notably the duration and territorial scope of the guarantee as well as the name and address of the guarantor' (Art 6(2), second indent). Moreover, the consumer is entitled to request that the guarantee is made available to him in writing, or in another durable medium available and accessible to him (Art 6(3)). Member States are given the option to require that guarantees are drafted in one or more of the official languages of the European Community (Art 6(4)). Finally, a failure to comply with the requirements on guarantees does not affect the validity of a guarantee and consumers can still rely on it (Art 6(5)).

3.6.3 Late payment of commercial debts

The *Late Payment of Commercial Debts* Directive[119] establishes that interest (set at seven percentage points above the central bank base rate (Art 3(1)(d)))[120] is payable either from the contractual date of payment (Art 3(1)(a)), or, if no date is fixed in the contract, after a period of 30 days from receipt of the invoice, or after 30 days from the date of receipt of the goods or services where the invoice date is uncertain, or where the invoice was sent before the goods or services were received (Art 3(1)(b)). Member States may extend the period, for particular categories of contract, to up to 60 days, but they must ensure that the parties to the contract do not exceed this additional period, or fix a substantially higher interest rate for any late payments (Art 3(2)).

The entitlement to interest applies to the extent that the supplier has completed his contractual and legal obligations, and he has not received the due amount, except where the recipient is not responsible for the delay in payment being made to the supplier (Art 3(1)(c)).[121] In

---

119 R Schulte-Braucks and S Ongena, 'The Late Payment Directive – a step towards an emerging European private law?' (2003) 11 *European Review of Private Law* 519–44.
120 For Member States participating in monetary union, the European Central Bank's base rate applies; for others, it is the base rate of their domestic central bank (such as the Bank of England).
121 In C-306/06 *01051 Telekom v Deutsche Telekom AG*, not yet decided (Advocate-General's opinion of 18 October 2007), the ECJ has been asked to consider when a payment can be said to have been 'received' if the debtor has authorised a bank transfer, or whether it is necessary that the funds have been credited to the creditor's account.

addition to interest, reasonable compensation for any recovery costs incurred as a result of the late payment may be claimed by the supplier (Art 3(1)(e)).[122] The Directive also controls agreements regarding the due date for payment or the consequences of late payment which vary from the rules laid down in the Directive. Such variations will either not be enforceable, or give rise to a claim for damages, if this is regarded as grossly unfair to the creditor, taking into account the circumstances of the case including good commercial practice and the nature of the goods or services supplied (Art 3(3)). It is also relevant whether the debtor would have any objective reason to deviate from the rules on late payment set down in the Directive. This is an instance where EU law provides a means of controlling the fairness of a contractual term in a non-consumer context.

3.6.4 Specific terms

3.6.4.1 Retention of title clause

The *Late Payment* Directive requires that the Member States ensure that a clause which retains title to goods until paid for is effective if agreed prior to delivery of the goods. However, this seems to be limited to requiring Member States to recognise a retention of title clause; the precise conditions, particularly their effectiveness as against third parties, are matters for national law.[123] Member States are also given permission to adopt or retain rules dealing with any 'down payments' made by the recipient of the goods (Art 4).

3.6.4.2 Restraint of trade clause

In the *Commercial Agency* Directive, it is provided that an agent may be subject to a restraint of trade clause after the contractual relationship has otherwise come to an end. The clause must be in writing and relate to the geographical area or group of customers, and the goods covered

---

122   It seems that national law may have some control over the costs that can be recovered: in C-235/03 *QDQ Media SA v Lecha* [2005] ECR I-1937, the cost of using a legal representative to lodge an initial claim for interest was not recoverable under applicable national law, and the ECJ held that the Directive could not be used as basis to override the national rule.

123   C-302/05 *Commission v Italy* [2006] ECR-10597.

by the agency agreement, and may only be of a duration of no more than two years (Art 20). It must be emphasised that this rule is limited to the specific context of commercial agency and does not constitute a general standard for restraint of trade clauses.

3.7 PERFORMANCE

There is greater regulation of aspects of the performance of contractual obligations in the *acquis*, although this is the case predominantly in the consumer *acquis*. Some of the performance rules are, in essence, simple information rules, but others do effectively prescribe how the parties to the contract should perform their respective obligations.

3.7.1 Information

A basic information rule can be found in the *Distance Selling of Financial Services* Directive: a consumer can, at any time during the contractual relationship, request a paper version of the terms and conditions of the contract. The consumer is also entitled to change the means of distance communication to be used, provided that this is not incompatible with the contract or the nature of the financial service contracted for (Art 5(3)).

3.7.2 Timing and substitute performance/variation

3.7.2.1 Distance Selling

The *Distance Selling* Directive contains a number of provisions on the performance of a contract falling within its scope. Thus, the supplier is required to perform his obligations within 30 days of the consumer placing his order, unless the parties have agreed a different period (Art 7(1)). If this is not possible because the goods or services are unavailable, the consumer is entitled to a refund of any prepayments within 30 days (Art 7(2)). Although the Directive does not make this explicit, the contract is, presumably, terminated in such circumstances. Alternatively, if the contract between supplier and consumer so provides and the consumer was informed about this in a clear and comprehensible manner, the supplier may provide substitute goods or services which are of equivalent value. If the consumer still wishes to exercise his right of withdrawal, having received a substitute, the cost of returning the goods will have to be borne by the supplier (Art 7(3)).

3.7.2.2 Package Travel

The *Package Travel* Directive deals with a number of aspects of contract variation, both on the part of the consumer and trader. Thus, a consumer is entitled to transfer his package to another person eligible to use the package by giving reasonable notice to the retailer or organiser, in which case both the consumer and transferee will be liable for the cost of the package and any additional expenses arising from the transfer (Art 4(3)). Prices may not be varied, except where the contract expressly provides for upward or downward adjustments, including precisely how such variations are to be calculated, which are due to changes in transportation costs, exchange rates, or relevant dues, taxes and chargeable fees (Art 4(4)(a)). The price may not be varied in the 20-day period before departure (Art 4(4)(b)).

If, prior to the consumer's departure, the organiser needs to make significant changes to essential parts of the package, he must notify the consumer. The consumer then has the choice to withdraw from the package, or to accept a variation to the package (Art 4(5)). If the consumer withdraws or if the package is cancelled by the organiser, he may either take a substitute package of equivalent or higher value (or a package of lower value together with a partial refund), or receive a full refund of all sums paid by him. Additional compensation may be payable to the consumer in accordance with national rules, except where the package was cancelled because the minimum number of bookings required had not been reached and the consumer was aware of this, or the cancellation is the result of *force majeure* (Art 4(6)).

Similarly, if a significant part of the package is not provided once the consumer has departed, or if the organiser discovers that he will not be able to provide a significant proportion of the package, the organiser is required to make alternative arrangements. These have to be provided at no extra cost to the consumer, but the consumer may be entitled to compensation if the value of what is provided by way of substitution is lower than the package contracted for. If no alternative arrangements can be made, the organiser has to arrange for transport back to the point of departure at no extra cost to the consumer (Art 4(7)).

More generally, the Directive specifies that the retailer or organiser is liable to the consumer for the proper performance of the contract, including those elements which are to be provided by a third party (Art 5(1)). This effectively broadens the basis of liability beyond the immediate obligations assumed by the party with whom the consumer has contracted.

3.7.3 Sale of goods

A Directive which goes to the heart of many consumer contracts is the *Consumer Sales* Directive.[124] The central requirement of the Directive is that the seller must deliver goods which are in conformity with the contract (Art 2(1)). Art 2(2) creates a rebuttable presumption that the goods do conform to the contract if certain requirements are satisfied. These are that:

(a) the goods comply with the description given by the seller and possess the qualities of the goods which the seller has held out to the consumer as a sample or a model;

(b) the goods are fit for any particular purpose required by the consumer, provided that the consumer has made this purpose known at the time of concluding the contract, and the seller has accepted this;

(c) the goods are fit for those purposes for which goods of the same type are normally used;

(d) the goods show the quality and performance which are normal in goods of the same type and which the consumer can reasonably expect, given the nature of the goods and taking into account any public statements on the specific characteristics of the goods made about them by the seller, the producer or his representative, particularly in advertising or labelling.

In respect of the public statements referred to in Art 2(2)(d), the seller will not be liable if he can show that (a) he was not, and could not reasonably have been aware of the statement; or (b) at the time of conclusion of the contract the statement had been corrected; or (c) the consumer's decision to buy the goods could not have been influenced by the statement.

Furthermore, there will be deemed to be no lack of conformity if, at the time the contract was concluded, the consumer was aware of it, or could not reasonably have been unaware of the matters which would otherwise mean that the goods were not in conformity.[125] The seller is

---

124 Directive 99/44/EC.
125 Cf C Twigg-Flesner, 'Information disclosure about the quality of goods – duty or encouragement?' in G Howells, A Janssen, and R Schulze (eds), *Information Rights and Obligations* (Aldershot: Ashgate, 2005).

also not liable for any lack of conformity which 'has its origin' in materials supplied by the consumer (Art 2(3)).

Art 2(5) extends the conformity requirement by treating a lack of conformity resulting from incorrect installation of the goods as a lack of conformity in the goods in certain situations, including where the consumer has installed the goods himself and there was 'a shortcoming in the installation instructions'.[126]

3.7.4 Consumer credit – early repayment

The *Consumer Credit* Directive contains a provision on the early repayment of a credit. A consumer is entitled to make partial or full repayment, and, where this is done, is entitled to a reduction in the overall cost by deducting the interest yet to be paid as well as any costs that would arise during the remaining part of the agreement (Art 16(1)). Where the agreement is subject to a fixed borrowing rate, and provided that the reference interest rate of the relevant central bank is lower than it was when the credit agreement was made, the credit provider is entitled to additional compensation (Art 16(2)). If more than one year has passed since the agreement was made, the compensation may be no more than 1% of the amount repaid early; otherwise, only 0.5% may be charged by way of compensation (Art 16(2)). National law may set a threshold which the early repayment must reach before compensation can be claimed, but this may be no higher than €10,000 in any 12-month period (Art 16(4)).

3.7.5 Commercial agency: performance and remuneration

The *Commercial Agents* Directive states that both agent (Art 3(1)) and principal (Art 4(1)) are under an obligation to act dutifully and in good faith, which is effectively imposing an obligation to act in good faith in the performance of contractual obligations (but limited to the specific context of commercial agency contracts). It also entails an obligation

---

126 Although the Directive refers to installation instructions, it does not consider operating instructions in any way. Inadequate operating instructions are not obviously a source of non-conformity under the Directive. Cf Council Resolution of 17 December 1998 on operating instructions for technical consumer goods (1998) OJ C 411/1 inviting the Commission to consider the adoption of standardised operating instructions. An Annex to the resolution provides 'indications for good operating instructions for technical consumer goods'.

to keep each other informed of relevant information (Arts 3(2)(b) and 4(2)(b)).

As far as the agent's remuneration is concerned, he is entitled to the level of remuneration customary where he is active; in the absence of customary practice, there should be reasonable remuneration (Art 6(1)). Often, remuneration will be based partly or wholly on commission, and the Directive provides a fairly detailed set of rules setting out the entitlement of a commercial agent to receive commission. These provisions are protective of the agent, and seek to ensure he receives commission where transactions are concluded as a result of his actions (Art 7(1)(a)), or with a customer previously acquired for similar transactions by the agent (Art 7(1)(b). Furthermore, where the agent is in charge of a particular geographical area or group of customers and transactions are entered into with a customer from that group or area, he is also entitled to commission (Art 7(2)), even if he had no active involvement in attracting that customer.[127] It may be difficult to establish that a particular customer was from the agent's geographical area, particularly in the case of a company operating in different places; whilst the place where the company carries on its commercial activity is the key factor, it may also be relevant where negotiations should have taken place, where the goods were delivered, and from where the order was placed.[128]

The right to receive commission may extend beyond the termination of the agency agreement (Arts 8–9). Commission becomes payable once the transaction arranged by the agent has been executed (Art 10), and there are provisions protecting the agent if the principal fails to execute the transaction when he should have done so (Arts 10(2) and 11, second indent).

Commercial agency contracts may be of indefinite duration, or for a fixed period; however, if the parties continue to perform after the fixed period has expired, the contract is deemed to be converted into one of indefinite duration (Art 14). Such contracts can be terminated by giving notice, and the number of months of notice which are required are set and are correlated to the number of years the contract has existed (Art 15). Contracts which have been in place for three years or more will be subject to a notice period of three months, although Member States are given the option to extend the correlational approach up to the sixth year of the contract, reaching a maximum notice period of six months

---

127 C-104/95 *Georgios Kontogeorgas v Kartonpak AE* [1996] ECR I-6643.
128 *Ibid.*

(Art 15(3)). These notice requirements are binding, although the parties may agree longer periods, provided that the notice period available to the principal is not shorter than that for the agent (Art 15(4)).

3.7.6 Payment services – information and performance

The *Payment Services* Directive requires that information is provided[129] once a payment order has been executed, again distinguishing between single transactions and those made in the context of a framework contract. In respect of a single transaction, the payee (that is, the recipient of the funds) has to be given information which provides a reference number for the transaction, the amount of the payment, any charges, the applicable exchange rate and the date the payment was credited (Art 39). The same information has to be given where the payment was made in the context of a framework contract (Art 48). In addition, under a framework contract, it is possible to request the terms and conditions regarding the contract at any time (Art 43). Changes to the contract have to be notified no later than two months before they are to take effect, with the exception of changes to exchange or interest rates (Art 44).

The Directive also includes more detailed rules than previously found in EU law regarding the authorisation of payment transactions, including an obligation to repay unauthorised payments (Arts 51–63). In addition, there are several provisions dealing with the performance of a payment transaction. Many of these deal with the time orders have been received and the time within which such orders have to be executed (Arts 64–73). A final section deals with the respective liabilities of the payment service provider and the user. Thus, a payment service provider is generally responsible for the correct execution of a payment transaction and must recredit the account with the value of the payment if it has not been executed properly; in addition, steps must be taken to trace the payment made (Art 75).

A framework contract may be terminated by the user at any time, unless the contract contains a notice period; in that case, this may not exceed one month. If the contract is intended to last for more than 12 months, or for an indefinite period, no charges may be imposed for terminating the contract once 12 months have expired. Similarly, a payment service provider may terminate the contract on giving two months' notice, if a term to that effect is included in the contract (Art 45).

---

129 The related provisions on cost, form and burden of proof were noted above at 3.4.2.

3.8 REMEDIES FOR NON-PERFORMANCE

Finally, an area in which there has been more limited EU action is that of remedies for non-performance of a contractual obligation. There are notable exceptions to this, both with regard to consumer sales contracts generally, as well as package travel contracts.

3.8.1 Damages

As already noted, the *Package Travel* Directive imposes liability on the retailer or organiser for the proper performance of the contract. A consumer is entitled to compensation for damage[130] resulting from a failure fully to perform the contract by the retailer or organiser, except where neither is at fault (Arts 5(1) and (2)). This is one of the very few instances in EU law where there is a specific entitlement to monetary compensation.

3.8.2 Remedies for non-conforming goods

The *Consumer Sales* Directive contains a detailed system of remedies for circumstances where the seller has failed to perform his obligation to deliver goods in conformity with the contract. In such a situation, the consumer is entitled to invoke the various remedies made available under Art 3. The consumer is only entitled to claim a remedy from the final seller, rather than an intermediary or the producer directly (Art 3(1)).

The seller's liability is restricted to any lack of conformity manifesting itself within two years of delivery of the goods (Art 5(1)). By way of derogation, Member States may provide that, in the case of second-hand goods, a consumer and seller may agree on a reduced period of seller's liability, but this may be not less than one year (Art 7(1)). Furthermore, where a lack of conformity becomes apparent within six months of delivery of the goods, it is rebuttably presumed that the goods were not in conformity with the contract at the time of delivery (Art 5(3)). This presumption does not apply where it would be incompatible with either the nature of the goods or the nature of the lack of conformity. Member States are given the option to provide that

---

130 It has been held by the ECJ that this includes non-material damage: C-168/00 *Simone Leitner v TUI Deutschland GmbH & Co KG* [2002] ECR I-2631. See further Chapter 2, p 47.

a consumer must inform the seller of the lack of conformity within a period of two months from the date on which he discovered this lack of conformity (Art 5(2)).

The seller can offer the consumer any of the four remedies of repair, replacement, price reduction or rejection (Recital 12). If he chooses not to accept this offer, Art 3 applies. This divides the four remedies into a two-stage hierarchy. The relationship between them is one of the most difficult and controversial aspects of the Directive. In the first instance, the consumer is entitled to require the seller to repair or replace the goods. If neither of those is available, or if the seller fails to complete the required remedy as specified, the buyer can resort to the remedies of rescission or price reduction. The objective is to hold both parties to their bargain, so primacy is given to requiring the seller to cure his defective performance.

Initially, the choice is between repair and replacement. Repair is defined as 'in the event of lack of conformity, bringing consumer goods into conformity with the contract of sale' (Art 1(2)(f)). Repair and replacement must both be provided free of charge.[131]

However, a consumer cannot require the seller to repair or replace the non-conforming goods if, in either case, the remedy is impossible or disproportionate (Art 3(3) final part). It will therefore be necessary first to consider whether it is possible to provide the remedy chosen by the consumer and second, whether it is disproportionate in comparison to another remedy. The impossibility of repair may depend, for example, on the availability of spare parts. Moreover, it is suggested that the replacement of second-hand goods will generally be impossible (cf Recital 16).

The more significant consideration is likely to be whether a remedy is 'disproportionate'. This will be so if the remedy 'imposes costs on the seller which, in comparison with the alternative remedy, are unreasonable' (Art 3(3)). A basic difference in cost between the two remedies is not sufficient; rather, the costs of one remedy must be *significantly* higher to be regarded as unreasonable (Recital 11).

In assessing whether the costs of a particular remedy are unreasonable, three factors are relevant:

(1)   the value the goods would have had if they had been in conformity with the contract;

---

131 Art 3(4) provides that 'free of charge' refers to 'the necessary costs incurred to bring the goods into conformity, particularly the cost of postage, labour and materials'.

(2) the significance of the lack of conformity; and
(3) whether the alternative remedy could be completed without significant inconvenience to the consumer.

This is an objective test, requiring consideration of the cost to the seller of providing the given remedy and the benefit to the buyer,[132] as well as the cost/benefit balance of the comparator remedy.

If the goods are of low value, the availability of repair might be limited. Where the cost of providing repair would, because of the cost of labour and parts required, exceed the market value of the goods themselves, repair would probably be disproportionate, and replacement would offer a better solution. Conversely if the goods are of high value, even an expensive repair might not be disproportionate.

Similarly, where there is only a small difference in value between the goods as delivered and their market value, replacement might be regarded as disproportionate, especially if repair could be effected easily and at low cost.

The cost of the chosen remedy must also be weighed against the significance of the lack of conformity. Thus, if the effect of the particular lack of conformity is to make the goods useless, expensive repair may be justified, if the (conforming) goods are of high value. Conversely, replacement may be more appropriate if the goods are of low value.[133] In some cases the lack of conformity may be so severe that there is little point in attempting repair. In contrast, if a particular lack of conformity is very slight, repair may be more appropriate than replacement.

Finally, the degree of inconvenience that may be caused to the consumer by the provision of the particular remedy must be considered. This seems to be the only factor where the consumer's interests matter. Its effect may be that the consumer can insist on a remedy which would otherwise be considered disproportionate.

Any repair or replacement must be provided within a reasonable time and without any significant inconvenience to the consumer (Art 3(3)), taking into account the nature of the goods and the purposes for which the consumer required the goods. If the seller fails to do so, the

---

132 R Bradgate and C Twigg-Flesner, *Blackstone's Guide to the Sale of Consumer Goods and Associated Guarantees* (Oxford: OUP, 2003), chapter 4.
133 On the other hand a relatively minor lack of conformity might not justify expensive repair. This would be especially so if comparison with the remedies of price reduction and rescission were permitted.

consumer may demand either rescission of the contract or reduction of the price (Art 3(5)). In addition, if neither repair nor replacement produces the desired result, or neither is available, it may be possible for the consumer to ask for a price reduction (effectively a partial refund) or, ultimately, rescission (full refund) (Art 3(5)).

Rescission will not be available where the lack of conformity is minor (Art 3(6)). Moreover, where the consumer does exercise his right of rescission, he should be given a refund of the purchase price, although Member States may provide that account may be taken of the use the consumer has had of the product (Recital 15).

3.8.3 Connected lender liability

A provision dealing with the person against whom a remedy may be sought, rather than a specific remedy as such, is provided in the *Consumer Credit* Directive. Where goods or services, which are financed through a linked credit agreement, are not provided fully, or where they are not in conformity with the contract, the consumer may be able to ask for a remedy from the credit provider, provided that attempts to seek a remedy from the supplier of the goods or services have been unsuccessful (Art 15(2)).

3.8.4 Commercial agency – termination payments

The *Commercial Agency* Directive contains provisions dealing with the termination of the agency contract. Here, the commercial agent is entitled either to an indemnity or to compensation. At the time of adopting the Directive, Germany and France had in place two rather different systems for dealing with the financial consequences of terminating an agency contract, and in order to reach agreement on the Directive, it became necessary to include both systems, leaving each Member State to choose one or the other.[134] The first system is to indemnify the agent (Art 17(2)). The indemnity should reflect the number of new customers secured by the agent, and it should be equitable having regard to all the circumstances. It is subject to a cap based on the

---

134 Early experience with the Directive suggested that there were difficulties with interpreting and applying either provision, although the Commission has not put forward any proposals for updating the Directive (cf Commission, *Report of the application of Art 17 of Council Directive on the co-ordination of the law of the Member States relating to self-employed Commercial Agents* (COM (96) 364 final).

average annual remuneration of the agent calculated over a five-year period (or a shorter period if the contract was of shorter duration). The alternative system is the compensation system (Art 17(3)). It is intended to compensate the agent for the damage suffered because of the termination, particularly the loss of commission and the inability to amortise the costs and expense incurred during the performance of the contract.

However, no payment is made to an agent where the principal terminated the agency agreement because the agent was in default, justifying immediate termination; where the agent has terminated the contract (unless the principal was at fault, or the termination was on grounds of age, infirmity or illness); or where the agent has assigned his rights and duties under the agreement to another person (Art 18). It is not permissible for the parties to derogate from Arts 17 and 18 if this would be detrimental to the agent (Art 19); consequently, it is not permissible to calculate an indemnity on the basis of criteria other than those in Art 17(2), except where such alternative criteria would always be more favourable to the agent.[135]

The ECJ has made it clear that whilst the Directive specifies that each Member State must provide for either compensation or an indemnity, there is no specific requirement under European law with regard to the method used for calculating either, and Member States have some discretion.[136]

3.9 BEYOND CONTRACT LAW: ENFORCEMENT BY INJUNCTION

This chapter is primarily concerned with charting the impact of EU law on domestic contract law rules. However, it would be wrong to ignore one other significant contribution made by EU law, both in the context of specific directives such as those on *Unfair Contract Terms* (Art 7) and

---

135 C-465/04 *Honeyvem Informazioni Commerciali Srl v Mariella De Zotti* [2006] ECR I-2879 (in the context of a collective agreement setting out different criteria which were less favourable in the circumstances of the case).

136 C-381/98 *Ingmar GB Ltd v Eaton Leonard Technologies Inc* [2000] ECR I-9305, para 21 and C-465/04 *Honeyvem Informazioni Commerciali Srl v Mariella De Zotti*, para 35. It will be interesting to see how the court will respond in a case pending at the time of writing, which asks two specific questions about factors which might be relevant to the calculation of an indemnity: C-348/07 *Turgay Semen v Deutsche Tamoil GmbH* (2007) OJ C 235/10.

Late Payment (Art 3(4) and (5)), but also more generally in Directive 98/27/EC on injunctions for the protection of consumers' interests.[137] The combined effect of these provisions is that enforcement of all the consumer protection directives are not only a matter for individual consumers seeking to enforce their contract with a trader, but may also be undertaken by appropriate organisations. Indeed, in the context of unfair terms, the ECJ has held that, in certain circumstances, national courts faced with a consumer dispute may be required to adopt a pro-active approach: in *Oceano Grupo Editorial SA v Quintero*, the ECJ held that a domestic court could decide, of its own motion, that a term in a consumer contract is unfair and refuse to apply it:

> In disputes where the amounts involved are often limited, the lawyers' fees may be higher than the amount at stake, which may deter the consumer from contesting the application of an unfair term . . . there is a real risk that the consumer, particularly because of ignorance of the law, will not challenge the term pleaded against him on the grounds that it is unfair . . . (para 26).

The wider policing mechanisms introduced by the EU are a significant feature of consumer contract law, and have certainly had a noticeable impact in many Member States, but it is beyond the scope of this book to examine this in greater depth.

3.10 CONCLUSION

This chapter has attempted to sketch the impact of EU legislation on contract law. Much of the legislation affects consumer law and may therefore be regarded as a derogation from general contract law. Outside the consumer field, EU legislation deals with specific issues, and does not (yet) explicitly affect general contract law.

What may appear as a disjointed approach in this chapter is a reflection of the fragmentary nature of the *acquis*, as well as the lack of overall coherence. Over a period of more than 20 years, directives have been adopted dealing with particular issues, but little regard has been had to the relationship between the various measures. The result is a patchwork of measures which do not fit together well. Importantly, whilst there is *acquis* that touches on all aspects of contract law, it does

---

137 (1998) OJ L 166/51.

so in specific contexts, and there has not (yet) been any EU legislation that directly affects the general law of contract. However, the effect of the EU's activity is that it has established a competence to regulate aspects of contract law, at least in some circumstances. There is a need to review the legislation adopted thus far, and steps to that effect have already been taken. Moreover, it does raise the question whether the EU can, and should, do more in the field of contract law. These issues are addressed in later chapters.

4   Impact on national law

4.1 INTRODUCTION

The previous chapters concentrated on the framework at the European level within which the process of Europeanisation occurs. It was seen there that this is largely done through the adoption of directives, and supplemented by relevant judgments of the European Court of Justice. The overview of the core *acquis* in the contract law field revealed that EU law permeates most areas of contract law, albeit only with regard to consumer contracts, or other particular types of contract.

The reliance on directives means that Europeanisation involves a considerable amount of interaction between the national jurisdictions of the 27 Member States and the European level, and the adoption of a harmonising measure by the European institutions is only the first step. The effectiveness of Europeanisation depends almost entirely on the correct implementation into national law of the various directives discussed previously. Every Member State is under an obligation to ensure that steps are taken fully to implement a harmonising measure into their domestic laws. This obligation may be divided into two distinct stages, ensuring that (1) the relevant legal framework meets the requirements of the harmonising measure; and (2) the application of the domestic rules giving effect to a harmonising measure does not undermine the effectiveness of the European measure.

The purpose of this chapter is therefore to consider the impact of the harmonisation programme on domestic contract law, focusing in particular on English law. In considering the impact of EU law on domestic contract law, three broad areas merit consideration. First, there is the process of implementing the various directives into domestic law. In Chapter 2, it was seen that Member States have some freedom in the methods they choose in order to give effect to a directive in their national law. English law is different from many other EU countries because its contract law is largely uncodified, and this chapter will focus on the approach taken in this jurisdiction. Second, it is necessary to consider how the domestic courts have interpreted and applied legislation which implements an EU directive. Finally, at a more general level, it may be considered to what extent the Europeanisation process has affected domestic contract law generally, for example, by considering whether it has resulted in a change to established principles or doctrines. It is not possible within the confines of this book to undertake a full survey of the impact of all the directives on domestic law; instead, a number of key issues are identified, and particular areas are selected by way of illustration.

4.2 IMPLEMENTATION INTO DOMESTIC LAW – GENERAL CONSIDERATIONS

For the Europeanisation process to work, Member States need to take care when implementing directives into national law. In Chapter 2, it was seen that the results-focused nature of a directive leaves a degree of freedom to the Member States in choosing the method of implementation. Exclusive reliance on case law is unlikely to be acceptable even in a jurisdiction such as England, making it necessary to adopt or amend legislation. However, there is a reasonable leeway in drafting the implementing legislation in that it is not obligatory to retain the text of a directive verbatim in domestic law. Rather, terminology and a drafting style appropriate to each national law can be chosen, provided that the overall aim of the directive, as well as the need to ensure that rights can be easily identified, are not undermined. Where there is pre-existing legislation in the field covered by a directive, it may be sufficient to amend or even retain this, as long as it meets the requirements of the directive.

A problem is the piecemeal approach of EU legislation, causing EU matters to appear in unexpected areas.[1] As seen in the previous chapter, directives deal with particular issues, and introduce provisions for a limited range of contracts. This will inevitably pose a risk to the coherence and consistency of national law, and it will have to be considered carefully whether legislation should be adopted in separate

---

1 T Wilhelmsson, 'Jack-in-the-box theory of European Community law', in LD Eriksson and S Hurri (eds), *Dialectic of Law and Reality* (Helsinki: Faculty of Law, 1999).

provisions and limited to the scope of the directive, or whether there should be wider changes to national law.[2]

Having considered these fundamental questions, there are then the following matters each Member State needs to consider as part of the implementation process.

4.2.1 Minimum harmonisation

Some of the directives in the contract law field are minimum harmonisation measures. As explained earlier,[3] Member States retain the freedom to adopt provisions which offer greater protection, for example to consumers, than required under the directive, provided that they are compatible with the Treaty.[4] Consequently, a Member State has to consider whether it wishes to exceed the minimum standard and provide a higher level of protection. In practice, it will often be the case that the minimum harmonisation principle facilitates the retention of existing rules, rather than the introduction of rules which are more protective than the corresponding directive. Minimum harmonisation might, on occasion, encourage a slapdash approach to implementation, relying on existing provisions without giving sufficient consideration as to how existing and new rules fit together.[5]

The exact implications of a minimum harmonisation clause for the residual legislative freedom of the Member States in the field occupied by a directive remain something of a grey area.[6] One difficulty with exceeding a minimum standard is that it has never been explored by the ECJ just how much leeway there is for national law to depart from the core of a directive. Rott has argued that the freedom of the Member State may be more limited than is often thought, particularly with regard to those aspects of a directive which were the focus of protracted negotiations during the legislative procedure.[7] For example, Rott suggests

---

2 WH Roth, 'Transposing "pointilist" EU guidelines into systematic national codes – problems and consequences' (2002) 6 *European Review of Private Law* 761–76.
3 Chapter 2, p 41.
4 See, eg, C-441/04 *A-Punkt Schmuckhandels GmbH v Schmidt* [2006] ECR I-2093 on the compatibility of a total prohibition of selling jewellery door-to-door.
5 An example from English law is the implementation of the Consumer Sales Directive (99/44/EC).
6 This might be one of the reasons behind the increasing shift towards abandoning minimum harmonisation.
7 P Rott, 'Minimum harmonisation for the completion of the internal market? The example of consumer sales law' (2003) 40 *Common Market Law Review* 1107–35.

that the provisions of the Consumer Sales Directive (99/44/EC) on the goods' conformity with the contract and the consumer's remedies in case of non-conformity should be transposed into domestic law without altering their substance. With regard to the remedies, this implies that the strict hierarchy should be maintained and that changes to this, as well as making available other remedies such as damages concurrently with the Directive's remedial hierarchy, is not permissible.[8] Although his arguments are persuasive, Rott relies on case law developed in the context of the Product Liability Directive (85/374/EEC),[9] which does not contain a minimum harmonisation clause, and therefore has been held to be of a full harmonisation standard. Consequently, there may be more flexibility with minimum harmonisation measures than suggested by Rott.

4.2.2 Regulatory options

Aside from minimum harmonisation clauses, directives also frequently include regulatory options, that is, provisions which grant Member States permission to introduce a particular provision, without making it mandatory for all countries to do so. A decision will therefore have to be taken whether a particular option should be utilised and the relevant provision be transposed into national law. For example, in the Consumer Sales Directive (99/44/EC), there are four separate regulatory options: exclusion of second-hand goods sold at public auction (Art 1(3)); obligation on consumer to notify lack of conformity within two months (Art 5(2)); a reduced period of liability for second-hand goods (Art 7(2)); and a language requirement for guarantees (Art 6(4)). In respect of each of these options, Member States can choose whether to introduce a corresponding provision into their domestic law.[10]

4.2.3 Matters left for Member States to resolve

A third feature of many directives is that they leave certain matters for national law to decide. It is then for each Member State to come up with

---

8 *Ibid.*, pp 1123–29.
9 C-52/00 *Commission v France* [2002] ECR I-3827.
10 Evidence from the Member States suggests that the use of these options has varied: see H Schulte-Nölke, C Twigg-Flesner and M Ebers, *Consumer Compendium – Comparative Analysis* (2008), section H.

appropriate rules to ensure that national law responds to the obligation of introducing a rule. For example, Art 4 of the Doorstep Selling Directive (85/577/EEC) states that 'Member States shall ensure that their national legislation lays down appropriate consumer protection measures in cases where the information referred to in this Article is not supplied', but leaves it to the Member States to come up with appropriate measures.[11]

Indeed, deciding on appropriate sanctions for failing to comply with substantive provisions in directives is often left to the Member States. Thus, Art 20 of the e-Commerce Directive (2000/31/EC) states that 'Member States shall determine the sanctions applicable to infringements of national provisions adopted pursuant to this Directive . . .', adding that such sanctions '. . . shall be effective, proportionate and dissuasive'. Similar provisions can be found in many other directives.[12]

4.2.4 Ambiguities in a directive

A particular challenge for a Member State will arise if the text of a directive is ambiguous. Such ambiguities may arise both with regard to definitions of core terms and substantive rules. Moreover, although the directives in the field of contract law contain definitions of many of the terms used in these measures, specific *legal* concepts, such as 'damage' or 'breach of contract', remain undefined altogether. It might be assumed that these concepts are the same, or sufficiently similar, in all the Member States, but whilst it may be possible to provide a translation of the word(s) that make(s) up a particular legal concept, the substance is likely to be different.[13] This can make it more difficult for a Member State to identify what exactly a directive requires. In such a situation, Member States need to consider the respective merits of copying out the provision of a directive to demonstrate compliance with EU law, at least at the formal level of the legislative text, against those of attempting to clarify the law by adopting more

---

11 These may, of course, be subject to review by the ECJ, as has indeed been the case with this particular provision: see Chapter 3, p 72.

12 This is in line with the case law developed by the ECJ on effectiveness and national remedies: see Steiner, Woods and Twigg-Flesner, *EU Law*, 9th edn, chapter 8, section 8.5.

13 See A Gambaro, 'The plan d'action of the European Commission – a comment' [2003] *European Review of Private Law* 768–81.

detailed rules and increasing the risk of state liability for incorrect implementation.[14]

Furthermore, when adding to provisions of a directive in domestic law, Member States need to be mindful of the overarching obligation under EU law to ensure that the effectiveness of a directive is not undermined. One example where the ECJ took a dim view of a Member State's decision to add to a directive is *Cofidis SA v Fredout*[15] in the context of the Unfair Contract Terms Directive. A French court requested a preliminary ruling on whether a domestic law prohibition that prevented a national court, on expiry of a limitation period, from ruling on the unfairness of a contract term was precluded by the Directive. The ECJ, having considered the *Oceano* judgment,[16] held that a limitation period on the court's power to set aside an unfair term, whether of its own motion or based on a plea by the consumer, would undermine the effectiveness of the relevant provisions of the Directive. In particular, such a period would enable a seller or supplier to wait until that limitation period had expired before commencing legal action which sought to rely on the terms that might otherwise be unfair.[17]

It is clear, therefore, that the obligation of implementing a directive requires a significant amount of care to be successful. The number of issues that have to be considered may raise concern about the overall effectiveness of the practice of Europeanisation by directives – there are several systemic flaws which can make it difficult to attain the goal of a more integrated common market.

4.3 POST-IMPLEMENTATION ISSUES

Although a review and adjustment of domestic legislation in the field occupied by a harmonising measure is essential to ensuring consistency

---

14 Although if a directive is ambiguous and a Member State implements it in a manner which is reasonably consistent with what the directive is capable of meaning, it is likely that a claim in state liability would be unsuccessful: C-392/93 *R v HM Treasury, ex parte British Telecommunications plc* [1996] ECR I-1631 and C-319/96 *Brinkman Tabakfabriken v Skatteministeriet* [1998] ECR I-5255.

15 C-473/00 *Cofidis SA v Jean-Louis Fredout* [2002] ECR I-10875, paras 32–3.

16 C-240-244/98 *Oceano Grupo Editorial SA v Rocio Quintero and others* [2000] ECR I-4941; see Chapter 3, p 100.

17 In basing its decision on the general principle of effectiveness, the ECJ had to distinguish its earlier jurisprudence on time limits, such as C-33/76 *Rewe* [1976] ECR 1989 and C-261/95 *Palmisani* [1997] ECR I-4025.

and compliance at a technical level, this alone is unlikely to be sufficient to ensure the full and effective operation of a directive in the domestic legal context. The subsequent application of the law, particularly by the courts, is just as relevant in this regard. Domestic courts need to ensure that they interpret the national implementing legislation in such a way as not to undermine the objective pursued by the relevant directive.

4.3.1 Autonomous interpretation of EU law

A long-established principle of EU law is the obligation on national courts to adopt an 'autonomous interpretation' of European legislation. This means that the approach to interpreting domestic legislation implementing an EU directive must reflect the European origins of the legislation by not relying on established national law, or the national laws of another Member State, in interpreting such a provision.[18] Thus, the court has observed that

> ... [t]he need for uniform application of Community law and the principle of equality require that the terms of a provision of Community law which makes no express reference to the law of the Member States for the purpose of determining its meaning and scope must normally be given an autonomous and uniform interpretation throughout the Community; that interpretation must take into account the context of the provision and the purpose of the legislation in question.[19]

This has been justified on the following basis:

> The reason for this approach is that only autonomous interpretation can achieve the full effectiveness of a directive, as well as its uniform application by the Member States.[20]

A problem with the obligation of autonomous interpretation is that the meaning given to the same term in the context of several directives may

---

18 See also J Mance, 'Is Europe aiming to civilise the common law?' [2007] *European Business Law Review* 77–99, p 96.
19 Case C-287/98 *Luxembourg v Linster* [2000] ECR I-6917; see also Case 327/82 *Ekro v Produktschap voor Vee en Vlees* [1984] ECR 107, para 11.
20 C-151/02 *Landeshauptstadt Kiel v Jaeger* [2003] ECR I-8389, para 58.

vary as between these measures.[21] Although there will be a European meaning in the particular context, there may not be a single European interpretation.[22]

In essence, therefore, the interpretation of legislation implementing an EU directive should not follow whatever approach may already have been established in a particular domestic law previously.[23] Instead, a separate 'European' interpretation should be adopted. This is perhaps less of a challenge in those areas where a directive introduces provisions which are new to a particular jurisdiction,[24] but where existing domestic provisions or established domestic terminology is used, this may be more difficult. Indeed, reliance on existing provisions/terminology may cause greater confusion for domestic law, because of the need for autonomous interpretation in respect of aspects falling within the scope of the relevant EU measure. Often, existing rules will have a wider scope, which may result in different interpretations having to be adopted based on whether a particular situation falls within the ambit of EU law or not.

The domestic courts are, of course, not entirely left to their own devices, and can seek a preliminary ruling from the ECJ under Art 234, which would provide guidance on the interpretation of a particular provision.[25] However, such references can take up a significant amount of time, which may delay the resolution of a dispute by such an extent that the parties might prefer to abandon their case altogether, or proceed without seeking further guidance.

4.3.2 Challenges for national courts

Although the principle of autonomous interpretation seems easy enough to state, it may be challenging for national courts to honour it in practice. In particular, whilst *interpretation* needs to be autonomous (that

---

21 Contrast the meaning of 'damage' in the context of Directive 85/374/EEC on product liability, as interpreted by the ECJ in C-203/99 *Veedfald v Arhus Amtskommune* [2001] ECR I-3569 with the meaning given to the same term in the Package Travel Directive in C-168/00 *Simone Leitner v TUI Deutschland* [2002] ECR I-2631.

22 Cf S Whittaker, 'The terminology of civil protection: rights, remedies and procedures' in B Pozzo and V Jacometti, *Multilingualism and the Harmonisation of European Private Law* (The Hague: Kluwer, 2006).

23 See also C-296/95 *R v Commissioners of Customs and Excise ex parte EMU Tabac SARL* [1998] ECR I-1605.

24 Although cf the response by the English courts under the Commercial Agents Regulations. See 4.5.2, below.

25 See further, Chapter 2, p 43.

is, European), national courts enjoy more discretion with regard to the *application* of the legislation to specific cases.

In dealing with the challenges for national courts regarding correct interpretation, an initial distinction needs to be made between the situation where a directive has (in a formal sense) been correctly transposed into domestic law, and where there are shortcomings in the implementing legislation.

Assuming that a directive has been correctly implemented into domestic law, the obligation of ensuring an autonomous European interpretation is clear. Whether the courts will in fact do so may depend on whether the directive was implemented by adopting new legislation, or if existing law was deemed sufficient to give effect to the requirements of a directive. Where existing legislation was regarded as sufficient, the problems of interpretation are similar. A domestic court who can look to an established line of cases applying the domestic legislation may not realise that established domestic law is now 'polluted' by a harmonising measure, and that this may necessitate a different approach to interpreting and applying such legislation.

A further factor is the terminology employed in the national legislation. Where new legislation has been adopted, but the terminology resembles familiar domestic concepts, there is a risk that existing practice will be maintained, and the legislation will be interpreted by following the established understanding, which would undermine the correct interpretation of the directive.

Even where the terminology that is used in domestic law is new and therefore unfamiliar, especially because national law is a verbatim implementation of a directive, there is a risk either that a domestic court may come up with an interpretation which would not be shared by the ECJ, or that a court may consider how the courts in other Member States have approached this issue and follow their lead. In the latter case, whilst a comparative approach may be welcomed by some, it does not inevitably guarantee the correct and effective application of a harmonising measure.

The task for the domestic courts may be made more difficult if there is a defect in the formal implementation of a directive into domestic law, for example because a Member State has taken no steps to implement a directive, or the implementing legislation contains gaps or other defects. In other areas of EU law, the doctrine of direct effect may assist.[26] This permits a domestic court to consider the text of a directive

---

26 Case 41/74 *Van Duyn v Home Office* [1974] ECR 1337.

itself, where there has been no, or a defective, implementation of a directive, and permit an individual to enforce rights conferred by that directive. This doctrine only applies to provisions which are sufficiently clear and precise, unconditional, and leave no room for discretion in implementation.[27] Moreover, it can only be invoked in circumstances where an individual is seeking to enforce rights against a public body ('vertical direct effect').[28] It cannot therefore be invoked where an individual is seeking to rely on a directive as against another individual ('horizontal direct effect'). The ECJ has time and again denied the availability of direct effect in such circumstances.[29]

However, in order to fill this possible gap in the protection of individuals, the ECJ has developed the principle of indirect effect, or consistent interpretation, which can be invoked both when domestic legislation has been expressly adopted to implement a directive, and where pre-existing legislation is deemed to be sufficient. In the seminal *Marleasing* decision,[30] the ECJ established that domestic courts are obliged to interpret domestic legislation, in so far as possible, in accordance with corresponding EU legislation.[31] This obligation applies to the domestic law in the field covered by the Directive, irrespective of whether it was adopted before or after the directive, except where national law cannot reasonably be interpreted in this way.[32]

Where the principle applies, it may allow a person to enforce particular rights against another person, although it must be emphasised that this method of interpretation may not result in the creation of entirely new obligations on an individual, nor produce a form of 'indirect horizontal direct effect'. In the context of contract law, the principle may therefore be of limited assistance.

As can be seen, there are strict obligations on the national courts to ensure that national legislation is interpreted in a European sense. However, it is equally clear that when it comes to the *application* of the law in particular cases, national courts enjoy a greater degree of

27 C-441/99 *Riksskatteverket v Soghra Gharehveran* [2001] ECR I-7686.
28 Case 152/84 *Marshall v Southampton & South West Hampshire Area Health Authority (Teaching)* [1986] ECR 723; C-188/89 *Foster v British Gas plc* [1990] ECR I-3461.
29 In the context of contract law directives, see C-91/92 *Faccini Dori v Recreb SRL* [1994] ECR I-3325 and C-192/94 *El Corte Ingles SA v Rivero* [1996] ECR I-1281.
30 C-106/89 *Marleasing SA v La Comercial Interacional de Alimentacion SA* [1990] ECR I-4135.
31 On the potential of this decision for the Europeanisation of private law, see M Amstutz, 'In-between worlds: *Marleasing* and the emergence of interlegality in legal reasoning' (2005) 11 *European Law Journal* 766–84.
32 C-334/92 *Wagner Miret v Fondo de Garantira Salaria* [1993] ECR I-6911.

discretion. The ECJ has, particularly in recent times, drawn a clear distinction between interpretation and application. For example, as noted earlier, in *Freiburger Kommunalbauten,*[33] the interpretation of the unfairness test in the Unfair Contract Terms Directive was held to be a matter for the ECJ, but the application to the facts of the case was a matter for national law.[34] This neatly demonstrates that the ECJ's role is limited and that national courts retain some discretion regarding the application of EU-based rules. Whilst this might pose a risk of divergent outcomes in similar cases, it also reflects the recognition of national (and even local) factors which influence the outcome of particular cases.

4.4 IMPLEMENTING EU LAW IN THE UK

Having considered the general issues that arise with regard to the implementation of directives, the specific approach taken in the UK will now be examined.[35] First, the UK's general approach to implementing EU directives will be outlined. This will be followed by an analysis of how the English courts have handled the interpretation of implementing legislation in two key areas: unfair terms and commercial agency.

4.4.1 Framework for implementation

EU directives, particularly in the field of contract law, have been implemented in regulations under s 2(2) of the European Communities Act 1972 (ECA), as amended. Many of the directives in question deal with matters on which there is no pre-existing domestic legislation, and their implementation consequently occurs through free-standing regulations.[36] However, where there already is legislation in place, the

---

33 C-237/02 *Freiburger Kommunalbauten GmbH Baugesellschaft & Co KG v Hofstetter* [2004] ECR-I 3403; see p 47.
34 See also case C-465/04 *Honeyvem Informazioni Commerciali Srl v Mariella De Zotti* [2006] ECR I-2879 in the context of commercial agency, discussed below.
35 See also S Whittaker, 'Form and substance in the reception of EU Directives into English contract law' (2007) 3 *European Review of Contract Law* 381–409. On the implications for codified systems, see Roth (2002), *op. cit.*, and for a Dutch perspective M Loos, 'The influence of European consumer law on general contract law' (2007) 15 *European Review of Private Law* 515–31.
36 Eg, with respect to doorstep selling or distance selling.

UK has generally attempted to amend this legislation to bring it into line with its obligations under EU law.[37] One obvious example where the implementation of a directive resulted in the adoption of regulations that operated alongside pre-existing legislation is the field of unfair contract terms, where the Unfair Contract Terms Act 1977 was retained when the Unfair Terms in Consumer Contracts Regulations 1999 were adopted. Eventually, the Law Commission was asked to propose new legislation that would combine the two measures into one more coherent piece of legislation, but its proposals[38] have yet to be enacted.

Section 2(2) ECA enables the adoption of orders, rules, regulations or schemes to implement directives or any other EU obligations, as well as to deal with 'matters arising out of or related to any such obligation' (s 2(2)(b) ECA). On the one hand, this power is broad in that it can be used to enact provisions which would otherwise have to be adopted by primary legislation (that is, an Act of Parliament), including amendments to existing primary legislation. On the other, the use of s 2(2) ECA has historically been problematic, because the power it granted was limited to measures necessary to give effect to EU obligations. This meant that wider reforms to domestic law to ensure that the EU-derived provisions fit better with existing law could not be undertaken by using s 2(2) ECA, and primary legislation was necessary. This explains the retention of two separate measures dealing with unfair contract terms, for example. The relevant directive only deals with unfair terms in consumer contracts, whereas the earlier Unfair Contract Terms Act 1977 also applies to non-consumer contracts, as well as terms which have been negotiated.

This position has now been modified by the Legislative and Regulatory Reform Act 2006 (LRRA). The LLRA empowers the government to adopt regulations which can remove or reduce any burden resulting from existing legislation, for example where the legislation imposes unnecessary costs or administrative inconvenience, or is a general obstacle to efficiency, productivity or profitability (s 1(3) LLRA); this includes burdens which are caused by legislation which is difficult to understand (s 1(4) LLRA). Until the LLRA was enacted, it would frequently have been impossible to implement EU legislation under s 2(2) ECA and amend related domestic law to reduce the overall burden, because the relevant procedure to be followed under the ECA

37 Eg, on timeshare and sale of goods.
38 Law Commission, *Unfair Terms in Contracts – Report 292* (London: TSO, 2005).

could be different from that under other legislation.[39] The changes
introduced by the LLRA make it possible to combine the order-
marking powers under the ECA and the LLRA, even where different
procedures need to be followed for particular provisions.[40]

However, these changes are only a limited improvement: they only
operate where there is scope for reducing any burden as a result of the
enactment of legislation. Perhaps the combination of the two unfair
terms regimes could be undertaken on this basis, if only because
revised legislation might be better understood. But if the intention is to
broaden the scope of legislation beyond what is required by an EU
directive, then primary legislation will almost certainly still be needed,
unless such an approach can be shown to reduce the overall burden.
Thus, with respect to the extension of the UK's rules on doorstep selling contracts to circumstances where a trader's visit was solicited,[41] the
enactment of a new enabling power in the Consumers, Estate Agents
and Redress Act 2007 was required.[42]

4.4.2 Minimum harmonisation

With regard to minimum harmonisation directives, the general approach
in the UK is to adhere to the minimum standard only and not to engage
in what is known as 'gold-plating'.[43] However, in the field of consumer
law, it has generally sought to maintain existing levels of consumer
protection, and a degree of gold-plating has been accepted.

An example of heavy reliance on a minimum harmonisation clause is
the implementation of the Consumer Sales Directive (99/44/EC). The
decision was taken to retain the existing Sale of Goods Act 1979, but to
add the remedial regime from Art 3 of the Directive[44] to the legislation.
Thus, instead of introducing the 'conformity with the contract' test, the

---

39 Statutory instruments may be adopted either by the negative resolution procedure
(the instrument will enter into force unless Parliament resolves not to pass it), or the
affirmative resolution procedure (requiring a vote by Parliament to give effect to the
instrument).
40 For further discussion of the LRRA, see, eg, P Davis, 'The significance of parliamentary procedures in control of the Executive: a case study: the passage of Part 1 of
the Legislative and Regulatory Reform Act 2006' [2007] *Public Law* 677–700.
41 See Chapter 3 on the exclusion of such visits from the scope of the Directive, and
below for a more detailed account of the Directive's implementation into UK law.
42 See s 59 of the Act.
43 Department for Business, Enterprise and Regulatory Reform, *Transposition Guide:
How to Implement European Directives Effectively*, September 2007, para 3.24.
44 See Chapter 3, at 3.8.2.

existing implied terms that goods must correspond with their description,[45] be of satisfactory quality[46] and reasonably fit for any particular purpose made known to the seller[47] were retained on the basis that these fulfilled the same purpose. More controversially, the right to terminate the contract of sale for breach of the implied terms was also kept, and exists alongside the new remedies.[48] The retention of existing provisions was generally justified on the basis that they met or exceeded the minimum standard set by the Directive. This may be so, but it seems that the existence of the minimum standard was used as a smoke-screen to avoid having to consider more carefully how the requirements of the Directive could be integrated into domestic law. As a result, the remedies available to consumers are complex and difficult to understand. Unsurprisingly, the government has been urged to amend the legislation, possibly by asking the Law Commission to propose a better system of remedies, as was indeed done in late 2007 (no proposals made as yet).[49]

4.4.3 Open issues

The implementation of the Doorstep Selling Directive is a good example of how the UK dealt with aspects in respect of which action was required without there being specific instruction in the Directive itself. As seen in the previous chapter, the Doorstep Selling Directive only requires that consumers are given a right of withdrawal for contracts to which the Directive applies, and that consumers are adequately informed about this right. This is the full extent of the 'result' to be achieved.[50] Many matters related to both the right of cancellation and the obligation to provide information about this right are left for the Member States to address. Thus, it is for domestic law to provide 'appropriate consumer protection measures' (Art 4, final sentence) if the consumer is not given the requisite information about the right of cancellation. The procedure for exercising the right of withdrawal is also for the Member States to decide upon (Art 5(1)), as are the legal

---

45 Section 13(1), Sale of Goods Act 1979.
46 Section 14(2), Sale of Goods Act 1979.
47 Section 14(3), Sale of Goods Act 1979.
48 For a detailed analysis of the implementation of the Directive into English law, see R Bradgate and C Twigg-Flesner, *Blackstone's Guide to Consumer Sales and Associated Guarantees* (Oxford: OUP, 2003).
49 See *Davidson Review – Final Report* (London: Better Regulation Executive, 2006) paras 3.10–3.23.
50 Cf Art 249 of the Treaty.

effects of exercising the right to cancel, especially with regard to the return of any prepayments and goods supplied under the contract (Art 7).

The Directive was implemented into UK law in the Consumer Protection (Cancellation of Contracts Concluded away from Business Premises) Regulations 1987 (SI 1987/2117). This was one of the first contract law directives, and the text of the Regulations differs significantly from that of the directive in that the language is more familiar to an English lawyer. For present purposes, the focus is on how the UK dealt with the various aspects that needed to be regulated at national level without there being prescriptive rules in the Directive itself. Thus, with regard to a failure to provide information about the right of withdrawal at the correct time, the Regulations provide that the contract is not enforceable against the consumer.[51] This appears to be a permanent consequence, and even if the consumer is subsequently informed about this right, the contract remains unenforceable. In light of how later directives deal with this issue,[52] the retention of this approach is surprising. In addition to the unenforceability of the contract, criminal sanctions for failing to provide information about the right of withdrawal were introduced.[53]

The right of withdrawal itself has to be exercised by giving notice in writing to the trader.[54] The Regulations provide a model cancellation form, but its use is not mandatory.

National law also has to address the legal effects of the consumer's decision to withdraw from the contract. The main consequence is that the contract is treated as if it had never been entered into by the consumer.[55] Regulations 5–8 deal with the related consequences of withdrawal. Any money paid by the consumer must be repaid, and if the consumer has in his possession any goods supplied under the contract, he will have a lien (a security interest) over those goods with regard to any money that is repayable to him.[56] If the contract includes a credit element, this will be deemed to continue until the consumer has repaid the whole or a portion of the credit either within one month of cancelling, or, where the credit is repayable by instalments, before the date on

---

51 Regulation 4(1).
52 Generally, the withdrawal period starts to run once the information has been provided, even if this is done a long time after the conclusion of the contract.
53 Regulations 4A–4H, added in 1998.
54 Regulation 4(5).
55 Regulation 4(6).
56 Regulation 5.

which the first instalment is due.[57] Regulation 7 obliges the consumer to 'restore' the goods to the trader and to take reasonable care of them until this has happened, which means that they must be available for collection from his home. The consumer may return the goods himself, but he is not obliged to do so; where he does, he needs to take reasonable care to ensure that the goods are received and not damaged in transit.[58]

The duty to restore does not apply to goods which are perishable; goods which by their nature are consumed by use and were so consumed by the time the contract was cancelled; goods supplied in an emergency, or goods incorporated into land or another thing not part of the contract. Where this is the case, the consumer has to pay for the goods and any services provided in connection with the goods in accordance with the term of the contract. This seems surprising as the effect of the withdrawal is that the contract never existed, yet the consumer is obliged to pay at the contract price. Hellwege argues that the better solution would be to require the consumer to pay for the value of the goods,[59] rather than their contract price, although this may be unacceptable if the contract price is lower than the value of the goods.

Finally, if the consumer has provided goods in part exchange and the trader has already received them, the trader must return them in a condition 'substantially as good as when they were delivered to the trader' within 10 days from when the contract was cancelled. If this is not possible, the consumer is entitled to receive a sum of money equal to the value given to the part-exchange goods.

From this brief overview of the UK's implementation of the Directive, it can be seen that a very short instruction in a directive can bring about a detailed set of national rules. In view of the limited guidance given in the Directive, it is not surprising that there is a considerable degree of variation across the Member States, particularly with regard to the effects of withdrawing from a contract.[60]

---

57 Regulation 6.
58 Presumably, this means that they should be sent in appropriate packaging, and, possibly, by recorded delivery, although there is no express obligation to that effect in the Regulations.
59 P Hellwege, 'Consumer Protection in Britain in Need of Reform' (2004) 63 *Cambridge Law Journal* 712–41, p 731.
60 See H Schulte-Nölke, C Twigg-Flesner and M Ebers, *Consumer Compendium – Comparative Analysis* (2006), section A.

4.4.4 Evaluation

The implementation of contract-law-related measures into domestic law is problematic, not least because the directives frequently deal with isolated and specific issues which have some impact on general contract law, but do not require a fundamental change. On one view, the UK, and English law in particular, can absorb EU contract law measures with a degree of ease, because most areas of contract law remain common law based and therefore uncodified. Most other European jurisdictions have a codified system of contract law, and greater effort may be required to slot EU-derived rules into the system of such codes. However, whilst free-standing legislation can be enacted to satisfy EU obligations, there is a risk that separate measures may be insufficiently co-ordinated with one another, which might result in unnecessary incoherence in domestic law. Hellwege, for example, has argued that the introduction of a right of withdrawal in various consumer protection measures lacks coherence as between these measures, as well as with wider principles of contract law and restitution,[61] although this view seems to be influenced by a desire for a more systematic and rigidly coherent approach more familiar to other jurisdictions. However, unnecessary discrepancies within national law may cause problems, and greater thought may need to be given to the relationship between new and existing implementing measures in related areas of contract law.

4.5 INTERPRETATION AND APPLICATION BY NATIONAL COURTS

The role of the domestic courts has already been outlined in general terms. In addition to their obligation to ensure that domestic legislation is interpreted in an EU-law-compliant manner, the courts may also be called upon to consider the wider implications of particular implementing measures for contract law generally. Unfortunately, there are few reported cases of relevance. One example for a situation where a domestic court had to deal with the impact of EU-based legislation on contract law was *Commissioners of Customs and Excise v Robertson's Electrical Ltd*.[62] Here, the Scottish Inner House had to consider the effect of a right of withdrawal under the legislation implementing the

---

61 Hellwege, *op. cit.*
62 [2006] SCLR 493.

Distance Selling Directive (97/7/EC) in the context of determining the tax point for charging value added tax (VAT). It was argued that a contract in respect of which there was a right of withdrawal was equivalent to a contract for the supply of goods on approval,[63] which would mean that the tax point was the end of the withdrawal period. This was rejected by the Court, which held that the existence of a right of withdrawal does not change the fundamental nature of the transaction; rather, it is a concluded contract with a 'statutory right to annul it'.[64] The legislation did not address this particular issue, and so it was for the court to provide clarification.

On the limited evidence available,[65] the English (and Scottish) courts recognise the European background to domestic law and generally seek to respect the principle of autonomous interpretation.[66] For example, when the Court of Appeal had to consider,[67] in light of the definition of 'goods or services', whether the legislation implementing the Unfair Terms Directive (93/13/EEC) applied to a situation in which a local council provides housing to tenants, Laws LJ was quick to emphasise the European origins of the legislation.[68] He undertook an extensive review of the Directive's legislative history, as well as other language versions of the Directive,[69] and discovered that the equivalent phrase in other versions of the Directive was capable of including both immovables and movables. Laws LJ rejected the suggestion that the legislation only applied 'to "contracts for goods and services as an English lawyer would understand those terms" '[70] by saying:

> European legislation has to be read as a single corpus of law binding across the member states. And the proposition leads to absurdity ... In our domestic law, these distinctions [between movables and immovables] have a long history and a present utility. In the

63 There is no transfer of property in such circumstances until the goods supplied have been approved.
64 Para [17] of the judgment.
65 The number of reported cases involving EU contract law measures in the UK is rather small.
66 It would appear that this is not so in many other Member States – see L Niglia, 'The non-Europeanisation of private law' (2001) 4 *European Review of Private Law* 575–99.
67 *The London Borough of Newham v Kathu, Zeb and Iqbal, and the Office of Fair Trading (Interested Party)* [2004] EWCA Civ 55 (24 February 2004).
68 Para 57.
69 Notably the French, Italian, Spanish and Portuguese versions.
70 Mr Underwood, counsel for the public authority, cited by Laws LJ at para 78.

context of a Europe-wide scheme of consumer protection, they could be nothing but an embarrassing eccentricity.[71]

This approach is commendable, because it reflects a clear recognition of the EU law background of the legislation and the need to avoid maintaining an interpretation that might correspond with a domestic understanding, but would undermine the Europeanisation objective. However, this particular example also illustrates the difficulties for the national courts – the phrase 'goods or services' had to be interpreted in a manner that seems at odds with their natural, or even previously established legal, meaning.

The following section will examine in more depth how the English courts (and, in some instances, the Scottish courts) have dealt with both the interpretation and application of national legislation based on EU directives, focusing on the areas of unfair contract terms and commercial agency.

4.5.1 Example 1: unfair contract terms and good faith

The *Unfair Contract Terms* Directive (93/13/EEC) was implemented into domestic law in two attempts, first in the Unfair Terms in Consumer Contracts Regulations 1994, replaced with a new version in 1999.[72] As seen earlier, the Directive introduces a general test of fairness applicable to all non-negotiated terms in a consumer contract. One of the elements of that test is the criterion of 'good faith', a concept which had not previously found its way into English contract law.[73] The implementation of the Directive resulted in an intense debate about the meaning, scope and implications of the 'good faith' principle, and whether the courts would be able to apply this concept sensibly. Early signs (albeit at County Court level) were not promising.[74]

---

71 Para 78 of his judgment.
72 The 1994 Regulations had some shortcomings, leading to their replacement with the Unfair Terms in Consumer Contracts Regulations 1999 (SI 1999/2083). On the 1994 Regulations, see R Brownsword and G Howells, 'The implementation of the EU Directive on unfair terms in consumer contracts – some unresolved questions' [1995] *Journal of Business Law* 243–63.
73 With the exception of the Commercial Agency Directive.
74 See the discussion of *Gosling v Burrard-Lucas* [1999] *Current Law* para 197, *Broadwater Manor School v Davis* [1999] *Current Law* para 208 and *Falco Finance v Gough* [1999] *CCLR 16* in R Bradgate, 'Experience in the United Kingdom', in *The Integration of Directive 93/13/EEC into the National Legal Systems* (European Commission, 1999).

This changed when the House of Lords was given an opportunity to consider the test in *Director-General of Fair Trading v First National Bank*.[75] The key issue in this case was the fairness of a term inserted by the respondent bank into its loan agreements which permitted it to charge further interest on the outstanding part of a loan, even after a court had, in default proceedings, made an order regarding the repayment of the loan. The judge in the High Court concluded that the term was fair,[76] but the Court of Appeal disagreed.[77] Both courts focused on whether the obligation to pay post-judgment interest contained in the term challenged was unfair to the consumer. The House of Lords, concluding that the term was not unfair, took a different approach: it was found that the legislative framework on consumer credit agreements[78] did not allow for the County Court to award statutory interest on a judgment debt for agreements subject to the Consumer Credit Act 1974. The bank could therefore only charge interest after such a judgment if the loan agreement contained a term to that effect. Consumer credit law did not include anything that prohibited an agreement to charge further interest after a judgment. Whilst such a term and its consequences would cause surprise to a consumer, as well as entail potentially serious financial consequences, the problem was with consumer credit legislation rather than the term itself.

Nevertheless, the Law Lords took the opportunity to express their views on the unfairness test generally, as well as the notion of good faith specifically. Lord Bingham considered the 'significant imbalance' and 'good faith' elements in turn. With regard to the former, he said:

> The requirement of significant imbalance is met if a term is so weighted in favour of the supplier as to tilt the parties' rights and obligations under the contract significantly in his favour. This may be by the granting to the supplier of a beneficial option or discretion or power, or by the imposing on the consumer of a disadvantageous burden or risk or duty ... This involves looking at the contract as a whole. But the imbalance must be to the detriment of the consumer ...[79]

---

75 [2001] UKHL 52; [2001] 1 All ER 97, HL.
76 [2000] 1 WLR 98.
77 [2000] 2 WLR 1353, CA.
78 In particular, the County Courts (Interests of Judgment Debts) Order 1991.
79 Para 17.

In dealing with the 'good faith' criterion, Lord Bingham returned to his *obiter* in *Interfoto Library Ltd v Stiletto Visual Programmes Ltd*,[80] a case under the Unfair Contract Terms Act 1977. Based on this, he suggested that good faith was about

> . . . fair and open dealing. Openness requires that terms should be expressed fully, clearly and legibly, containing no concealed pitfalls or traps. Appropriate prominence should be given to terms which might operate disadvantageously to the customer. Fair dealing requires that a supplier should not, whether deliberately or unconsciously, take advantage of the consumer's necessity, indigence, lack of experience, weak bargaining position . . . Good faith in this context is not an artificial or technical concept; nor, since Lord Mansfield was its champion, is it a concept wholly unfamiliar to British lawyers. It looks to good standards of commercial morality and practice . . .[81]

Bingham concluded that the fairness test 'lays down a composite test, covering both the making and the substance of the contract . . .'.[82] Lord Steyn agreed that the fairness test had both a procedural and a substantive element.[83] 'Good faith' is an objective standard which demands open and fair dealing.[84] The 'significant imbalance' criterion relates to the substantive unfairness of a term.[85] To this, Lord Millett added:

> It is obviously useful to assess the impact of an impugned term on the parties' rights and obligations by comparing the effect of the contract with the term and the effect it would have without it. But the inquiry cannot stop there. It may also be necessary to consider the effect of the inclusion of the term on the substance or core of the transaction; whether if drawn to his attention the consumer would be likely to be surprised by it; whether the term is a standard

---

80 [1989] QB 433. He noted that good faith 'does not simply mean that [parties] should not deceive each other . . . its effect is perhaps most aptly conveyed by such metaphorical colloquialisms as "playing fair", "coming clean" or "putting one's cards face upwards on the table". It is in essence a principle of fair and open dealing . . .' (p 439).
81 Para 17.
82 *Ibid.*
83 Para 36.
84 Para 36.
85 Para 37, referring to H Collins, 'Good faith in European contract law' (1994) 14 *Oxford Journal of Legal Studies* 229.

term, not merely in similar non-negotiable consumer contracts, but in commercial contracts freely negotiated between parties acting on level terms and at arms' length and whether, in such cases, the party adversely affected by the inclusion of the term or his lawyer might reasonably be expected to object to its inclusion and press for its deletion. The list is not necessarily exhaustive; other approaches may sometimes be necessary.[86]

The speeches of the Law Lords constitute the authoritative statement on the unfairness test in English law, and subsequent cases have followed it. However, some of Lord Bingham's reasoning might suggest that he is adopting an 'English' interpretation of the 'good faith' test, rather than one that respects the need for an autonomous European reading. Whilst his earlier observations in *Interfoto* were based on an assessment of how good faith is used generally in those jurisdictions familiar with the concept, this does not mean that this corresponds with the European interpretation that might be adopted by the ECJ, and lingering doubts remain as to whether this was the correct approach.[87]

4.5.2 Example 2: commercial agency

The attempts by the English (and Scottish) courts to apply the legislation implementing the Commercial Agency Directive (86/653/EEC) show that the courts can struggle to understand concepts introduced through the process of Europeanisation into domestic law. The Directive was implemented into national law in the Commercial Agents (Council Directive) Regulations 1993,[88] largely by copying out the text of the Directive. As explained earlier, Art 17 of the Directive gives Member States a choice as to what should happen when an agency contract terminates, that is, whether the agent should receive an indemnity or compensation. UK law has given effect to both possibilities: compensation is the default position, but the parties are able to specify in their contract that an indemnity should be provided on termination instead. Either concept was new to domestic law: the protection of a commercial agent on termination of the agency relationship was limited to damages for breach of contract, where the termination constituted such a

---

86 Para 54.
87 See below for a discussion of the refusal to request a preliminary ruling under Art 234 in this case.
88 SI 1993/3053.

breach. If an agency contract had simply expired, there was no entitle-ment to any form of payment from the agent's principal.

This changed with the coming into force of the Commercial Agents Regulations. Now, on termination of the relationship, the agent could demand compensation (or an indemnity). Such compensation should cover the damage suffered as a result of this termination. The courts soon realised that 'termination' in this context did not only refer to termination of the contract as a result of a breach, but also the mere expiry of the agreement (for example, where it was a fixed-term agree-ment or where appropriate notice was given).[89] So compensation is not equivalent to the award of damages for breach of contract, but it was not at all clear what the purpose of awarding compensation would be, and how the amount the agent is to receive should be calculated. This section will examine how the UK courts have sought to deal with the application of these provisions. The focus is not on the detailed criteria developed, but rather the process by which the courts have arrived at these.

As noted earlier, the notions of compensation and indemnity have their origins in French and German law respectively, and whilst they are different, their common objective is to reward an agent for the work undertaken in using their skill and expertise to create a customer base for the principal from which orders will continue to be received.[90] This, too, was something which the domestic courts readily accepted.[91] In *Lonsdale v Howard & Hallam*,[92] Lord Hoffmann said that 'the agent is treated as having lost something of value for this termination and is entitled to compensation for this loss'.[93] He continued:

> As this part of the Directive is based on French law, I think that one is entitled to look at French law for guidance, or confirmation, as to what it means . . . The French jurisprudence . . . appears to regard the agent as having had a share in the goodwill of the principal's business which he has helped to create. The relationship between principal and agent is treated as having existed for their common benefit . . . The agent has thereby acquired a share in the goodwill,

---

89 See, eg, *Tigana Ltd v Decoro Ltd* [2003] EWHC 23; *King v Tunnock* [2000] Eu LR 531.
90 S Saintier, 'The principles behind the assessment of the compensation option under the agency regulations: clarity at last?' [2007] *Journal of Business Law* 90–98, p 92.
91 Eg, in *Moore v Piretta PTA Ltd* [1999] 1 All ER 174 and *Barret McKenzie v Escada (UK) Ltd* [2001] ECC 50.
92 *Lonsdale v Howard & Hallam Ltd* [2007] UKHL 32; [2007] 4 All ER 1.
93 Para 8 of the judgment.

an asset which the principal retains after termination of the agency and for which the agent is therefore entitled to compensation . . .[94]

Whilst this provides a useful explanation of the underlying purpose of the compensation provision in the Directive/Regulations, Lord Hoffmann's comments raise an important fundamental question: he immediately turns to French law to identify the rationale for the provision on compensation. However, UK law is not based on French law, but rather a European directive. It may therefore be asked to what extent it is permissible to consider other national laws in trying to give substance to an unfamiliar concept. The reason to be cautious is the principle of 'autonomous interpretation' mentioned earlier, according to which principles and concepts introduced by EU legislation should be treated as European concepts. Consequently, the fact that a provision in a directive was inspired by a particular national rule does not invariably mean that all the other Member States are bound by that national law, unless the directive explicitly states as much. Indeed, Member States should avoid following another national law so as not to undermine the need for an autonomous interpretation.

This does not mean, however, that Lord Hoffmann's approach is wrong. It seems perfectly possible for a UK court to consider the position in another jurisdiction in order to assist with establishing the overall purpose of a specific provision. However, identifying that purpose on the basis of the national law which clearly inspired the European provision does not mean that the criteria for its application should also be drawn from that jurisdiction. This is indirectly supported by the ECJ's observations in *Honeyvem v De Zotti*,[95] made in the context of the indemnity provision in Art 17(2) of the Directive, that '. . . Member States may exercise their discretion as to the choice of methods for calculating the indemnity . . .'.[96] On the one hand, the ECJ does not say that German law[97] must be followed, but on the other, the Court also does not expressly rule this out. This leaves open the possibility that courts in other jurisdictions *could* adopt the French or German approach respectively, but they are *not obliged* to do so.

The UK courts have not adopted a consistent approach in this matter. Initially, the courts were quick to look to either French or German

---

94 Para 9.
95 Case C-465/04 *Honeyvem Informazioni Commerciali Srl v Mariella De Zotti* [2006] ECR I-2879.
96 Para 35.
97 Which was the inspiration for the indemnity provision.

law. In *Moore v Piretta Ltd*,[98] the only reported case on the indemnity
provision, Judge Mitting QC said:

> ... the primary purpose of the directive is the harmonisation of
> Community law by requiring all member states to introduce rights
> and duties similar to those already subsisting in at least two of
> the member states of the Community, the Federal Republic of
> Germany and France ... Consistent with the purpose of achieving
> harmony between member states, it is in my judgment permissible
> to look into the law and practice of the country in which the
> relevant right originated ... and *to use them as a guide to their
> application.*[99]

Although Mitting QC did not follow German law entirely in his
assessment of the indemnity due to the agent in that case, the relevant
German law was clearly a material factor. Although the judge did not
go so far as to say that following German law was obligatory under the
Directive, his words appear to reflect the assumption that the harmonising purpose of the Directive means that, in principle, German law
should be followed.

In Scotland, Lord Hamilton in *Roy v MR Pearlman Ltd*[100] agreed
with Mitting QC's approach and rejected arguments by counsel that
French law was irrelevant to the interpretation and application of
the Regulations. He also did not accept that considering French law
required expert evidence to be provided, regarding this approach as
'in the nature of a comparative law exercise, for the purposes of
which a Scottish court is entitled to have direct regard to sources of
foreign law'.[101]

Similarly, the Scottish Court of Session in *King v Tunnock Ltd*,[102] this
time dealing with the compensation provision, was urged by counsel
not to follow French practice, but declined. Having emphasised that the
harmonisation of the law to ensure that conditions for commercial
agents are equivalent throughout the internal market was the aim of the
Directive, the Court observed that this would fail if national courts
applying the corresponding domestic rules came to different outcomes.
It then favourably considered submissions made about the relevant

98 [1999] 1 All ER 174.
99 [1999] 1 All ER 174, p 177, emphasis added.
100 [1999] 2 CMLR 1155.
101 P 1170.
102 [2000] IRLR 570.

French law,[103] and came to a conclusion squarely based on the general approach adopted by the French courts when applying the compensation provision.[104]

In these cases, no consideration was given to the principle of autonomous interpretation. In *King*, counsel made strong representations about the approach that should be adopted, but the Court chose to follow the French approach. But doubts about the correctness of this approach were soon expressed by other courts. In *Jeremy Duffen v FRA Bo SpA*,[105] Judge Hallgarten in the Central London County Court urged caution:

> ... a better understanding of the regulations may be gained from having some idea of the principles applicable within the legal system or stems from which those regulations may have been derived. But at this point I hesitate ... It seems to me that once an English Court is diverted from the general into the particular, it will find itself drawn into attempting to mimic what a French Court would actually have done, a task which it is ill-equipped to perform.[106]

Thereafter, the tide began to turn. Bowers J in *Barrett McKenzie v Escada (UK) Ltd*[107] expressed his scepticism of the approach in *King v Tunnock* thus:

> ... how do we know in the United Kingdom, how do I know how the French would deal with this particular case? ... It does seem to me that it is important to realise we are dealing with United Kingdom legislation and, whilst this 'foreign animal' has been created that is unknown to common law, the compensation principles have in practical terms to be sufficiently United Kingdom based and developed so as to be interpreted and enforceable by United

---

103 The Court did express its agreement with a suggestion made by counsel that both parties might present an agreed statement from an expert as to the position under another Member State's law, suggesting perhaps a recognition of the practical difficulties associated with attempts to follow slavishly another jurisdiction's approach.
104 These judgments received favourable treatment by S Saintier, 'A remarkable understanding and application of the protective stance of the agency regulations by the English courts' [2001] JBL 540–53.
105 [2000] 1 Lloyd's Rep 180.
106 Pp 197–8.
107 [2001] ECC 50.

Kingdom judges, English judges, without requiring in any single case, it seems to me, an expert in French law to determine the case.[108]

Rather, what mattered in order to achieve harmonisation was to ensure that where there was a breach of a right, there would be a domestic remedy. It would be 'extraordinary ... for one Member State to be required to impose not just a remedy from Europe but in fact from another Member State'.[109] He explicitly disagrees with *King v Tunnock* by concluding that the Directive was concerned with establishing the entitlement to compensation generally but that the method of assessment was a matter for the domestic courts.[110]

This position has been endorsed by the House of Lords in *Lonsdale v Howard & Hallam*.[111] Lord Hoffmann rejected a submission that the Commission, in its report on the Directive[112] had, by commenting favourably on the French approach, endorsed this as the appropriate method of calculating the compensation payable. First, Lord Hoffmann – correctly – stated that the Commission's report did not, nor could it, contain any endorsement; it merely summarised the position as it obtained in national law at that time.[113] Second, both the English and French courts agreed on the purpose of the compensation provision, but differed with regard to the method of calculation. Following the *Honeyvem* case, that is a matter for each Member State.[114] Third, the market conditions for commercial agents in France and England are different,[115] further justifying varying national approaches in the method for calculating compensation. Taken together, this meant that the English courts were free to develop their own criteria for calculating compensation and were not bound to follow the methods developed in another Member State.[116]

---

108 Para 21.
109 Para 22.
110 Para 26.
111 *Lonsdale v Howard & Hallam Ltd* [2007] UKHL 32; [2007] 4 All ER 1.
112 Commission, *Report on the Application of Article 17 of Council Directive on the co-ordination of the laws of the Member States relating to self-employed commercial agents* COM (96) 364 final.
113 Para 16.
114 Para 17.
115 Para 18.
116 The remainder of Lord Hoffmann's speech was concerned with the factors that would be relevant in calculating compensation, the detail of which is not relevant for present purposes.

What lessons can be drawn from this discussion? There are several noteworthy points about the Europeanisation of contract law reflected in these decisions. It can be seen that the underlying purpose of Europeanisation, that is, to achieve greater harmonisation across the EU, may not permeate every last detail of the area concerned. Thus, the objective of providing for better protection for commercial agents pursued by the Directive can be attained without harmonising the method for calculating compensation. Of course, if the purpose of the Directive had been to harmonise not only the general protection of commercial agents, but also the method for calculating compensation (and indemnity), then a different approach by the national courts may have been required. The ECJ has made it clear that national courts retain significant discretion in this regard without undermining the Directive's overall aims. Furthermore, Europeanisation as a result of an EU measure does not mean that national legislation which may have inspired that measure becomes the yardstick which the courts in all the other jurisdictions are bound to follow. Quite unlike Lord Hamilton's view in *Roy v Pearlman*, this seems to be much less of a comparative law exercise than might be the case in other areas.

4.5.3 Domestic courts and Article 234 references

In Chapter 2, it was seen that national courts can (and, in some instances, must) request a preliminary ruling from the ECJ on the interpretation of particular questions of EU law. However, despite the fact that there are now many directives in the contract law field, with some in place for more than 20 years, the number of preliminary rulings requested from the national courts of all the Member States remains small.[117] There may be various reasons for this.[118] Many of the directives concerned are consumer law measures, and there appears to be a considerable degree of variation between the Member States in the number of reported cases involving consumer claims.[119] Moreover, if a case does reach a court, there may not necessarily be a recognition that the

---

117 Although it is difficult to give a precise number because of the various issues raised by cases that have been referred (eg, some involve questions of fundamental EU law, such as direct effect or state liability), there are probably fewer than 30 preliminary rulings on contract law directives.

118 Cf Niglia, *op. cit.*, pp 583–4.

119 H Schulte-Nölke, C Twigg-Flesner and M Ebers, *Consumer Compendium – Comparative Analysis.*

dispute turns on a question of EU law that needs to be clarified through a preliminary ruling. But even where there is awareness of the relevance of EU law, there may be a reluctance to refer questions to the ECJ because of the not inconsiderable delay this would cause to resolving the dispute before the national court – many cases now take at least two years before the ECJ hands down its judgment. Furthermore, there may also be an element of protectionism involved, in that contract law – as all areas of private law – is a central feature of each national legal system, and by not referring matters to the ECJ, national courts retain an element of control even in those areas where Europeanisation has already occurred.

The number of English cases involving legislation giving effect to an EU directive in the field of contract law is small. The main areas where a body of case law has developed are those already considered, unfair contract terms and commercial agency. In both areas, the courts have had to consider whether to request a preliminary ruling from the ECJ on the interpretation of the corresponding directives. In almost all cases, the courts (including the House of Lords) concluded that this was not necessary.

A somewhat pointed observation about the (lack of a) need for a reference was made by Staughton LJ in *Page v Combined Shipping and Trading Co Ltd*:[120]

> It may well be that ... we shall have to refer the problem to the European Court, and it will take another two years after that before a decision emerges as to what the regulation really means. Maybe the parties will think there are better methods of spending their time and their money than disputing that for a long period of time.[121]

Such an observation might reflect a more widespread feeling that the delays associated with the preliminary reference procedure make it deeply unattractive, which would have significant implications for the future harmonious Europeanisation of contract law. Rather than prolong the dispute by an undefinable period for the ECJ to answer the questions referred, national courts may seek to resolve any questions of EU law on the basis of previous ECJ jurisprudence, or on the basis of the legislation itself.

120 [1997] 3 All ER 656.
121 *Ibid.*, p 661.

So why have the courts decided that references were not necessary? In *Lonsdale v Howard & Hallam Ltd*,[122] the House of Lords was invited to ask for a preliminary ruling on the scope of the compensation provision in Art 17(3) of the Commercial Agency Directive, because there had been differences of opinion between the domestic courts involved in earlier cases in this field. Having reviewed both the Directive and the existing ECJ case law, Lord Hoffmann concluded that there was no need for a reference because the Directive was clear on what was required and ECJ case law had established that the method of calculating the amount of compensation to be awarded was within the discretion of the domestic courts. The real problem in the earlier cases had been the exercise of that discretion, which had caused uncertainty. It was for the House of Lords as the highest national court to resolve that uncertainty, rather than the ECJ.[123]

Similarly, in *Director-General of Fair Trading v First National Bank*, Lord Bingham of Cornhill made the following observations about the Directive and its implementing regulations:

> One of [the Directive's] objectives was partially to harmonise the law in this important field among all member states of the European Union. The member states have no common concept of fairness or good faith, and the Directive does not purport to state the law of any single member state. It lays down a test to be applied, whatever their pre-existing law, by all member states. If the meaning of the test were doubtful, or vulnerable to the possibility of differing interpretations in differing member states, it might be desirable or necessary to seek a ruling from the European Court of Justice on its interpretation. But the language used in expressing the test . . . is in my opinion clear and not reasonably capable of differing interpretations . . .'[124]

Lord Bingham acknowledged that the fairness test needs to be interpreted autonomously, rather than on the basis of any existing domestic principles. Lord Steyn similarly noted that 'the concepts of the Directive must be given autonomous meanings so that there will be uniform application of the Directive so far as is possible'.[125] However,

---

122 [2007] UKHL 32; [2007] 4 All ER 1.
123 *Ibid.*, paragraph 40 of the judgment.
124 Para 17 of his speech.
125 Para 32.

Lord Bingham also immediately ruled out any need for a preliminary reference under Art 234 to obtain a guidance from the European Court of Justice on the interpretation of the fairness test, by stating that the language is clear and not capable of differing interpretations. It has been suggested that the lack of a common understanding and the need for consistent, autonomous interpretation necessitated that a preliminary ruling was sought,[126] but if – as here – the criteria of the test appear clear to the court, there is no need. Of course, referring a question to the ECJ would have created an opportunity to seek a 'European' interpretation of 'unfairness' and 'good faith', particularly in view of the previous divergences between the Member States regarding their notions of fairness. Nevertheless, if the House of Lords was happy that the test was sufficiently certain,[127] then no guidance from the ECJ was needed.

In both instances, the House of Lords therefore asserted its competence to deal with the case without seeking guidance from the ECJ, ostensibly in accordance with established EU law that references are not necessary where the interpretation of EU law is clear, and where the matter involves merely a question of application.

4.6 IMPACT ON CONTRACT LAW GENERALLY

So far, the analysis in this chapter has focused on how the UK ensures that there is legislation which implements directives, and how the courts ensure that they interpret and apply this legislation in accordance with relevant European principles. However, Europeanisation reaches beyond these aspects, and also requires consideration of how contract law generally has been affected by the various directives. Teubner famously argued that the effect of some harmonising measures may be to introduce 'legal irritants' into national law which take on a life of their own after implementation and may ultimately result in new divergences between the Member States.[128]

To some, there may be a simple answer: most of the directives are only concerned with consumer law (whether in the narrow or wider

---

126 M Dean, 'Defining unfair terms in consumer contracts – crystal ball gazing?' *Director General of Fair Trading v First National Bank plc*' (2002) 65 *Modern Law Review* 773.

127 For example, Lord Hope said that 'the Directive provides all the guidance that is needed as to its application' (para 45).

128 G Teuber, 'Legal irritants: good faith in British law or how unifying law ends up in new divergences' (1998) 61 *Modern Law Review* 11–32.

sense[129]), which seeks to modify general rules of contract law in order to protect consumers. There are no directives which go to the heart of the general law of contract – that is, there has been no legislation on how contracts are concluded, how they are to be performed, vitiating factors, remedies and so on.

This might be too narrow a view, however. Whilst it is correct that the various consumer-specific measures have left the common law of contract largely unaffected, this does not mean that their impact might not eventually be felt there, too. Three aspects have been singled out by way of example: pre-contractual information duties, specific performance and good faith.

4.6.1 Pre-contractual information duties

Pre-contractual information duties are in widespread use in EU contract law directives (both in the consumer field and beyond). In contrast to other European jurisdictions,[130] English contract law is traditionally reluctant to impose pre-contractual information duties. With the exception of a small category of contracts *uberrimae fidei*,[131] English contract law does not have a general duty of disclosure in the pre-contractual context, reflecting its adversarial rather than co-operative ethic.[132] Not providing relevant information is therefore not in itself a legal wrong,[133] and *caveat emptor* remains the basic principle. Instead, the provision of information in the pre-contractual stage is controlled primarily through the doctrine of misrepresentation, but this generally depends on some information having been given by one of the parties. If the information given before a contract was concluded is a statement of *fact* rather than simply one of opinion,[134] but incorrect to such an extent as to constitute an actionable misrepresentation, the contract is voidable and may be rescinded, and damages may be claimed.[135] The information given must be untrue; if it is ambiguous, the person supplying the information will

---

129 As explained in the previous chapter, some directives with consumer contract provisions do not fall within the responsibility of DG SANCO, but other DGs, and are therefore often not regarded as consumer law at all.

130 See JHM van Erp, 'The pre-contractual stage', in A Hartkamp *et al.* (eds), *Towards a European Civil Code*, 3rd edn, Nijmegen: Ars Aequi, 2004.

131 Mainly contracts of insurance.

132 Cf Lord Ackner in *Walford v Miles* [1992] 2 AC 128.

133 *Keates v Cadogan* (1851) 10 CB 591; *Bradford Third Equitable Benefit Building Society v Borders* [1941] 2 All ER 205.

134 Eg *Esso Petroleum Co Ltd v Mardon* [1976] QB 801.

135 The latter are largely governed by the Misrepresentation Act 1967.

be liable if there was an intention to convey an untrue meaning which is understood in that way by the recipient, but not if his interpretation was honestly held.[136] A misrepresentation can arise where the conduct of one of the contracting parties suggests something which is not, in fact, true.[137] An active attempt to conceal information could amount to a misrepresentation,[138] as could partial non-disclosure.[139] Also, a statement which is literally true but still misleading because not all the relevant information has been given could amount to a misrepresentation.[140] The same holds in respect of a statement which, whilst true when given, becomes false before the contract is concluded.[141] The misrepresentation must be *material*, that is, affect the decision of a reasonable person to conclude the contract on the particular terms. Finally, the recipient of the information must rely on it in concluding the contract. What therefore matters is actual reliance on the misrepresentation,[142] although if a reasonable person would have relied on the wrong information, it is presumed that the particular claimant did, too.[143] Materiality and reliance are separate requirements and both need to be established.[144]

With the introduction of express pre-contractual information duties in so many areas, it may be the case that the reluctance of English law to impose such duties may slowly be eroded more generally. As yet, there is no obvious sign that this may happen, but that is not to say that it will remain so for ever.[145]

---

136 The circumstances in *Sykes v Taylor-Rose* [2004] EWCA Civ 299 illustrate this. The vendor of a house had to complete a standard questionnaire for the buyer, which asked, *inter alia*, if there was any other information which, in the vendor's view, the purchaser might have a right to know. The vendor did not disclose that a murder had taken place in the house previously. This was only discovered by the purchaser subsequently, after watching a television documentary, which also suggested that there might still be undiscovered body parts hidden in the house. A claim in misrepresentation failed, because the answer to the question had been given honestly.
137 *Spice Girls Ltd v Aprilia World Service BV* [2002] EMLR 27.
138 *Schneider v Heath* (1813) 3 Camp 506.
139 *Peek v Gurney* [1871–73] All ER Rep 116.
140 *Notts Patent Brick and Tile Co v Butler* (1866) 16 QBD 778.
141 *With v O'Flanagan* [1936] Ch 575. See R Bigwood, 'Pre-contractual misrepresentation and the limits of the principle in *With v O'Flanagan*' (2005) *Cambridge Law Journal* 94–125.
142 *Museprime Properties Ltd v Adhill Properties Ltd* [1990] 2 EGLR 196.
143 *Smith v Chadwick* (1884) 9 App Cas 187.
144 *Pan Atlantic Insurance Ltd v Pine Top Insurance Ltd* [1995] 2 AC 501.
145 C Twigg-Flesner, D Parry, G Howells and A Nordhausen, *An Analysis of the Application and Scope of the Unfair Commercial Practices Directive* (London: DTI, 2005), pp 49–61 (available at http://www.berr.gov.uk/files/file32095.pdf (last accessed 9 November 2007)).

4.6.2 Specific performance

A second area where English law may come under pressure, this time as a result of the Consumer Sales Directive (99/44/EC), is the remedy of specific performance. As seen earlier, the primary remedies under the Directive are to have non-conforming goods repaired or replaced. This is in contrast to English law, which grants a consumer an immediate right to terminate the contract.[146] Requiring a seller to repair or replace goods is equivalent to ordering specific performance of the contract of sale. In English law, specific performance is rarely granted. The courts have only exercised their discretion to award this remedy where the contract was for goods which are (almost) unique,[147] but not for ordinary items of commerce.[148] Generally, there will be no order for specific performance where another, more appropriate remedy is available, which in most cases will be damages.[149]

There is therefore a very obvious clash between the reluctance of English law to order specific performance and the Directive's focus on repair and replacement as the main remedies in consumer sales contracts. The implementation of the Directive might therefore have necessitated a fundamental change to English practice, albeit confined to the context of consumer sales. Whilst making specific performance more widely available may be a positive step, doing so merely for one particular type of contract seems unattractive.[150] The solution adopted in the implementing legislation has been to give the courts the power to order specific performance of either repair or replacement in the context of consumer sales,[151] but the court is also able to order an alternative remedy if this is more appropriate.[152] This seems to reflect the existing approach of English law, and does not give full effect to the requirements of the Directive.[153] It remains to be seen if, over time,

---

146 Subject to various limitations which are not relevant for present purposes. See, eg, Bradgate and Twigg-Flesner, *op. cit.*, chapter 4.

147 *Behnke v Bede Shipping Co* [1927] 1 KB 640.

148 *Cohen v Roche* [1927] 1 KB 169.

149 *Co-operative Insurance Society v Argyll Stores (Holdings) Ltd* [1998] AC 1.

150 Cf H Beale and G Howells, 'EU harmonisation of consumer sales law – a missed opportunity?' (1997) 12 *Journal of Contract Law* 21–46, p 33.

151 Section 48E(2), Sale of Goods Act 1979.

152 Section 48E(3) and (4).

153 A Johnston and H Unberath, 'Law at, to or from the centre?' in F Cafaggi, *The Institutional Framework of European Private Law* (Oxford: OUP, 2006), p 187.

there will be a shift towards a greater willingness to award specific performance.[154]

4.6.3 Good faith

Moving beyond particular rules, English law may also find itself under pressure at the level of principle. Unlike most other jurisdictions within Europe,[155] English law does not recognise a general principle of good faith. Indeed, such a principle (in the context of negotiating in good faith) was famously rejected by Lord Ackner in *Walford v Miles* as 'repugnant to the adversarial position of the parties when involved in negotiations'.[156] Instead, English law continues to rely on individual doctrines and rules in response to particular problems. However, EU legislation does rely on good faith in several instances, most prominently in the context of unfair terms and commercial agency, and it has found its way into domestic law in those particular areas. As familiarity with the concept develops, the debate over the acceptance of a good faith principle in English contract law increases.[157] As will be seen in the following chapter, the hand of English law may be forced by imminent developments at the European level: the Lando PECL, which contain a general principle of good faith and fair dealing in Art 1:106, will form the basis of the so-called Common Frame of Reference on European Contract Law, and the *Green Paper on the Review of the Consumer Acquis* raises the possibility of introducing a general principle of good faith for consumer contracts.[158] Such developments may eventually result in the creeping development of a general good faith principle in English contract law.

---

154 A further pressure may come from an altogether different direction. Should the UK ever decide to ratify the United Nations Convention on the International Sale of Goods, there would be a similar remedial scheme for international commercial contracts (cf Art 46), although there is a provision to the effect that specific performance would only have to be awarded if this was also available under national law (Art 28).

155 M Hesselink, 'The concept of good faith', in A Hartkamp *et al.* (eds), *Towards a European Civil Code*, 3rd edn (Nijmegen: Ars Aequi, 2004).

156 [1992] AC 128, p 138.

157 It is impossible within the confines of this book to do this debate any justice. A good starting point is R Brownsword, *Contract Law – Themes for the Twenty-first Century*, 2nd edn (Oxford: OUP, 2006), chapter 6.

158 See Chapter 5.

4.7 CONCLUSION

The preceding discussion demonstrates that the process of formal Europeanisation by the EU is shaped by several restrictions imposed by the Treaty itself, and depends on a significant degree of interaction between the European level on the one hand, and the domestic one on the other.

As seen in the previous chapter, Europeanisation by directive is essentially a form of piecemeal harmonisation which may lead to greater approximation between the laws of the Member States, but it can also result in a disruption to unity of domestic law.[159] This chapter has sought to identify the main challenges, as well as to consider how the implementation of directives is handled in the UK. On the whole, the UK seeks to comply at a formal level, but may be criticised for not taking sufficient care in considering the relationship of implementing legislation with related areas of domestic law. The attitude of the English courts with regard to the interpretation of domestic legislation enacting EU directives reveals that they are more able than might have been expected to interpret EU-derived legislation in a manner that seeks to be consistent with the need for autonomous interpretation, whilst closely safeguarding the responsibility of the national courts to apply the legislation to the circumstances of individual cases.

---

159 W van Gerven, 'The ECJ case law as a means of unification of private law', in A Hartkamp *et al.* (eds), *Towards a European Civil Code*, 3rd edn (Nijmegen: Ars Aequi, 2004).

5 The way forward

5.1 INTRODUCTION

The previous chapter focused on the extent of the EU's legislative activity in the field of contract law. From this, it can be seen that it has done little more than to create 'islands' of Europeanisation in the domestic contract law field, but – perhaps with the exception of consumer contracts – there has been little interference with the fundamental aspects of the contract law system in the European jurisdictions so far. However, in 2001, the European Commission kick-started a process which could eventually lead to much greater Europeanisation of domestic contract laws. Work is now underway on preparing the groundwork for future action in the field of contract law. Two major initiatives merit closer examination: the creation of a 'Common Frame of Reference' (CFR) on European contract law, and a major review of the *acquis communautaire* in the consumer law field. Although these were initially launched as independent projects, both are now interlinked. The purpose of this chapter is to examine the background to the current process, starting with the Commission's 2001 Communication and subsequent documents. The work that is now ongoing will then be discussed, followed by a consideration of what may happen in the immediate future.[1]

---

1 See also M Röttinger, 'Towards a European Code Napoléon/AGBG/BGB? Recent EC activities for a European contract law' (2006) 12 *European Law Journal* 807–27.

5.2 THE COMMISSION'S TRILOGY ON EUROPEAN CONTRACT LAW

The basis of developments are three Commission documents, published in 2001, 2003 and 2004 respectively. They are well known and examined in many contributions to the literature, and a brief account here will suffice. The Commission's *Communication on European Contract Law*[2] was intended to provoke debate and invite evidence on the necessity of further EC action in the field of contract law. In particular, the Commission identified shortcomings both in the quality of the various harmonisation directives adopted so far[3] and in their implementation into national law. The Commission set out four possible courses of action, some of which might overlap.

(1) No EC action (that is, the 'do nothing' option).
(2) Promote the development of common contract law principles, for improving EU legislation, as guidance to domestic courts applying a foreign law, and as a template for domestic legislators when adopting legislation in the contract law field.[4]
(3) Improve the quality of legislation already in place, by improving the coherence of the terminology used; and revising current exceptions from the scope of existing directives to increase coherence in the scope of application of the *acquis*.[5]
(4) Adopt new comprehensive legislation at EC level, resulting in 'an overall text comprising provisions on general questions of contract law as well as specific contracts'.[6] This could be purely optional, to be selected by the parties; an 'opt-out' or default framework, which would apply unless the parties excluded it; or a non-excludable framework – effectively replacing national contract laws.[7]

In February 2003, the Commission presented the follow-up document

---

2 COM (2001) 398 final, 11 July 2001. See also 'On the way to a European contract code?' (editorial comments) (2002) 39 *Common Market Law Review* 219–55.

3 The Annex to the *Communication* contains a long list of measures which arguably have some effect on contract law, or even private law generally, although quite what that relationship might be is not always apparent (see N Reich, 'Critical comments on the Commission Communication "On European contract law"' in Grundmann/Stuyck (2002)).

4 Paras 52–55.

5 Paras 57–60.

6 Para 61.

7 Para 66.

A More Coherent European Contract Law – An Action Plan.[8] At that point, the Commission had received 181 responses to its *Communication,*[9] from which it derived broad support for options (2) and (3), but few respondents were in favour of option (1), and the majority opposed option (4). Specific suggestions for further action were presented for further consultation, and subsequently confirmed in *European Contract Law and the revision of the acquis: the way forward.*[10] First, the quality of the *acquis* in the field of contract law should be improved, with a view to ensuring greater consistency. The main tool in this process would be a CFR on European contract law, providing common principles and terminology. Separate research on the implementation of eight consumer law directives across all the Member States had been commissioned,[11] and any proposals for reform will be based on the CFR.[12] The Commission envisages three possible purposes for this CFR: (a) to help with reviewing existing legislation, and proposing new measures, especially by providing common terminology and rules on fundamental concepts; (b) to promote convergence between domestic legal systems both within and outside the EU;[13] and (c) to consider the usefulness of an optional instrument on contract law.[14]

Second, the elaboration of EU-wide standard contract terms would be promoted. In particular, the Commission planned to facilitate the exchange of information, perhaps via a Commission-hosted website, and to offer guidance on the use of standard terms and conditions within the EC's legal framework, particularly on unfair contract terms and competition law.[15]

Finally, there would be 'further reflection' on non-sector-specific measures such as an optional instrument on contract law. In particular, the suitability of the CFR for such an instrument would be considered.[16]

---

8 COM (2003) 68 final.
9 Cf M Kenny, 'Globalization, interlegality and Europeanized contract law' (2003) 21 *Penn State International Law Review* 569–620.
10 COM (2004) 651 final, 11 October 2004. See D Staudenmeyer, 'The way forward in European contract law' [2005] *European Review of Private Law* 95–104.
11 See below.
12 *The Way Forward*, pp 2–5.
13 Whatever 'convergence' might mean in this context: cf R Brownsword, *Contract Law – Themes for the Twenty-First Century* (Oxford: OUP, 2006), pp 173–4; also D Kennedy, 'Thoughts on coherence, social values and national tradition in private law' in M Hesselink (ed), *The Politics of a European Civil Code* (The Hague: Kluwer, 2006).
14 Para 62.
15 Paras 81–88.
16 Page 5.

Several parallel initiatives in the field of contract law have therefore emerged from the process launched with the *Communication* in 2001: work on EU-wide standard contract terms, the CFR, the review of the consumer *acquis*, and further exploration of the scope for an optional instrument on EU contract law. All of these merit closer examination.

5.3 EU-WIDE STANDARD CONTRACT TERMS

In view of the fact that standard terms, that is, terms pre-drafted for repeated use in numerous similar transactions, are popular in certain industry sectors, and could usefully reduce transaction costs, the Commission intended to promote the establishment of such terms, with its role limited to that of facilitator, or 'honest broker'. There were plans for a website for exchanging information, but the Commission decided to refrain from drafting specific guidelines on the creation of standard contract terms. In addition, the Commission planned to identify legislative obstacles to the use of standard contract terms on an EU-wide basis, and to consider how to reduce or eliminate them.[17]

The Commission has since announced that it has abandoned plans to host such a website, partly because of the practicalities of keeping such a site up-to-date, but primarily because EU-wide standard contract terms would have to be compatible with the most restrictive national rules, making them unattractive to the vast majority of businesses.[18]

The pursuit of EU-wide standard contract terms may not be a good thing for other reasons. The standard terms would have to be drafted in one language, and then be translated into all the other official languages. Translating a set of standard terms from one language into another could be a very difficult enterprise, not only due to the inherent difficulties associated with translating any kind of text,[19] but also because of the additional difficulty posed by variations in legal terminology.[20] Second, the variations regarding the default rules applicable to certain types of contract in the domestic contract laws of the Member States could make standard contract terms difficult to agree upon, and

---

17 Pp 6–8.
18 *First Annual Progress Report on European Contract Law and the Acquis Review* COM (2005) 456 final, 23 September 2005, p 10.
19 See B Pozzo and V Jacometti, *Multilingualism and the Harmonisation of European Private Law* (The Hague: Kluwer, 2006).
20 S Whittaker, 'On the development of European standard contract terms' (2006) 2 *European Review of Contract Law* 51.

might make them rather unattractive.[21] Third, jurisdictions adopt different approaches to interpreting contracts,[22] creating some concern about the practical application of agreed standard terms. That, too, would reduce the effectiveness of such terms.[23] Finally, concerns have been expressed about the legitimacy of promoting EU-wide standard contract terms by sector on the basis that this is tantamount to placing law-making powers in the hands of private actors.[24]

Whilst these reasons for being cautious about developments all sound plausible, it may be asked whether they are not overstating the problem. The development of *international* standard terms (particularly those developed by the International Chamber of Commerce, such as the INCOTERMS, or the UCP on documentary credits[25]) demonstrates that it seems entirely possible to prepare standard terms for use in international transactions. Rather strangely, the Commission largely fails to consider the activities of the various international organisations,[26] including the ICC.[27] The Commission has rightly been criticised for failing to recognise the significant work that has already been done in the field of international standard terms, and this failure might be the primary reason for the lack of support from businesses for the Commission's proposals in this regard.[28]

There is work which the Commission could undertake in this area to make the use of standard contract terms easier. In particular, the identification of legislative obstacles to the use of standard contract terms on an EU-wide basis, with a view to reducing or eliminating them,[29] remains necessary.

---

21 *Ibid.*, pp 61–3.
22 C Mitchell, *Interpretation of Contracts* (London: Routledge-Cavendish, 2007).
23 Whittaker, *op. cit.*, pp 63–7.
24 H Collins, 'The freedom to circulate documents: regulating contracts in Europe' (2004) 10 *European Law Journal* 787–803, p 801.
25 C Twigg-Flesner, 'Standard terms in international commercial law – the example of documentary credits', in R Schulze, *New Features of Contract Law* (Munich: Sellier, 2007).
26 The only reference is to an organisation called Orgalime, which is cited as an example of an organisation that has managed to produce standard terms for cross-border transactions.
27 Cf E McKendrick, *The Creation of a European Law of Contracts – The Role of Standard Form Contracts and Principles of Interpretation* (The Hague: Kluwer, 2004).
28 U Bernitz, 'The Commission's Communications and standard contract terms', in S Vogenauer and S Weatherill (eds), *The Harmonisation of European Contract Law* (Oxford: Hart Publishing, 2006).
29 First Annual Progress Report, pp 6–8.

5.4 THE COMMON FRAME OF REFERENCE

The main outcome of the current process will be the development of the CFR. An interim draft version (the DCFR, or 'academic CFR') was delivered at the end of 2007, with a final DCFR due in December 2008 (the pace of this project has been described as 'breathtaking'[30] by the co-ordinators of the research teams involved in its preparation).[31] In this section, the process will be examined more closely.

5.4.1 Nature and substance of the CFR

The nature of the CFR is an issue in respect of which there remains a degree of uncertainty. The Commission has stated that it regards the CFR as a 'non-binding' instrument,[32] which, presumably, means that it will have no independent legal status. But what will it contain? In terms of sources, the CFR should draw on domestic legislation and case law, as well as the existing *acquis* and international instruments such as the United Nations Convention on the International Sale of Goods (CISG), and provide general rules on all the fundamental aspects of contract law.

The Commission's initial conception of the CFR suggested that it should provide 'common terminology and rules'.[33] As such, the CFR would be a 'toolbox' to assist with improving existing legislation and for the adoption of future measures.[34] It should have three broad features: definitions of relevant legal terms, fundamental principles, and coherent model rules. This is to be done through some sort of amalgam drawing on the *acquis* and best solutions derived (or rather, divined) from the domestic laws of the Member States.[35]

The Commission envisages that the CFR would commence with a number of fundamental principles of contract law.[36] There should also be an indication of when there would be an exception to these

---

30 C von Bar and H Schulte-Nölke, 'Zum Stand der Arbeiten an einem Gemeinsamen Referenzrahmen für europäisches Schuld- und Sachenrecht' (2005) *Zeitschrift für Rechtspolitik* 165–8.
31 *Way Forward*, pp 10–13. As the review of the consumer *acquis* (see below) is also due to be completed by 2009, this timetable has to be rather flexible.
32 *Way Forward*, p 5 (section 2.1.3).
33 *Action Plan*, para 62.
34 *Way Forward*, p 3.
35 See 'Drafting the CFR', below.
36 See Annex I to *The Way Forward*.

principles. Three examples of such fundamental principles are given: (1) freedom of contract, (2) the binding force of contract (*pacta sunt servanda*); and (3) good faith. An exception to (1) would be mandatory rules of contract law (such as consumer law), and to (2) the existence of a right of withdrawal.

Unsurprisingly, there has been a lot of criticism of the fact that the tension between freedom of contract at one end of the spectrum and co-operation or fairness at the other appears to have been largely skimmed over by the Commission;[37] it does seem that a debate on where to strike the balance is necessary. The absence of a discussion of fundamental issues is a theme which permeates all the developments examined in this chapter and has given rise to repeated criticism.

An important contribution made by the CFR will be a single legal terminology with clear definitions.[38] One of the problems with the existing *acquis* is its use of legal terms of art which are not defined at the European level, and have very different connotations in the various national laws.[39] Although there will undoubtedly be a heated debate about the definitions eventually adopted, the CFR terminology will provide a reference point as to what otherwise undefined terms in EU legislation should mean. This will not solve all the problems, because the vagaries of translating legal terminology from one language into another,[40] even if the CFR terminology is intended to be neutral, is likely to create some variations.[41]

As far as definitions are concerned, there is also some uncertainty as to what is expected here. The Commission talks of 'some definitions of abstract legal terms of European contract law in particular where relevant for the EC *acquis*'.[42] As already seen, one of the difficulties with

---

37 Eg B Lurger, 'The future of European contract law between freedom of contract, social justice and market rationality' (2005) 1 *European Review of Contract Law* 442–68.

38 G Ajani and M Ebers (eds), *Uniform Terminology for European Contract Law* (Baden-Baden: Nomos, 2005).

39 B Pozzo, 'Harmonisation of European contract law and the need for creating a common terminology' (2003) 11 *European Review of Private Law* 754–67; also Pozzo and Jacometti, *op. cit.*

40 That is, from English into all the other official languages, as English has become the dominant language for the drafting process.

41 It has been suggested that the EU's aim of maintaining cultural and linguistic diversity is difficult to square with established practice and the desire for one common legal terminology: N Urban, 'One legal language *and* the maintenance of cultural and linguistic diversity?' (2000) 8 *European Review of Private Law* 51–57.

42 *Way Forward*, p 14.

the current *acquis* is that terms which appear in more than one directive are defined differently. The intention here might be a review of the various definitions already found in the *acquis*, with a view to coming to a single definition for each term applicable across the *acquis*.

However, it is not limited to that, because it is also suggested that there could be a definition of 'contract' itself. To this, it is added that 'the definition could for example also explain when a contract should be considered as concluded'.[43] That, however, is going to be very difficult to narrow down to a definition. A brief look at PECL shows that as many as 20 articles deal with aspects of contract formation. It might therefore be better to restrict a section on definitions to those terms that could easily be defined (such as 'consumer' or 'durable medium'), and to leave other matters for more detailed rules. Indeed, attempting to define 'contract' runs into the fundamental difficulty that the various jurisdictions within Europe each have their own conception of contract, as well as varying underlying philosophies.[44] In particular, there are differences in how the supply of certain public services, such as the public utilities, health care and education, are classified.[45]

In this context, it is also important to bear in mind the dual function performed by definitions in EU law. On the one hand, they explain what is meant by specific terms used in legislation, and also serve to determine the scope of application. On the other, definitions in EU legislation serve to define the 'occupied field', that is, the extent to which a particular area of law is 'Europeanised'. Matters not within the occupied field are within the competence of the national legislator. Whilst there can be little concern over the intention to arrive at common definitions for legal terms of art, it may be doubted whether the same can be said for more fundamental issues, including the notion of contract itself.

The main part of the CFR would comprise 'model rules' on contract law. A suggested structure of these model rules is given in Annex I to the *Way Forward*. These include aspects of contract formation, validity, authority of agents, interpretation, contents and effects, followed by

---

43 *Ibid.*
44 See L Miller, 'The Common Frame of Reference and the feasibility of a common contract law in Europe' [2007] *Journal of Business Law*, 378–411. Miller also examines different national conceptions of rules on non-performance, including the variations that remain after, or were created by, the Consumer Sales Directive (99/44/EC).
45 S Whittaker, 'Unfair contract terms, public service and the construction of a European Conception of Contract' (2000) 116 *Law Quarterly Review* 95–120; A Gambaro, 'The Plan d'Action of the European Commission – a comment' [2003] *European Review of Private Law* 768–81, p 773.

pre-contractual obligations, performance, plurality of parties, assignment and prescription. There should then be specific rules on sales and insurance contracts. There might also be a section dealing with service contracts. Moreover, it may be necessary to include provisions on the transfer of title to goods, and retention of title clauses. The publication of an interim version of the DCFR indicates that the final CFR could cover even more topics.[46]

The inspiration for CFR are undoubtedly the *Principles of European Contract Law*. One of the hallmarks of PECL is the combination of a stated principle with a detailed explanation, and, crucially, notes which explain how the various national contract laws relate to the principle. Following this approach for the CFR would undoubtedly make it more valuable as a toolbox, especially if it draws out both commonalities and significant differences in the national laws.

5.4.1.1 The relevance of consumer law

In the CFR, consumer contracts should be given 'specific attention'.[47] Indeed, the focus of EC legislation has been on consumer contract law, which is a derogation from general contract law principles. Whilst the CFR is intended to be a toolbox on all aspects of contract law, once drafted, its immediate use will be in the field of consumer contract law, rather than general contract law (to review and improve the *acquis*). The Commission has emphasised that it expects the CFR to be drafted on the basis of both domestic law and the *acquis*. With the *acquis* primarily comprising rules on consumer contract law, this means that there will have to be specific rules on consumer law issues in the CFR. These may be derived directly from the *acquis*,[48] although it is clear that the law as it is at present cannot simply be transposed into the CFR. This is because one of the concerns about the current *acquis* is its incoherence, and adjustments will have to be made to any *acquis*-derived rules to provide the 'best solution' the CFR is intended to provide.

This in itself will be a challenge, because decisions about the substance of consumer law are clearly policy-based, and are a conscious departure from general contract law in the interest of consumer protection. For example, it was clearly felt that when consumers conclude a contract at their doorstep, or via the internet, the general rule that a

---

46 See below, p 157.
47 *Way Forward*, p 11.
48 See below, p 153.

contract is binding once validly formed should be made subject to a right of withdrawal. Identifying the circumstances when protection is needed, and determining what that protection might be, therefore involve policy choices, which cannot necessarily be made at the drafting stage.[49] So, whilst the mechanism for exercising a right of withdrawal and its consequences might be set out in the (D)CFR, the circumstances where such a right should be made available must be left for those who make policy choices.

This challenge is further complicated by the fact that, according to the Commission's expectations about the structure of the CFR, circumstances in which there might be a departure from fundamental principles of contract law need to be identified clearly. Consumer-specific rules are usually such departures, and these will, presumably, have to be linked to relevant fundamental principles, together with possible justification for departing from them.

More than in respect of other aspects of the CFR, what is needed here is not so much one 'best solution', as might be expected, but rather a number of options. The CFR could include several possible solutions to particular consumer protection problems, identify the underlying policy choices, and then leave it to the legislature to express its preference for one solution when adopting new legislation.

5.4.2 Purpose(s) of the CFR

There are a number of different possible uses for the CFR. According to the *Action Plan*, its primary function will be as a toolbox for improving the *acquis*, but this could mean several different things.

In providing model rules, the CFR might provide a blueprint for future legislation, whether entirely new measures, or improvements of existing ones. As explained further below, the CFR should point out those areas where there may be more than one answer to a particular problem, and offer several approaches which are then selected by the EU legislator.[50] The relevant model rules from the CFR could be adopted expressly in new legislation, or be incorporated by reference to the relevant parts of the CFR.[51]

---

49 See below, p 155.
50 H Beale (2007), 'The future of the Common Frame of Reference' (2007) 3 *European Review of Contract Law* 257–76, pp 268–69.
51 See H Beale, 'The European Civil Code movement and the European Union's Common Frame of Reference' (2006) 6 *Legal Information Management* 4–11.

Assuming that the model rules CFR are accompanied by detailed notes on the corresponding domestic rules, it will have a second important function: when drafting legislation, the EU legislator can identify what each national law might understand by a particular rule. Thus, both substantive similarities expressed in doctrinal forms which differ as between the Member States and identical terminology with different substantive meanings could be identified in these notes.[52] This will be particularly important where European legislation is proposed which would impact on a matter where there are significant differences between the Member States. A particular concept or model rule might be understood in different ways at national level, and the CFR could assist the EU legislator by identifying these different conceptions. This should enable the legislator to draft rules which are sufficiently precise, thereby avoiding unnecessary ambiguity. In a sense, the CFR would be a translation tool, creating awareness of what different national laws understand by particular concepts and rules. As the CFR will contain a 'best solution' model rule, it will be possible to identify those jurisdictions which do not have this rule.[53] As an example, one only needs to recall the *Leitner* case,[54] which revealed that some Member States, including Austria, did not include non-pecuniary loss within the notion of 'damages'. Had there been a reference point to illustrate these differences, an express provision could have been included in the Directive and thereby have avoided the uncertainty which eventually produced the ECJ's ruling.[55]

It may have a number of additional functions which could contribute to the further Europeanisation of domestic contract laws. Thus, the CFR could assist Member States faced with the task of implementing an EU directive into their domestic legal systems in trying to consider how the directive relates to neighbouring areas of contract law.[56] Hitherto, the transposition of directives has often been limited to doing whatever is necessary to comply with basic obligations under the EC Treaty, without spending too much time on dealing with any knock-on effects.[57] The suggestion appears to be that, by looking to the CFR, Member States could examine how the provisions from the directive relate to other areas of contract law, and further consider to what extent their domestic law might be at variance with the position under the

---

52 *Ibid.*, p 264.
53 *Ibid.*, p 268.
54 C-168/00 *Simone Leitner v TUI Deutschland* [2002] ECR I-2631.
55 H Beale (2006), *op. cit.*
56 *Way Forward*, p 5.
57 See Chapter 4.

CFR. This approach, if carried out systematically, certainly has the potential of contributing to the evolution of a more coherent Europeanised contract law (albeit in the form of 'creeping Europeanisation').

It is also of concern, however: the adoption of a directive dealing with what might be a small aspect of contract law could mean that some Member States might feel compelled to adjust their domestic contract law in related areas in order to ensure that the transposition does not undermine the effectiveness of the directive. Depending on the subject matter of the directive, and the extent to which domestic law departs from the CFR, this may result in much further-reaching changes to domestic law than required by the directive. This might turn directives into a form of Trojan horse, driving a wider range of CFR-based rules into domestic law. This might not be palatable to a Member State for all sorts of reasons, for example, because the costs associated with changes to domestic law going beyond the immediate implementation of a directive might be too high, or because of a reluctance to accept further encroachment of European legislation into domestic law. It remains to be seen whether this purpose of the CFR would merely create an opportunity for a domestic legislator, or reflect an expectation to go further. This may depend on the reach of the general principle of effectiveness (*effet utile*) of EU law. In essence, this obliges Member States to ensure that EU rules are fully effective in national law and not restricted by provisions of national procedural or substantive law. On a broad interpretation, it might lead to the conclusion that a Member State is in breach of its EU law obligations by not adjusting the domestic legislation in areas linked to a directive in accordance with the CFR. However, if there is no legal obligation to follow the CFR, it will be difficult to see how a decision by a Member State not to make changes to related areas of law could contravene *effet utile*. Nevertheless, there is a lingering uncertainty.

A related purpose envisaged by the Commission is that Member States might look to the CFR when adopting legislation on contract law at the national level, where there is no corresponding EU legislation. As such, it would do no more than to offer a possible solution for a domestic legislator to consider, but it would leave the Member States free to adopt a rule that differs from the relevant CFR provision. Although not mentioned explicitly in the *Way Forward*, the CFR could similarly provide guidance to national courts when interpreting domestic law, particularly if that law contains a gap or is ambiguous (thereby supporting 'spontaneous Europeanisation'[58]).

---

58 See Chapter 1, p 11.

Beyond this, the CFR could assist the ECJ when it is dealing with a request for a preliminary ruling on the interpretation of particular provisions of EC contract law. This might ensure that a decision by the ECJ does not have the effect of creating varying meanings for particular concepts used in the *acquis communautaire*. At a more general level, the CFR could be of use in arbitration. It is suggested that arbitrators might be guided by the substance of the CFR in dealing with particular conflicts. Other potential uses are that the CFR could be incorporated into contracts which the Commission (and other EU bodies) enter into with its contractors.

5.4.3 Drafting the CFR: CoPECL research network

As mentioned earlier, the CFR is to combine 'best solutions' found in the domestic laws of the Member States and the existing *acquis communautaire* into a coherent whole.[59] It is therefore necessary to undertake a detailed comparative study of the contract laws of the Member States to analyse and evaluate the various rules on each aspect of contract law. From this, one (or more) best solutions need to be distilled.[60] To this, it is necessary to add aspects of the *acquis*, particularly rules on consumer contract law. This task is formidable and, were it to commence *de novo*, likely to require many years of thorough comparative law research. However, the Commission is, of course, aware of the significant amount of scholarly work that has already been undertaken, and it clearly sees no merit in starting afresh. In particular, the work of the Lando Commission has already gone a long way towards identifying best solutions based on the laws of the Member States. That work was initially based on a much smaller group of countries, and some revisions may be needed to take into account both developments in the countries which were subject of the original work and the new Member States that have joined the EU.[61] To this, solutions already in the *acquis* need to be added.

---

59 C von Bar, 'Coverage and structure of the academic Common Frame of Reference' (2007) 3 *European Review of Contract Law* 350–61.
60 The advantage of a 'best solution' approach may be neutrality: the solution adopted should be free from particular national restraints: MJ Bonell, 'The need and possibilities of a codified European contract law' (1997) 5 *European Review of Private Law* 505–18, p 511.
61 With regard to the latter, this task may not be as complicated as might be thought, because some of the new Member States have been inspired both by the Lando Principles, and the *UNIDROIT Principles on International Commercial Contracts*.

The initial task of creating a draft version of the CFR (the DCFR) has been given to the leading academic research groups. A research network has therefore been established within the context of the FP6-research programme. This research network comprises many of the leading European research groups on contract law, headed by the Study Group on a European Civil Code[62] and the Research Group on the Existing EC Private Law (Acquis Group).[63] Other groups participating in the network are the Project Group on a Restatement of Insurance Contract Law, the French Association Henri Capitant, the Common Core (Trento) Group, the so-called Database Group, as well as the Tilburg Group of economists responsible for preparing an impact assessment of the work undertaken, and the European Academy of Law in Trier.[64] Its task is to prepare the DCFR, which should be based on both domestic laws and the *acquis*.

At the same time, the Commission has established its network of stakeholders ('CFR-net'), and a programme of workshops on specific aspects of the draft CFR has been held. The research teams submit draft reports in advance of the workshops, and CFR-net participants are invited to prepare written comments after the relevant workshop has taken place.[65] Mance has noted that the balance of representation seems inadequate, with both some business sectors and geographical areas inadequately represented in this network.[66] Moreover, it is not entirely clear what purpose this network may serve; the input from stakeholders into a drafting process seems to be of limited relevance at the stage of producing a toolbox, and might be of more significance once specific legislation has been proposed.

For some, the leading role of the Study Group is of concern, because it seems to be in conflict with the Commission's position that it has no intention of proposing a civil code for the EU;[67] indeed, Kenny goes so far as to claim that 'the symbiotic relationship between Commission and Study Group . . . is clearly a central paradox in this initiative'.[68]

---

62 Under the leadership of Prof Christian von Bar (University of Osnabrück, Germany).
63 Co-ordinated by Prof Hans Schulte-Nölke (University of Bielefeld, Germany); its speaker is Prof Gianmaria Ajani (University of Turin, Italy).
64 The existence of only one network, and the exclusion of other leading academic groups and individuals, has been criticised in particular by S Grundmann, 'European contract law(s) of what colour?' (2005) 1 *European Review of Contract Law* 184–210.
65 For a detailed description of the process, see *First Annual Progress Report*, pp 3–6.
66 J Mance, 'Is Europe aiming to civilise the common law?' [2007] *European Business Law Review* 77–99, p 93.
67 *Way Forward*, p 8.
68 M Kenny, 'The 2004 Communication on European Contract Law: those magnificent men in their unifying machines' (2005) 30 *European Law Review* 724–42, p 733.

This might be one factor which contributed to the fact that progress at the initial round of CFR workshops was hampered by a degree of misunderstanding among CFR-net members about the purpose of the exercise. In particular, there was some confusion as to whether a 'European Civil Code' was on the agenda.[69] Moreover, the topics considered in the early workshops were on specialised areas (service contracts and long-term contracts) rather than general contract law. A later workshop to discuss the structure of the DCFR turned into a debate about its purpose and content instead, with the result that the primary focus of the CFR, which the Commission intends to produce by selecting parts from the DCFR, would be on general contract law and matters relevant to the *acquis*.[70] Following the initial series of workshops in 2005, the Commission adjusted its programme of workshops to focus on topics which will be of particular relevance to the review of the consumer *acquis*,[71] and after a series of workshops during the first half of 2006,[72] there has only been limited activity.

5.4.3.1 Incorporating the acquis – the work of the Acquis Group

It has already been noted that the DCFR should be based on a comparative analysis of the contract laws of the Member States to find 'best solutions', but that the *acquis* already in place should also be reflected in the DCFR. This is a major challenge, because the sources in the *acquis* are fragmented, and may not offer anything greatly coherent[73] – indeed, that is why one of the main objectives of the DCFR is to provide the tools for making the *acquis* coherent. This approach raises a serious question of legitimacy, as the CoPECL Network has, in effect, been tasked with presenting coherent rules that will be used to modernise the *acquis* in the DCFR. This is worrying as many *acquis* rules come from consumer law, which has clear policy implications.

There are, however, good reasons for taking account of the *acquis* in

---

69 Undoubtedly not helped by the fact that some of the work presented to the workshops was headed 'Study Group on a European Civil Code' – see Mance, *ibid.*, p 94.
70 H Beale, 'The European Commission's Common Frame of Reference project: a progress report' (2006) 2 *European Review of Contract Law* 303–14.
71 *First Annual Progress Report*, pp 5–6.
72 A summary of these is reported in the *Second Progress Report on the Common Frame of Reference* (COM (2007) 447 final), pp 3–8.
73 See, eg, T Wilhelmsson and C Twigg-Flesner, 'Pre-contractual information duties in the *acquis communautaire*' (2006) 2 *European Review of Contract Law* 441–70.

the (D)CFR.[74] The *acquis* comprises rules which have generally[75] met the broad agreement of the Member States, and therefore have some value as a core of European contract law, as well as a degree of European legitimacy.[76] The task of providing rules derived from the *acquis* is undertaken by the Research Group on the Existing EC Private Law, better known as the Acquis Group.[77] Its objective is to analyse the various directives, regulations and judgments by the ECJ in order to create a coherent set of rules on contract law.

The Acquis Group faces several challenges: as seen, the *acquis* has not had a significant effect on general contract. It is therefore difficult to derive principles or model rules on general contract law from much of the *acquis*, because the *acquis*, largely comprising consumer law, generally tends to provide rules which form an exception from a general principle. From the position of consumer law as a derogation, the task is to identify that hidden general principle which has been derogated from.[78] The Acquis Group therefore needs to decide whether one can identify unexpressed underlying principles which are sufficiently well reflected in existing law to be suitable for generalisation, a process which will not be without controversy.[79] In particular, the fragmentary nature of the *acquis* and the danger of turning an exception into a general rule through generalisation are of concern.[80]

Furthermore, many of the measures which constitute the existing

---

74 R Schulze, 'European private law and existing EC law' (2005) 13 *European Review of Private Law* 3–19.

75 It must be borne in mind that measures are generally adopted on the basis of Art 95 EC, and that only a qualified majority is required for legislation to pass. Not all the Member States have supported all the contract *acquis* measures. Moreover, the new Member States have not had an opportunity for voting on most of the *acquis*, because it predates their accession.

76 S Grundmann, 'The optional European Code on the basis of the Acquis Communautaire' (2004) 10 *European Law Journal* 678–711; Wilhelmsson and Twigg-Flesner, *op. cit.*, p 444.

77 H Schulte-Nölke, 'The Commission's Action Plan on European contract law and the research of the Acquis Group' [2003] *ERA Forum* 142–45.

78 See, in particular, K Riesenhuber, *System und Prinzipien des Europäischen Vertragsrechts* (Berlin: De Gruyter, 2003); also *System and Principles of EC Contract Law* (2005) 1 *European Review of Contract Law* 297–322.

79 See further, G Dannemann, 'Consolidating EC contract law: an introduction to the work of the Acquis Group', in Acquis Group, *Principles of the Existing EC Contract Law – Contract I* (Munich: Sellier, 2007).

80 H Collins, 'The alchemy of deriving general principles of contract law from European legislation: in search of the philosopher's stone' (2006) 2 *European Review of Contract Law* 213–226.

acquis adopt a minimum harmonisation standard. Whilst this may have been acceptable to all (or most) of the Member States as a minimum standard, it does not mean that it is the standard that should become the norm in the (D)CFR. In addition, the *acquis* measures were not designed to operate independently of domestic law; instead, they need to be applied as part of, and through interaction with, related national rules. Incorporating the *acquis* in the (D)CFR is therefore a task that needs to be handled with considerable care. It may be that the most appropriate way forward is to identify the particular contributions made by the *acquis*, but to return to the drawing board to develop provisions that could fit into the (D)CFR. Key areas are pre-contractual information duties, rights of withdrawal, unfair contract terms and non-discrimination, all hallmarks of the *acquis*.[81] Provisions on these clearly need to appear in the (D)CFR, but in its current form, the *acquis* is too incoherent to offer instant solutions. Some thought will therefore have to be given to the development of model rules from what is already in the *acquis*. Inspiration could be gained from the way the Member States have implemented these directives and their subsequent application by domestic courts, as well as additional guidance given by the ECJ.[82] However, this is a risky business and could easily result in creating provisions without clear foundations in the *acquis* or domestic law. Moreover, Collins suggests that as parts of the *acquis* are a hybrid of private law and regulatory measures, finding principles of contract law 'appears to be as futile as trying to distil beer from grapes, or as wishful as turning a toad into a handsome prince',[83] although he concludes that the character of modern private law generally has been infused with regulatory principles, making this process not impossible.

5.4.3.2 Policy choices

The CFR is intended as a toolbox for improving and developing legislation. However, during the drafting process, there will be instances when policy choices are identified, for example with regard to consumer protection.[84] These will need to be explained in the (D)CFR, and it would

---

81 Cf the topics covered in Acquis Group, *Contract I, op. cit.*

82 The *Consumer Compendium and Comparative Analysis*, prepared by H Schulte-Nölke with C Twigg-Flesner and M Ebers and published on the Commission's website, provides detailed information for most of the consumer *acquis* on the implementation, including use of the minimum harmonisation clauses.

83 Collins, *op. cit.*, p 220.

84 See above, p 147.

be wrong to skim over such choices by stating a single rule as 'the best solution'. Those preparing the (D)CFR need to 'recognise policy issues for what they are, and [set] out the arguments on each side. A failure to do that . . . would not only be an academic failure; it would be an improper abrogation of decision-making powers.'[85] The task of the scholars developing the toolbox is to identify policy choices and present a range of options. A decision on which of the various policy choices should be favoured is only needed once actual legislation is being considered.

5.4.4 A critical view

There is concern about the way the (D)CFR will be created. An exercise undertaken by academics (the CoPECL network), based on a comparative research and the *acquis* to provide 'best solutions', might sound like an ideal way to undertake the groundwork that is needed in order to create the (D)CFR. However, this approach has been criticised because it seems to have reduced the entire process to a technical matter without taking due account of the fact that there are economic, social and cultural factors which also affect the determination of whether a particular solution qualifies as a 'best' solution.[86]

Drawing on the work already undertaken by legal scholars alone might not have been the best means of creating the CFR: 'The coupling of a useful Commission project with a useful academic project which had its own direction and momentum has not proved entirely happy. Academic freedom has in some ways provided more a problem than an advantage.'[87] Indeed, the pace with which the project has proceeded, and the fact that insufficient room has been given for addressing fundamental questions about the project are of concern.[88]

---

85 Beale, 'What has been done, what is going on, what is to be expected: Common Frame of Reference, Optional Instrument and . . .?', paper presented at a seminar held in Sheffield in November 2004 (unpublished; on file with author), para 76.

86 Cf 'European contract law: quo vadis?' (editorial comments), (2005) 42 *Common Market Law Review* 1–7, p 6.

87 J Mance, 'Is Europe aiming to civilise the common law?' [2007] *European Business Law Review* 77–99, p 97.

88 M Kenny, 'Constructing a European Civil Code: quis custodiet ipsos custodes?' (2006) 12 *Columbia Journal of European Law* 775–808.

5.4.5 The interim DCFR (2007)

At the end of December 2007, the CoPECL research network submitted an interim version of the DCFR to the Commission, and the text of the definitions, principles and model rules (without any accompanying commentary or national notes) was made available to the public in book form.[89] This interim version also contains an introductory section in which the co-ordinators of the research network set out their approach towards creating the DCFR.[90]

The DCFR is divided into seven 'books' (reflecting the continental approach to civil codes) and two annexes (containing definitions and rules on computation of time respectively). It extends beyond what might be regarded as general contract law; indeed, its central section (Book III) deals with all types of obligations, not merely contract law. There are also 'books' on benevolent intervention in another's affairs, non-contractual liability (tort), and unjustified enrichment. Their immediate relevance to contract law, particularly EU contract-related legislation, is far from obvious. Indeed, it is the omission of provisions dealing with aspects of property law, such as the transfer of property in movables, that is surprising, because this would be of more immediate significance for cross-border contracting.[91]

Publication of the interim DCFR is intended to provide an opportunity for comments from scholars and stakeholders,[92] as well as to enable the network's own evaluation groups to undertake their work. The DCFR will be reviewed before a final version is submitted in December 2008. What is already clear is that the DCFR will be much broader than the Commission requires, and the co-ordinators have accepted, with some reluctance, the fact that not all parts of the DCFR will survive in the final 'Commission CFR'; nevertheless, a case is made in favour of adopting as broad a CFR as possible.[93]

---

89 Study Group on a European Civil Code/Research Group on the Existing EC Private Law (Acquis Group) (eds), *Principles, Definitions and Model Rules on European Private Law – Draft Common Frame of Reference* (Munich: Sellier, 2008) (*DCFR*).

90 *Ibid.*, pp 3–39.

91 Cf U Drobnig, HJ Snijders and EJ Zippo (eds), *Divergences of Property Law: An Obstacle to the Internal Market?* (Munich: Sellier, 2006).

92 An initial response analysing both the extent to which the *acquis* is reflected in the DCFR, as well as the potential significance of the DCFR for the *acquis* review, can be found in R Schulze (ed), *Common Frame of Reference and Existing EC Contract Law* (Munich: Sellier, 2008).

93 *DCFR*, pp 29–37.

5.4.6 Beyond the DCFR

The creation of the DCFR will only be the first stage on the way to a final CFR. The Commission has planned a follow-up process once the final version of the DCFR has been presented (at the end of 2008) that will encompass several stages. There will be a period of evaluation, during which the Commission intends to submit the DCFR to a practicability test.[94] In essence, this might involve preparing a revision to one (or more) of the directives in the consumer law field, using the provisions of the DCFR as a guide. There is no detail on the criteria the Commission might apply in this regard.

It is, however, clear that the Commission will concentrate on those aspects of the DCFR which will be directly relevant to the review of the consumer *acquis*, although this might also include aspects of general contract law as well as other areas where EU legislation is envisaged.[95] In fact, it seems impossible to ignore general contract law because consumer law is largely a derogation from general principles, and if the CFR is to serve its toolbox function, there needs to be clarity as to what the consumer *acquis* departs from.[96]

Following consultation with other European institutions and Member State experts, the Commission will present a revised, pared-down version of the DCFR (the 'Commission's CFR'). This will culminate in the adoption of a White Paper on the CFR, which will require the translation of the Commission's CFR into all the official languages of the EU. There will be a six-month period of consultation to enable stakeholders to comment on this version of the CFR, and to deal with any differences in the various language versions of the CFR. The latter aspect is crucial, and reflects a systemic problem of EU legislation that has not been addressed properly to date: the difficulties of translating legal terminology from one language into another.[97] Once this process is complete, the 'adoption' of the CFR by the Commission and its publication are scheduled for 2009.

The stages subsequent to the delivery of the DCFR will, it seems, be

---

94 *Way Forward*, p 12.

95 *Second Progress Report*, pp 10–11.

96 Eg, M Storme, 'Freedom of contract: mandatory and non-mandatory rules in European contract law' (2007) 15 *European Review of Private Law* 233–50, p 238.

97 See A Gambaro, 'The Plan d'Action of the European Commission – a comment' [2003] *European Review of Private Law* 768–81.

a political process involving the other European institutions,[98] Member States, and stakeholders. The reason for this is unclear – if the CFR is going to be a toolbox for improving existing legislation, or for adopting new legislation, then the political process will come into play once a formal legislative proposal has been made.[99] As long as the research network has identified the various policy options in the DCFR, no further decision is needed until specific legislation is being considered; only then will a decision on which of the various choices to adopt be required.

Less controversially, the Commission also promises that 'mechanisms for updating the CFR will be identified'.[100] This may be a somewhat aspirational statement, because keeping the CFR updated may be just as monumental a task as the initial drafting process. National contract laws would have to be monitored regularly to keep track of significant developments, and there would need to be some sort of threshold that would need to be reached before amendments are made to the CFR. However, regular updating is essential if the CFR is to remain useful. In particular, as national laws continue to evolve (albeit perhaps on more parallel tracks than before the CFR), the notes on the national rules accompanying each Model Rule will need to be amended to ensure that the CFR retains its toolbox function.

The CFR will be a crucial step in the Europeanisation process. However, the fact that there is still so much uncertainty about its substance and subsequent application, as well as the drafting process itself, is worrying. It is to be hoped that, once the draft CFR is available, the Commission will present a clear picture of what its intentions are.

5.5 AN OPTIONAL INSTRUMENT

The third aspect of the work ongoing at the European level is the 'reflection on the opportuneness' of a non-sector-specific measure, also known as an 'optional instrument'. Although there was wide opposition to option IV from the *Communication*, which considered comprehensive EU regulation of contract law, the possibility of broader

---

98 The European Parliament has called for the early involvement of the Parliament in this process, and has already resolved that it seeks a broad CFR that goes beyond consumer contract law: European Parliament Resolution of 12 December 2007 on European Contract Law (B6/0513/2007).
99 Cf H Beale (2007), *op. cit.*
100 *Way Forward*, p 13.

intervention in the sphere of contract law has not been taken off the table completely. The Commission holds back on any firm proposals, although it hints that it is thinking about a legal framework on contract law to operate alongside the existing domestic laws, possibly applicable only to cross-border transactions or through the parties' choice; largely based around default rules, with some mandatory rules; and based on the content of the CFR.

This is inevitably all rather vague at this stage, but it would be risky to come forward with concrete ideas about a more comprehensive intervention. There is, of course, concern that the optional instrument is really an obscure reference for a European contract code. Thus, Kenny argues that the 'Commission's linguistic contortions should be understood as a warning: what does the Commission mean by arguing for a frame of reference and an optional instrument, yet insisting that it is not to be understood as a nascent pan-European civil law?'[101] Unsurprisingly, it has been claimed that the optional instrument is really a 'camouflage for a European Contract Code'.[102] As things stand, the development of an optional instrument on general contract law seems a distant prospect. Instead, more concrete action in the field of financial services is a possibility. In its *First Progress Report*, the Commission noted that exploratory work in the field of financial services may lead to a so-called '28th regime' for life-insurance or savings products, and also potentially for mortgage credit.[103] And, as will be seen later, consumer law has emerged as the primary candidate for an optional instrument.

There are a number of different models for an optional instrument (OI). If the label currently used by the Commission is indicative of its thinking, then there is not going to be a framework on contract law which has to be adopted by the Member States instead of their domestic contract laws. Rather, the OI would exist alongside domestic laws and provide an alternative legal framework for contracting parties.[104]

Whatever the OI may become, it will be optional; that is, contracting parties may choose not to be bound by the OI. In the *Action Plan*, the

---

101 M Kenny, 'The 2003 Action Plan on European Contract Law: is the Commission running wild?' (2003) 28 *European Law Review* 538–50, p 550.
102 'European Contract law: quo vadis?' (editorial comments) (2005) 42 *Common Market Law Review* 1–7, p 3.
103 *First Annual Progress Report*, p 11.
104 *Action Plan*, para 92.

Commission suggested that this optionality could be for the parties to choose whether to 'opt in' or 'opt out' in respect of the OI. An 'opt-out' model would apply only to cross-border situations. This makes some sense: in a purely domestic context, it would be very unusual to have a conflict of laws, as both contracting parties will be based in the same jurisdiction and expect the contract law of that jurisdiction to govern their relationship. Although the notion of 'cross-border' has not been explored further by the Commission in its documents, it seems that this relates to contracts where goods or services cross borders, rather than a situation where the contracting parties are based in different jurisdictions. There would be a presumption that the OI applied to all cross-border contracts, unless the parties expressly chose not to apply it, but to subject their contract to a particular domestic regime.

The 'opt-in' model would, in essence, make the OI available as an alternative to existing domestic laws, but leave it up to the contracting parties to choose whether to use a national law or the OI. Their choice would be reflected through a choice of law clause in their contract. This suggestion does give rise to a possible problem: parties opting in would choose a non-national law, and that has raised concerns about the conceptual difficulties for private international law to accept the choice of a non-national law. This obstacle could, however, be overcome because the EC can adopt appropriate legislative provisions in the field of private international law to permit contracting parties to choose a non-national legal framework.[105] It is certainly true that there may be problems with trying to fit an optional instrument into the existing framework on private international law.[106] Nevertheless, Recital 16 of the Rome-I Regulation (which was agreed in December 2007) states that if the EU were to 'adopt in an appropriate legal instrument rules of substantive contract law, including standard terms and conditions, such instrument may provide that the parties may choose to apply those rules'. This seems to create the possibility of enabling the choice of an optional instrument as an alternative to national law. It does not go as far as Art 3(2) of the original proposal for the Rome-I regulation,[107] but

---

105 Von Bar and Schulte-Nölke, *op. cit.*, p 167.
106 D Staudenmeyer, 'The way forward in European Contract Law' [2005] *European Review of Private Law* 95–104, pp 100–03.
107 COM (2005) 650 final, Art 3(2): 'The parties may also choose as the applicable law the principles and rules of the substantive law of contract recognised internationally or in the Community . . .', which could relate to both the CFR and OI. See C von Bar (2007) *op. cit.*, p 352.

appears sufficient for creating the private international law basis needed for an OI.

5.5.1 Scope of the OI

There are then questions of scope: the OI could apply to all types of contract (that is, business-to-business (B2B), business-to-consumer (B2C), business-to-government (B2G) and private), or be more limited.

The Commission has indicated that, in view of the link of all of the activities in the sphere of European contract law with the internal market, the OI should also contribute to the operation of the internal market. In that context, B2C transactions are significant, and for this reason, the OI would almost certainly include provisions on consumer law.[108]

If the OI covers B2C transactions, then there would be mandatory provisions.[109] Assuming this to be so, then a further issue is what would happen to existing national mandatory rules in this field. The purpose of mandatory rules in private international law is to prevent the evasion of particular rules in one jurisdiction by choosing the law of another jurisdiction which does not provide similar rules. If the OI were chosen by the parties to a contract, then the expectation would be that only the mandatory provisions of the OI would be applicable. However, it seems that domestic mandatory rules would not be excluded through choosing the OI rather than another national law, unless the rules of private international law were amended in such a way that domestic mandatory rules of consumer law would not apply if the chosen 'law' is the OI. This issue underlines the importance of co-ordinating the Rome-I regulation with an eventual proposal for an OI.

As for the B2B context, the Commission is keen to rely on freedom of contract as a fundamental principle not just for the CFR but also the OI, and in B2B transactions, the parties would be free to modify the OI to suit their own needs.[110]

Whenever the OI were applied to B2B cross-border sales contracts, there would be the danger of treading on the toes of a well-established instrument dealing with cross-border sales between businesses: the

---

108 *The Way Forward*, p 19.
109 On the question of mandatory rules in an optional instrument, see H Heiss and N Downes, 'Non-optional elements in an optional European contract law' (2005) 13 *European Review of Private Law* 693–712.
110 *The Way Forward*, p 19.

CISG. To avoid this, the OI could merely copy out the CISG (which would add nothing). Alternatively, it could deliberately provide alternative rules which would compete with the CISG. The latter option seems undesirable, because it could cause difficulties for businesses contracting with both EU- and non-EU-based partners who might rely on the CISG for all types of transaction.

5.5.2 Substance

The development of the OI would not occur in isolation, but take into account the CFR. The Commission is careful in saying that the CFR 'would be likely to serve as a basis for discussions'[111] on the OI. If, as discussed above,[112] the CFR is a toolbox which presents options rather than one complete set of rules, then a subsequent step towards an OI will need to decide which of these options should be adopted, particularly in respect of matters which require clear policy choices.

There may also have to be a decision as to how broad a scope an OI might have: should it really be so bold as to cover general contract law, and thereby rival each of the domestic contract law systems? Or would it be better if it dealt with areas where there is a clear internal market reason, for example with regard to consumer law or financial services (particularly insurance)? These are questions which will undoubtedly be at the centre of the deliberations about an OI (or several OIs).

5.5.3 An 'optional instrument': is it needed?

Any proposal to adopt an optional instrument is likely to be controversial, because it would introduce a new system of contract law to sit alongside all the national regimes.

A '28th regime' might fail because it could add to the confusion already caused by the existing 27 regimes, adding just another layer of complexity. Certainly, the adoption of a 28th regime would not have the immediate effect of reducing transaction costs. The uncertainty that prevails about the contract rules in another jurisdiction would be no less acute with an entirely new legal framework. Indeed, in the short term, such a regime would create higher transaction costs because there

---

111 *The Way Forward*, p 19.
112 See 5.4.2.

would be greater unfamiliarity for lack of practical experience with the new rules, as well as uncertainty about its application across the EU.[113]

To this, one might respond that reliance on 'jurisdictional competition' is just as unlikely to provide an answer.[114] Moreover, if one is in favour of diversity and utilisation of choice of law by the parties to a contract, there seems to be no logical basis for rejecting the possibility of an optional instrument as an alternative choice to a domestic law.[115]

5.6 CFR AND OI: EVALUATION

5.6.1 Confusion reigns

There has been much speculation about what the CFR will look like and what its ultimate uses will be. As discussed above, the Commission's documents suggest that, one the one hand, it will be a 'toolbox' that can be used for improving the *acquis*; on the other, it might form the basis of an optional instrument. This 'tension between [its] twin aims'[116] is causing a degree of confusion regarding the substance of the CFR, and also its form. If it is solely to be a toolbox, its key function would be to provide coherent definitions and consistent terminology, and perhaps basic coherent rules on recurring themes (such as rights of withdrawal or pre-contractual information duties). The analysis of the laws of the Member State and the possible 'solutions' this may produce may lead to the identification of a 'best solution', but alternative solutions must not be omitted from the CFR; indeed, there may be more than one candidate for a 'best solution'. The CFR should not be a ready-made law of contract in a form that could be adopted 'as is'; rather, where necessary, it should identify the options that are available to both the EU and national legislators for developing the law. If it is to be the blueprint for an optional instrument, it will have to contain detailed model rules on general contract law, as well as some specific contracts.[117] But these two objectives are not necessarily separate – as Beale observes, even for the *acquis* review,[118] more detailed rules may be

---

113 Cf H Collins, *op. cit.*
114 Von Bar and Schulte-Nölke, *op. cit.*, p 168.
115 Beale (2004), *op. cit.*
116 H Beale, 'The European Commission's Common Frame of Reference project: a progress report' (2006) 2 *European Review of Contract Law* 303–14, p 305.
117 *Ibid.*
118 See below.

needed if the Commission is to press ahead with its proposal to convert the consumer law *acquis* to a maximum harmonisation system. Whether the DCFR, already available in interim form and to be finalised by the end of 2008, will form the appropriate basis for the development of such a CFR, remains to be seen.

5.6.2 The Social Justice Manifesto

Both the (D)CFR and OI are controversial, and sustained criticism comes in the shape of the *Manifesto* of the Study Group on Social Justice in European Private Law.[119] It claims that the process initiated by the European Commission is not merely concerned with improving the operation of the internal market; rather, it reflects a political goal of creating a union of 'shared fundamental values concerning the social and economic relations between citizens'.[120]

The *Manifesto's* concern is that the approach adopted by the EU towards greater Europeanisation of contract law is too technocratic a process and fails to address concerns over social justice.[121] According to the *Manifesto*, national private law reflects 'basic principles of justice and social ordering in a market society',[122] and is therefore not concerned with merely technical rules. The rules of contract law, and private law generally, reflect contemporary ideals of social justice. Any move towards a comprehensive European contract law system therefore needs to consider where the balance should be struck between party autonomy (freedom of contract) and principles of social solidarity.[123]

The *Manifesto* is critical of the drafting process for the CFR – which it assumes will lead to an optional instrument or even a Contract Code – regarding it as purely technocratic for its stated aim of promoting market integration.[124] The combination of legal experts and business interests promotes an integration agenda, which is largely concerned with rules which are uniform, transparent and effective, but there is no

---

119 Study Group on Social Justice in European Private Law, 'Social justice in European contract law: a manifesto' (2004) 10 *European Law Journal* 653–74 ('Manifesto'). The document needs to be read in full, and the following can only give a brief impression of its main points.
120 *Ibid.*, p 657.
121 For a critical assessment, see O Lando, 'Liberal, social and "ethical" justice in European contract law' (2006) 43 *Common Market Law Review* 817–33.
122 *Manifesto*, p 655.
123 *Ibid.*, p 656.
124 *Ibid.*, p 660.

scope for considering questions of social justice.[125] But, it is argued, if the CFR will become binding law at a later stage, the drafting process for the CFR should be a political process where questions of social justice can be presented and debated,[126] in order to give the entire process 'regulatory legitimacy'.[127]

These concerns have some force if the underlying assumption that the CFR will inevitably become an OI or even a full-blown Code is correct,[128] but it is far from certain that this will happen. If the (D)CFR does identify policy choices, then once binding legislation is envisaged, there will be scope for debating the conception of social justice it should embody. In this respect, the political scrutiny proposed by the Commission before a final CFR is adopted[129] might be of more concern if this results in addressing policy options at that stage.[130] But perhaps because of the uncertainties that surround the eventual fate of the CFR, a more political process to consider questions of social justice at an earlier stage would have been appropriate, and the failure to engage with such fundamental issues early on remains of concern.[131]

5.7 COMPETENCE – THE PERENNIAL PROBLEM

There are concerns about the EC's competence to become more proactive with regard to general contract law. The CFR is therefore looked at with considerable scepticism. If the CFR is to remain a simple recommendation, or perhaps some sort of inter-institutional agreement between the various EU institutions, then the question of competence may not be of great significance.[132]

But if it is to have uses beyond a 'toolbox', then questions of competence will become more significant. If there were to be an OI, some thought would have to be given to its legal form. If the OI were to be developed within the scope of the treaties, the choice of binding

125   *Ibid.*, p 663.
126   *Ibid.*, p 664.
127   *Ibid.*, p 670.
128   Beale (2007), *op. cit.*, pp 268–9.
129   See above, p 158.
130   Beale (2007), *op. cit.*, p 269.
131   See also U Mattei, 'Basics first please! A critique of some recent priorities shown by the Commission's Action Plan', in A Hartkamp *et al.*, *Towards a European Civil Code*, 3rd edn, Nijmegen: Ars Aequi, 2004.
132   Von Bar and Schulte-Nölke, *op. cit.*, p 167.

instruments would be between a regulation, decision or directive; alter-natively, there might be a non-binding recommendation. A directive, however, would make no sense: its objective is to specify a result only, with form and method of giving effect to this result left to the Member States.[133] The choice is therefore between a binding regulation and a non-binding recommendation. For an 'opt-in' model, both legal forms are possible, particularly if Recital 16 of the Rome-I Regulation is suf-ficient to include such an OI within its choice-of-law rules. An 'opt-out' model assumes a binding legal framework that would apply unless the parties decided against this, and a regulation would be the appropriate legal instrument to use.[134]

For a legally binding instrument, one needs an appropriate legal base in the Treaty.[135] Art 95 may be the obvious candidate, but – as seen in Chapter 2 – the threshold for basing legislation on this provision might be too high unless strong evidence of a beneficial effect on the establishment and functioning of the internal market is adduced.[136]

But there are other provisions in the Treaty which could also be a possible legal basis, whether for narrower fields, such as consumer pro-tection (Art 153),[137] or more widely, for example, the EU's residual power to act where there is no other suitable legal basis (Art 308), as well as the more recent Treaty provision on judicial co-operation in civil matters (Art 65).[138]

5.7.1 Article 65 – judicial co-operation in civil matters

Art 61 of the Treaty[139] sets out the aim of establishing an 'area of freedom, security and justice', the creation of which should include '. . . (c) measures in the field of judicial co-operation in civil matters

---

133 Art 249 EC; see Chapter 2, p 34.
134 *The Way Forward*, p 19.
135 See Chapter 2.
136 Whether surveys such as the one reported by S Vogenauer and S Weatherill, 'The EC's competence to pursue the harmonisation of contract law – an empirical contri-bution to the debate', in Vogenauer and Weatherill, *Harmonisation of European Contract Law* (2006) are sufficient is questionable for the reasons they themselves give (pp 138–9).
137 See Chapter 2, p 33.
138 Legislation has also been based on the power in Art 47(2) EC to adopt legislation to promote the freedom of establishment, but this provision is not discussed further here.
139 This will become Art 67 TFEU (with amendments) once the Lisbon Treaty comes into force.

as provided for in Art 65 . . .'. Art 65,[140] in turn, provides a basis for the adoption of 'measures in the field of judicial co-operation in civil matters having cross-border implications . . . necessary for the proper functioning of the internal market'.[141] This Article also provides a list of those areas which should be the focus of legislative activity, although that list is not exhaustive.[142] It includes 'eliminating obstacles to the good functioning of civil proceedings', which might appear to be concerned solely with matters of civil procedure.[143] However, at the European Council at Tampere in October 1999, it was concluded that the creation of a 'genuine European area of justice' did not only require improvements in access to justice and the mutual recognition of judicial decisions. The Council also resolved that 'as regards substantive law, an overall study is requested on the need to approximate Member States' legislation in civil matters in order to eliminate obstacles to the good functioning of civil proceedings'.[144]

That said, the use of Art 65 as an alternative legal basis for the adoption of legislation in the contract law field remains unexplored. It has been used as a basis for the adoption of the 'Brussels Regulation' (Regulation 44/2001), but not – as yet – for any matters of substantive law. However, the ongoing process of deeper Europeanisation may more appropriately be treated as a matter of justice,[145] and this legal basis may yet be considered for further legislation. Indeed, in its Hague Programme on freedom, security and justice, adopted in 2004, the Council explicitly refers to the need for improving the quality of Community law in the field of contract law through consolidation,

---

140 To become Art 81 TFEU, with amendments. Crucially, the opening paragraph will change to: 'The Union shall develop judicial cooperation in civil matters having cross-border implications, based on the principle of mutual recognition of judgments and of decisions in extrajudicial cases. Such cooperation may include the adoption of measures for the approximation of the laws and regulations of the Member States.' Whilst this removes the 'internal market' link of the current Art 65, it also seems to emphasise mutual recognition. Whether this might affect the use of Art 81 TFEU as discussed in this section remains to be seen.

141 For useful background, see G Betlem and E Hondius, 'European private law after the Treaty of Amsterdam' (2001) 9 *European Review of Private Law* 3–20.

142 Art 65 states that the measures adopted 'shall include' those listed in paras (a)–(c) of that Article, but it is not limited to those areas.

143 Eg J Mance, 'Is Europe aiming to civilise the common law?' [2007] *European Business Law Review* 77–99, p 81.

144 Para 39 of the Tampere Conclusions.

145 M Hesselink, 'European contract law: a matter of consumer protection, citizenship, or justice?' [2007] *European Review of Private Law* 323–48.

codification and rationalisation of legislation in force and developing a Common Frame of Reference.[146] This seems to assume that 'judicial co-operation in civil matters' extends as far as the approximation of substantive law (including contract law), which is a very generous reading of Art 65 and one likely to prove controversial.[147]

The availability of Art 65 for adopting measures on substantive contract law remains uncertain, although a close reading of the Hague Programme on justice suggests that serious consideration is being given to its use. It is arguable that differences in substantive law have the effect of creating obstacles to the functioning of civil proceedings,[148] thereby bringing Art 65 into play. This is strangely reminiscent of the simplistic reasoning deployed to invoke Art 95 in pre-*Tobacco Advertising* times, and it might be stretching the scope of this Article rather too far.

5.7.2 Article 308: residual competence

In addition to the legal bases in Arts 94 and 95, Art 308 provides a residual power for the EU to take action if this 'prove[s] necessary to attain, in the course of the operation of the common market, one of the objectives of the Community and this Treaty has not provided the necessary powers'.[149] This power was historically significant to deal with matters which were part of the Community's general aims, but for which there was no specific Treaty base. With the various additions made to the original Treaty by the amending treaties, this provision has become less significant. Its existence has sometimes given rise to 'competence creep', that is, concern that the Community would use it to claim competence in areas not explicitly conferred on it by the Treaty, on the basis that this would be necessary to pursue the Community's objectives. There is some uncertainty as to the significance to be attached to the reference to the common market in Art 308 – it has been suggested that the focus of the Article is on attaining the objectives of

---

146 *Hague Programme*, para 3.4.4 (under heading 'Judicial Co-operation in Civil Matters'). The Common Frame of Reference is discussed in chapter 5.
147 J Ziller, 'The legitimacy of codification of contract law in view of the allocation of competences between the European Union and its Member States' in M Hesselink (ed), *The Politics of a European Civil Code* (The Hague: Kluwer, 2006).
148 Tampere declaration 1999.
149 This will become Art 351 TFEU with amendments, once the Lisbon Treaty becomes effective.

the Community (which are not all tied to the internal/common market), and that the reference to the common market is all but redundant.[150]

The potentially wide scope of this Article is mitigated by the legislative procedure to be followed in this regard, which is requires unanimity to adopt legislation on this basis. However, it only specifies consultation of the European Parliament, but grants it no power of co-decision, which is of concern.[151]

Although it may be of more limited use today following the introduction of legal bases for action in specific areas in the various amending treaties, there are circumstances where Art 308 may still be significant. A key case in this regard is C-436/03 *European Parliament v Council of the European Union*.[152] Here, the ECJ had to consider the relationship between Arts 308 and 95 in the context of a challenge to the legality of Regulation 1435/2003 on the Statute for a European Co-operative Society (SCE).[153] This created a new legal structure, the European co-operative society, which is a new legal entity to be recognised in all the EU Member States. As initially proposed, the legal basis for the Regulation would have been Art 95, but the Council substituted Art 308, on the basis of which the Regulation was adopted. This was challenged by the Parliament, undoubtedly because its involvement under Art 308 is much more restricted. The Council's argument was that the Regulation creates a new European entity which exists alongside domestic co-operative societies. Measures based on Art 95 are intended to approximate domestic law and remove the barriers created by the divergence in domestic legislation, but because the SCE could not be created through domestic law, this did not involve the approximation of national law.

The ECJ emphasised that Art 308 could only be used where there is no other legal basis in the Treaty on which a measure can be adopted.[154] Art 95 was the appropriate base for measures which genuinely have as their object a contribution to the establishment and functioning of the internal market, and this includes circumstances where obstacles to the internal market are likely to be caused by the heterogeneous

---

150 Cf House of Commons European Scrutiny Committee, *Art 308 of the EC Treaty* (London: TSO, 2007). Note that Art 351 TFEU omits a reference to the common market, lending support to this analysis.

151 In the replacement of Art 308, the Parliament has to 'consent' to any measures adopted on the basis of Art 351 TFEU.

152 [2006] ECR I-3733.

153 (2003) OJ L 207/1.

154 Para 36 of the judgment.

development of domestic laws.[155] As the Regulation did not aim to approximate domestic laws on co-operative societies, but rather to create a new type of co-operative society, Art 308 was the correct legal basis.[156] This was so notwithstanding the fact that the SCE Regulation referred back to national law for certain operational rules affecting the SCE.[157]

From this judgment, it is clear that Art 95 can only form the basis of legislation approximating the national laws (which includes the replacement of divergent national rules with a uniform Community procedure enacted by way of regulation[158] and the creation of a monitoring agency[159]), but not for the creation of new, supranational legal forms. For this, Art 308 is the appropriate legal basis.[160]

This is likely of relevance to the future Europeanisation of contract law, and the adoption of an optional instrument, in particular. Art 95 may be difficult to justify as a legal basis if there is no obvious harmonisation of national laws.[161] If one then pursues the reasoning in *Parliament v Council*, the creation of a European Contract Regulation on the basis of Art 308, to co-exist with national contract laws, seems to be a possibility, although the almost complete exclusion of the European Parliament from the legislative procedure, as well as the need for unanimity, would make this unlikely.

5.7.3 Conclusions on legal basis

Finding a legal basis for wider action is difficult. Certainly, a broad harmonisation of national contract law seems to be beyond the competence of the EU. More targeted action, as well as the adoption of an optional instrument, might be possible; however, it might still require the use of an alternative to Art 95. It remains to be seen if Art 65 can fulfil this role; alternatively, Art 308 is a contender, but its use would

---

155 Paras 37–38.
156 Para 44.
157 Para 45.
158 C-66/04 *United Kingdom v Parliament and Council* [2005] ECR I-10553.
159 C-217/04 *United Kingdom v Parliament and Council* [2006] ECR I-3771.
160 The ECJ *inter alia* referred to its *Opinion 1/94* [1994] ECR I-5267, where it held that Art 308 would be the appropriate basis for the creation of a new intellectual property right which would exist in addition to national rights.
161 Although J Rutgers, 'An optional instrument and social dumping' (2006) 2 *European Review of Contract Law* 199–212, pp 207–8, argues that an optional instrument could be based on Art 95 because it would not create entirely new rights, but enhance existing (national) contract laws.

create serious political difficulties because of the limited role of Parliament (which has been driving the entire process), and the requirement of unanimity. The changes made by the Lisbon Treaty are not sufficient to alter the basic limitations of the various candidates for a legal basis for more detailed legislation on EU contract law.

5.7.4 An alternative? The open method of co-ordination

Instead of binding harmonisation, it has been argued by van Gerven that, if there is a desire to pursue a greater degree of convergence in the field of contract law, or private law more generally, a more successful approach might be to utilise the so-called 'open method of co-ordination' (OMC), rather than binding legislation.[162] Instead of adopting directives or regulations, Member States agree on broad objectives, leaving it to each Member State to take appropriate action in response. The Commission assumes a co-ordinating role and monitors progress towards the agreed objectives. This approach has the advantage of giving greater leeway to the Member States for taking action, but also the drawback that there will not be the same enforcement principles that apply in the context of binding legislation. Although a firm Treaty basis for this can be found in the context of social rights (Art 137(2)(a)), its use on a wider basis has been recommended.[163] As the experience with this approach is limited, it is difficult to assess whether it could be a viable alternative to formal legislation in the field of contract law.

5.8 REVIEW OF THE CONSUMER *ACQUIS*

A more concrete step towards further Europeanisation, and the one most likely to produce results in the short term, is the *Green Paper on the Review of the Consumer Acquis* in February 2007.[164] The *Green Paper* is the final step in the Commission's 'diagnostic phase' of EU

---

162 W van Gerven, 'Bringing (private) laws closer at the European level' in F Cafaggi, *The Institutional Framework of European Private Law* (Oxford: OUP, 2006).

163 *White Paper on European Governance* (COM (2001) 428 final).

164 COM (2006) 744 final. The Commission published a summary of the responses in October 2007. An analytical report of all the responses, prepared by the Consumer Policy Evaluation Consortium, was published in November 2007. Both documents can be accessed on DG SANCO's internet site.

consumer law,[165] which also included the Consumer Compendium,[166] several CFR stakeholder workshops and surveys of consumer and business attitudes.[167] The Compendium, in particular, found that, despite the Europeanisation efforts so far, there continues to be a noticeable difference between domestic laws caused by incoherence and ambiguity in the *acquis*; regulatory gaps in the *acquis* addressed differently by the Member States, and use of the minimum harmonisation clause by the Member States.

The *Green Paper* makes a number of different types of proposal, with 30 questions in total. There are some matters regarding the approach to be adopted in future legislation, whereas others deal with specific issues of individual directives. For present purposes, the broader questions are of immediate relevance.[168]

5.8.1 General issues

5.8.1.1 From vertical to horizontal

It has been seen in previous chapters that the process of Europeanisation has resulted in a patchwork of measures which lack coherence both within themselves and with related measures. Consequently, a shift from the present *vertical* to a broader *horizontal* approach is suggested.[169] The Commission is understandably reluctant to undertake a separate revision of each directive; quite apart from the additional legislative time this might take, it would multiply the risk of defective implementation, which is already of some concern with the present *acquis*.

The favoured approach is the horizontal one, although vertical measures[170] may still be used 'where necessary'.[171] All those aspects common to several directives, such as key definitions ('consumer', 'professional' or even 'durable medium'), together with provisions of broad

---

165 *Green Paper*, p 4.

166 See H Schulte-Nölke, C Twigg-Flesner and M Ebers (eds), *Consumer Compendium – Comparative Analysis*.

167 A report on the implementation of the Distance Selling Directive (97/7/EC) was issued in September 2006 (see COM (2006) 514 final), and a report on the Consumer Sales Directive (99/44/EC) in May 2007 (COM (2007) 210 final).

168 For comments on the detail, see C Twigg-Flesner, 'No sense of purpose or direction?' (2007) 3 *European Review of Contract Law* 198–213.

169 As usual, 'no legislative action' was also mooted, but clearly not pursued seriously.

170 There would still be a need to adopt or retain legislation on specific topics, notably the Timeshare Directive (94/47/EC), which do not have broad horizontal application. A proposal for a new timeshare directive was presented in June 2007.

171 *Green Paper*, p 8.

application (sales, unfair terms, withdrawal rights) could be absorbed in a single horizontal Instrument. This would be done with a 'better regulation' objective firmly in mind, and the Commission has argued that simplification and rationalisation of the *acquis* in a horizontal instrument would have that effect and thereby 'reduce the volume of the *acquis*'.[172] However, the immediate beneficiary of such a step would be neither business nor consumers, but the Member States (particularly those who favour the copy-out approach to implementation), assuming that the horizontal instrument would be another directive. However, the *Green Paper* leaves open the question of the legal nature of the horizontal instrument, and instead of it being another directive, it could be a regulation instead. This would be more likely to produce regulatory simplification,[173] although it could have a significant impact on national contract law, because Member States would have limited control over the integration of the regulation-based rules into domestic law.

The *Green Paper* then considers the potential scope of the horizontal instrument: (1) domestic and cross-border contracts; (2) cross-border only; and (3) distance selling (domestic and cross-border) only. Neither option (2) nor (3) seem to appeal to the Commission, primarily because of the resulting legal fragmentation depending on the type of consumer transaction that would result from this. However, the Commission may be overstating the problems associated with such an approach: whilst the existence of two parallel frameworks increases the risk of confusion for those consumers who engage in cross-border (or distance) contracting, the wider impact of extending any new rules to all consumer transactions might confuse a greater number of consumers – after all, the majority of consumer contracts remain domestic (even local) matters.[174] A detailed horizontal instrument for cross-border transactions might be more desirable, and less difficult to achieve, than instinctively thought.[175]

172 *Green Paper*, p 9.
173 Cf footnote 12 in *A Europe of Results – Applying Community Law* (COM (2007) 502 final): 'Replacing directives with regulations can, when legally possible and politically acceptable, offer simplification as they enable immediate application and can be directly invoked before courts by interested parties.' See also Commission Working Document *Instruments for a Modernised Single Market Policy* (SEC(2007) 1518).
174 Indeed, in view of the market integration objective, it may be asked whether the focus is really on consumers at all. Instead, it may matter more whether a cross-border framework would assist business in offering their goods and services in a cross-border context. See Beale (2007), *op. cit.*, p 271.
175 Eg, N Reich, 'A European contract law, or an EU contract law regulation for consumers?' (2005) 28 *Journal of Consumer Policy* 383–407; also H Rösler, *Europäisches Konsumentenvertragsrecht* (München: Beck, 2004).

5.8.1.2 *From minimum to maximum harmonisation*

According to the *Green Paper*, the use of minimum harmonisation is a problem for the operation of the internal market, because of the uncertainty about the exact level of consumer protection in each Member State. The Commission has therefore expressed its clear preference for maximum harmonisation in reviewing the consumer *acquis*. What remains unclear is how high a level of protection would be adopted under a maximum harmonisation approach. It may be of concern for Member States for two, conflicting, reasons: first, the remaining divergence caused by minimum harmonisation suggests that many Member States regard the level of consumer protection established in the *acquis* as inadequate, and those Member States which have exceeded the minimum requirements are unlikely to agree to a simple removal of the minimum clauses purely for the sake of regulatory simplicity. The level of protection may therefore need to be raised. That leads to the second reason: some of the Member States have only adopted the minimum standard, and many have used regulatory options in some directives, whereas others have not. The benefits of raising the level of protection and removing options will therefore need to be accepted by those Member States who prefer a lower level of consumer protection.

The Commission acknowledges that 'it may be difficult to achieve full harmonisation on all aspects',[176] but fails to explore which aspects might be controversial and how it might tackle national concerns. Indeed, the Commission does not present any realistic alternatives to maximum harmonisation. It only considers minimum harmonisation with either a mutual recognition clause or country of origin provision in the *Green Paper*, but not the status quo.[177] Neither is supported, because national laws would still vary between the Member States. Moreover, under a mutual recognition approach, a judge dealing with a cross-border dispute would need to examine both the law in the consumer's Member State and in that of the business to see if there are

---

176 *Green Paper*, p 10.
177 The ECJ's observations in case C-376/98 *Germany v Parliament and Council (Tobacco Advertising)* [2000] ECR I-8419 (paras 101–04) on minimum harmonisation might suggest that minimum harmonisation without a 'market access' clause may not be in accordance with Art 95. See H Micklitz, 'Minimum/maximum harmonisation and the internal market clause', in G Howells, H Micklitz and T Wilhelmsson, *European Fair Trading Law* (Aldershot: Ashgate, 2006). For a contrary view, S Weatherill, 'Minimum harmonisation as oxymoron?' in H Micklitz, *Verbraucherrecht in Deutschland* (Baden-Baden: Nomos, 2005).

stricter consumer protection rules in the consumer's State, and then establish whether these would be an unjustified obstacle to trade – which would be unworkable in practice.

The long-running debate about the respective merits of maximum and minimum harmonisation is largely ignored,[178] despite the fact that the scholarly literature on this issue has burgeoned.[179] The Commission's case in favour of full harmonisation does not convince; in particular, it fails to address objections such as concerns over lost diversity.[180]

5.8.1.3 Legal basis (again)

Questions of competence permeate the Europeanisation of contract law, and yet this issue is not addressed at all in this *Green Paper*. However, the reasoning is couched in terms of internal market objectives, and Art 95 must be the preferred legal basis. This is worrying, because under a full harmonisation approach, Member States would not be able to derogate from a harmonised standard in the interest of consumer protection. The safeguard clause in Art 95 permits derogations only in certain circumstances,[181] but these do not include consumer protection.[182] As seen earlier, Art 153(3)(b), although little-used so far, could be an alternative legal basis. The fact that Art 153(3)(b) could not be a legal basis for full harmonisation measures, because Art 153(5) contains a Treaty-based minimum harmonisation clause, might explain why nothing is said in the *Green Paper* about the appropriate legal base.[183]

---

178 It is clear from the *EU Consumer Policy Strategy 2007–2013* (COM (2007) 99 final, 13 March 2007), that the Commission has already settled for (targeted) full harmonisation: see p 7.

179 See, eg, G Howells, 'European consumer law – the minimal and maximal harmonisation debate and pro-independent consumer law competence', in S Grundmann and J Stuyck (eds), *An Academic Green Paper on European Contract Law* (The Hague, Kluwer Law International, 2002, and 'The rise of European consumer law – whither national consumer law?' (2006) 28 *Sydney Law Review* 63–88.

180 T Wilhelmsson, 'Private law in the EU: harmonised or fragmented Europeanisation' (2002) *European Review of Private Law* 77–94.

181 See Art 95(5) EC.

182 See H Micklitz, N Reich and S Weatherill, 'EU Treaty revision and consumer protection' (2004) 27 *Journal of Consumer Policy* 367–99.

183 Cf the opinion of the Economic and Social Committee (2007) OJ C 256/27, calling for the adoption of consumer legislation in its own right and not merely as part of the internal market programme.

In addition to these general issues, the *Green Paper* then deals with a range of more specific issues. Several of these have a horizontal flavour, whereas others are on specific provisions in the various directives. Some of the former are singled out for particular consideration here.

5.8.2 Specific points

5.8.2.1 Good faith and fair dealing

It is suggested that the horizontal instrument could include a general obligation on professionals to comply with the principles of good faith and fair dealing from the pre-contractual stage through to performance.[184] The introduction of a general principle might be controversial, particularly for lawyers with a common law background.[185] The brief explanation in the *Green Paper* indicates that a good faith principle would be (1) a general principle underpinning many of the more specific rules in the *acquis* and therefore provide guidance for the interpretation and application of these rules; (2) a gap-filling mechanism for the courts to resolve ambiguities or gaps in the *acquis* (effectively a safety net), rather than a free-standing basis for creating additional obligations; and (3) applied in interpreting contract terms. The *Green Paper* offers a choice between imposing this duty only on professionals, or also on consumers.[186] The Commission acknowledges that a general principle could reduce legal certainty, and also produce divergent results between Member States, but it has already adopted a similar approach in the UCPD.[187]

5.8.2.2 Information duties

The *Green Paper* does not deal with the current information duties as such, but it invites suggestions for the remedies to be made available if there is a failure to provide information. The focus is on extending the period during which a right of withdrawal, where this exists, can be exercised. No other specific remedies are mentioned.

---

184 *Green Paper*, p 17.
185 For a more positive position, see R Bradgate, R Brownsword and C Twigg-Flesner, *The Impact of Adopting a Duty to Trade Fairly* (London: Department of Trade and Industry, 2003) (available at http://www.dti.gov.uk/files/file32101.pdf; last accessed 4 April 2007).
186 See B Heiderhoff and M Kenny, 'The Commission's 2007 Green Paper on the Consumer Acquis: deliberate deliberation' (2007) 35 *European Law Review* 740–51.
187 See Chapter 3, p 53.

5.8.2.3 *Right of withdrawal*

With regard to the right of withdrawal, three issues are raised:

(1) The existence of differing periods in the Member States because of minimum harmonisation. To deal with this, a single withdrawal period is proposed; alternatively, two separate standard periods could be adopted.[188]

(2) The modalities of withdrawal. It is asked whether there should there be a uniform procedure, or whether there should effectively be a ban on particular formalities to permit as many different means of withdrawing as possible. Alternatively, Member States could retain their discretion regarding formalities.

(3) Should consumers be charged for certain matters when exercising their right of withdrawal?

As the right of withdrawal is such a central feature of the *acquis*,[189] it seems likely that there will be a more consistent approach across the range of areas where this right is made available.[190]

5.8.2.4 *General contractual remedies*

As already seen, the *acquis* lacks remedies for breach of contract (with some exceptions, such as consumer sales), leaving this as a matter for national law. The *Green Paper* raises the possibility of introducing a set of general contractual remedies for consumer cases, as well as a general right to damages. Clearly, if pursued, this proposal would have a major impact on national contract laws.

5.8.3 Evaluation

Overall, the *Green Paper* is slightly odd, because it omits discussion of some fundamental issues, and yet goes into detail on others. At a more general level, the lack of any reference to competence and legal basis is worrying. Even more surprising is the fact that there is no information

---

188 Cf P Rekaiti and R van den Bergh, 'Cooling-off periods in the consumer laws of the EC Member States. A comparative law and economics approach' (2000) 23 *Journal of Consumer Policy* 371–407.

189 Chapter 3, p 71.

190 Cf G Howells, 'The right of withdrawal in European consumer law', in H Schulte-Nölke and R Schulze (eds), *European Contract Law in Community Law* (Cologne: Bundesanzeiger, 2002).

about the link between the *acquis* review and the CFR, despite the significance of the CFR for this review.[191] Admittedly, it has been noted that the CFR 'will not, and cannot, be an appropriate instrument for giving answers to all the questions which will be posed in the all-encompassing review of the *acquis*',[192] but greater clarity about its relevance is needed. The proposal of sweeping changes towards maximum harmonisation and a horizontal regulation without a more thorough debate about the values of EU consumer law is also of concern.

That said, it may be that consumer law is the one area where there will be more detailed Europeanisation activity. Indeed, it has been argued that the idea of a horizontal instrument proposed in the *Green Paper* and the idea of an optional instrument might be combined and offer businesses operating across the EU the choice whether to sell their goods or services on the basis of law of the consumer's habitual residence,[193] or the optional instrument instead.[194]

For the time being, however, it seems that what will emerge will be another directive adopted on the basis of Art 95: the Commission intends to submit a proposal for a Framework Directive on Consumer Contractual Rights at the end of 2008.[195] This could be a lot less ambitious than what might have been expected in light of the CFR project and the *Green Paper*.

5.9 CONCLUSIONS

These are interesting times in the story of the Europeanisation of contract law. There is undoubtedly some concern about the current activities, particularly with regard to the absence of a thorough debate on the appropriateness and necessity of the development of the CFR, and, indeed, the move towards an optional instrument. Kenny, in

---

191 However, the *Second Progress Report* states that 'the relevant CFR findings will be incorporated where appropriate into the EU consumer contract law acquis review . . .' (p 10).

192 'European contract law: quo vadis?' (editorial comments) (2005) 42 *Common Market Law Review* 1–7, p 4.

193 As apparently made possible in the Rome-I Regulation (see Chapter 1, p 6).

194 H Schulte-Nölke, 'EC law on the formation of contract – from the Common Frame of Reference to the "blue button" ' (2007) *European Review of Contract Law* 332–49.

195 Commission Legislative and Work Programme 2008 (COM (2007) 640 final), p 28.

particular, laments the lack of answers to a number of fundamental questions, including how agreement on the one set of rules that is business-friendly might be obtained.[196] However, perhaps some of the concerns are fuelled by the fear of a significant EU invasion into general contract law, which, as things appear at present, seems highly unlikely. One may see further Europeanisation of consumer contract rules, and – with the help of the CFR – a better understanding of the context within which the European rules are intended to operate. However, until the CFR is complete and the Commission has put forward firm proposals for further action, many such concerns may be misplaced.

---

196 M Kenny, 'The 2004 Communication on European Contract Law: those magnificent men in their unifying machines' (2005) 30 *European Law Review* 724–42, p 741.

6 Towards a European contract code? Concluding thoughts

6.1 INTRODUCTION

This book has sought to examine the various aspects of the Europeanisation of contract law. Although still largely a piecemeal framework dealing with discrete issues, the development of a Common Frame of Reference may herald a more co-ordinated and broader intervention by the EU in the contract law sphere. Whether this will eventually produce an optional instrument on contract law, or even lead to a contract code for Europe, remains to be seen. In this concluding chapter, the main strands of the debate about deeper Europeanisation, including a European code, are raised, but it is beyond the scope of this book to cover this fully.[1]

6.2 A EUROPEAN CONTRACT CODE?

The Commission's activities discussed in the previous chapter have prompted a major academic discourse on the desirability, or otherwise, of a European contract code, or, indeed, a 'European civil code'.[2] The Commission has attempted to dispel any such speculation by firmly rejecting the suggestion that there are plans for harmonising all of

---

1 A reader interested in more depth on this topic is advised to consult the many contributions to journals such as the *European Review of Private Law* or *European Review of Contract Law*, as well as the excellent collection of essays in S Grundmann and J Stuyck (eds), *An Academic Green Paper on European Contract Law* (The Hague: Kluwer Law International, 2002).
2 See, seminally, A Hartkamp and others (eds), *Towards a European Civil Code*, 3rd edn (Nijmegen: Ars Aequi, 2005).

domestic contract law. It has stated that it is not 'the Commission's intention to propose a "European civil code".[3] And yet, the debate over greater harmonisation, even the creation of a European contract code, lingers on – undoubtedly not helped by the ambiguity surrounding the objectives of the CFR project. Getting a grip on this debate is difficult because of its multi-faceted nature, with different background assumptions, particularly about the nature and function of law, influencing the positions adopted in this debate.[4] Whilst this chapter cannot offer a full account of all the arguments in this debate, the following paragraphs offer a flavour.[5]

6.2.1 The economic argument

The economic case concentrates on market integration, that is, making the internal market work more smoothly. The fundamental argument that is often advanced in favour of greater harmonisation, or even unification of contract law, is that the diversity between the domestic contract laws effectively constitutes a non-tariff barrier to trade between the Member States.[6] The existence of numerous different contract laws within the EU creates additional information costs for businesses seeking to engage in cross-border transactions. Compliance with different, and possibly contradictory, laws also increases costs, although this is likely to be a problem for small and medium-sized enterprises (SMEs), rather than large multinational companies.[7] A unified legal framework would reduce transaction costs considerably and, consequently, a European contract code is needed for business.

Of course, the replacement of existing national law with a uniform European framework would itself create costs,[8] not only in reaching

---

3 *The Way Forward*, p 8.
4 T Wilhelmsson, 'The legal, the cultural and the political – conclusions from different perspectives on harmonisation of European contract law' [2002] *European Business Law Review* 541–55.
5 The constitutional limitations on the EU for imposing a full code were already considered in the previous chapter and are not repeated here.
6 Eg, Commission documents; O Lando, 'Why does Europe need a civil code?', in Grundmann and Stuyck (eds), *op. cit.*
7 See H Wagner, 'Economic analysis of cross-border legal uncertainty', in Smits, *op. cit.*, p 43.
8 See eg G Wagner, 'The virtues of diversity in European private law', in Smits, J (ed), *The Need for a European Contract Law* (Groningen: Europa Law Publishing, 2005), p 4.

agreement on a single code,[9] but also in adopting related areas of national law as well as the considerable amount of re-training that would be required. Admittedly, whilst such costs may be substantial, they would also be transitional, and after a period of adjustment, there would be a cost saving flowing from the harmonisation of the legal framework across the EU.[10] But agreeing on common rules itself would not ensure uniformity. There would be no guarantee of common interpretation,[11] that is, sufficient certainty that these rules will also be applied uniformly in all the Member States, unless a new EU-wide court system were established.[12]

A practical difficulty with economic arguments is the difficulty of compiling the quantitative data needed properly to compare the benefits and costs.[13] An *ex ante* assessment is hampered by a lack of clarity as to what degree of unification is envisaged and what the substance of those rules would be.

Moreover, it remains at least uncertain whether the existence of diverse contract laws in itself is a real barrier to trade, particularly if one focuses on the law itself, rather than the context within which it operates.[14] There is certainly clear evidence to suggest that the law itself is not inevitably the deciding factor in business relations.

Collins urges caution in this regard by emphasising that the notions of 'barriers or obstacles to trade' and transaction costs ought not to be conflated.[15] Obstacles to trade effectively prevent cross-border trade because they prevent a business from selling its goods or services in the manner adopted for its home jurisdiction when seeking to sell in another territory. Transaction costs, on the other hand, are simply the costs associated with entering into a contract. Undoubtedly, the higher transaction costs associated with cross-border contracting may make

---

9 R van den Bergh, 'Forced harmonisation of contract law in Europe: not to be continued' in Grundmann and Stuyck (eds), *op. cit.*

10 H Collins, 'Transaction costs and subsidiarity in European contract law', in Grundmann and Stuyck (eds), *op. cit.*, p 276.

11 R van den Bergh, 'Forced harmonisation of contract law in Europe: not to be continued' in Grundmann and Stuyck (eds), *op. cit.*, p 257.

12 H Collins, 'Transaction costs and subsidiarity in European contract law', in Grundmann and Stuyck (eds), *op. cit.*, p 276.

13 For a fuller discussion of this issue, see J Haage, 'Law, economics and uniform contract law: a sceptical view', in Smits (ed), *op. cit.*

14 J Smits, 'Diversity of contract law and the European internal market', in Smits (ed), *op. cit.*

15 Collins, 'Transaction costs and subsidiarity in European contract law', in Grundmann and Stuyck (eds), *op. cit.*

such trade less attractive, but it does not form a barrier to trade as such. According to Collins, there are only two circumstances where the law forms a real obstacle to trade. The first situation arises where what is being sold by the business is the contract itself, such as an insurance policy.[16] Variations in the domestic legal frameworks on such contracts can form a real obstacle to trade, because a business may not be able to sell its contracts in another Member State. The second instance is where marketing techniques are regulated differently and a business may not be able to utilise its established marketing techniques when moving into a new jurisdiction. In respect of such genuine barriers to trade, action to harmonise may be justified. Beale has argued with some force that, whilst further harmonisation of certain aspects of contract law may be needed, there is no need for a full-blown unification attempt.[17] Instead, he argues that harmonisation should be restricted to what he calls 'hidden traps', that is, domestic rules which produce different substantive outcomes that could be detrimental to the contracting parties who are unaware of them.[18]

Diversity in national contract laws generally, therefore, does not constitute a barrier to trade. Instead, the barrier is more psychological; that is, there is a perception that businesses do not engage in more cross-border trade because of the differences in the law; but it is no more than that.[19]

Concerns about over-emphasising the role of law in the process of building the internal market are not restricted to the specific question of a full-blown European code; one can also raise objections in the context of targeted directives seeking to harmonise national laws in the interests of the internal market. Particularly in commercial contract law, which is largely unaffected by national mandatory rules that could prove problematic, the economic case for intervention fails to take into account the fact that in business relations, the law is not usually the dominating factor.[20] The formalist focus on clear and certain legal rules in the context of Europeanisation may therefore be misguided.[21] However, what

---

16 *Ibid.*, p 271.
17 H Beale, 'Finding the remaining traps instead of unifying contract law', in Grundmann and Stuyck (eds), *op. cit.*
18 *Ibid.*, p 70.
19 *Ibid.*, p 272.
20 T Wilhelmsson, 'The legal, the cultural and the political – conclusions from different perspectives on harmonisation of European contract law' [2002] *European Business Law Review* 541–55, p 543.
21 H Collins, 'Formalism and efficiency: designing European commercial contract law' (2000) 8 *European Review of Private Law* 211–35.

will matter is the ability of businesses to use their standard form contracts across Europe, without having to make changes in light of particular national mandatory rules which invalidate certain terms.[22] Ensuring that there is appropriate EU-wide regulation of this aspect would be more significant, and it is to be regretted that the EU's work on standard contract terms never turned to this issue before it abandoned all activities in this field.[23]

6.2.2 Arguments from culture

6.2.2.1 Common–civil law divide

In Chapter 1, it was noted that the legal landscape in Europe is characterised by a significant divide between two legal cultures, the civil and the common law.[24] Space precludes a detailed consideration of this difference. Put very simply, the civil law tradition is based around a civil code[25] which provides abstract legal norms, clearly defined areas of law, and a rather rigid approach to legal classification. The legal system is generally regarded as complete and does not contain any gaps. A new problem needs to be resolved within the existing framework of legal principles, as contained in the code. Legal thinking is more abstract. Sytematisation and classification of legal rules is the focus of the civil lawyer. The English common law, on the other hand, is found in continuously evolving case law, and cases are vital (despite the various statutory interventions). Its thinking is concrete and based around actual cases. It shirks away from generalisation, preferring instead a gradual development through resolution of individual disputes. It does not seek to plan ahead for all future eventualities, and is generally more responsive. If a particular solution to a legal problem is seen as desirable, there is no need to consider how this might affect the overall system of the law. In short, in the civil systems, law is regarded as a science, whereas the common law is better seen as art.

The existence of these two legal cultures is often mentioned as a principal obstacle to the creation of a European civil code. The very

---

22 H Collins, 'The freedom to circulate documents: regulating contracts in Europe' (2004) 10 *European Law Journal* 787–803.

23 See Chapter 5, p 143.

24 Note the earlier reservations about this distinction, and the separate position of the Nordic legal systems in this regard.

25 On civil codes, see S Grundmann and M Schauer (eds), *The Architecture of European Codes and Contract Law* (The Hague: Kluwer Law International, 2006).

notion of a code, with its focus on systematisation, is an anathema to the common law.[26]

The most vociferous opponent of greater European harmonisation efforts is Pierre Legrand, whose work is well known and controversial for its clear opposition, based primarily on the fundamental differences between the two legal families. His arguments are complex and occasionally overstep the boundaries,[27] but provide much food for thought. In arguing against the suggestion that there is considerable convergence between the legal families,[28] he highlights the concern with formal rules[29] and insufficient consideration of the cultures within which such rules operate. Because of such cultural variations, congruence in the content of specific legal rules does not mean that there is real convergence, as these rules will be understood differently. His concern about the focus on rules should be taken seriously – not merely in the debate about a civil code, but also in the context of the ongoing developments.[30] Whilst many of Legrand's concerns focus on the common–civil law divide (although even he concedes that 'there can be no sharp and fixed distinctions between legal traditions'[31]), his observations about different legal cultures also apply within the context of the civil law family itself, as even here there are different cultural factors at play. Overall, he argues that the focus in the debate centres too heavily on rules with insufficient regard for legal cultures and traditions, and that the real obstacles towards greater convergence are largely ignored, possibly because they are essentially insurmountable.[32]

Yet, some have argued that whilst there may be differences between the common and civil law worlds, there is also a lot of similarity between them, not least because of common historical roots.[33] That may be true in respect of specific doctrines, but that does not inevitably

---

26 For an English view on the difficulties of codification, see A Tettenborn, 'From chaos to cosmos – or is it confusion?' [2002] *Web Journal of Current Legal Issues*.

27 He has singled out Professor von Bar for a personal attack in P Legrand, 'Antivonbar' (2005) 1 *Journal of Comparative Law* 13–40. The risk of such a confrontational approach is that many of his arguments are overlooked out of concern about his style.

28 P Legrand, 'European legal systems are not converging' (1996) 45 *International and Comparative Law Quarterly* 52–81.

29 Benchmark (i) in Brownsword's classification: see Chapter 1, p 9.

30 See Chapter 5.

31 Legrand (2005), *op. cit.*, p 20.

32 P Legrand, 'Against a European civil code' (1997) 60 *Modern Law Review* 44–63.

33 Eg, R Zimmermann, 'Roman law and the harmonisation of private law in Europe', A Hartkamp *et al.*, *op. cit.*

mean that there is sufficient commonality to justify the imposition of a single European rule. Lando goes beyond a focus on legal rules by arguing that the differences of legal method between the various European systems are overstated, and that even the common law, in the shape of textbooks, pursues a degree of systematisation.[34] He asserts that the conflict between the common law and civil law should not be exaggerated and that there is more cultural congruence than often assumed. He has even gone as far as to assert that 'the legal values of the European brotherhood of lawyers are very similar',[35] drawing on his experiences within the Lando Commission (a rather small, self-selecting sample).[36]

The extent to which the common–civil law debate is a true obstacle to greater Europeanisation remains insufficiently explored to come to firm conclusions. Legrand's extreme opposition may have prompted active disengagement by scholars in the field, although the debate is shifting towards the cultural dimension.[37] What is needed is greater understanding of what is meant by culture, and an acceptance that culture should not be an absolute bar to Europeanisation,[38] but should certainly act as a brake.

6.2.2.2 Lack of a European legal culture

One step up from the concerns about cultural variations between the Member States (whether in terms of legal traditions or more widely),[39] is the question whether the foundations of a common European culture have emerged to form the basis for greater Europeanisation. Some assistance is offered by Tuori's analysis of European law.[40] He suggests that law can be divided into three levels. The surface level

---

34 O Lando, 'Culture and contract laws' (2007) 3 *European Review of Contract Law* 1–20.
35 O Lando, 'Optional or mandatory Europeanisation of contract law' (2000) 8 *European Review of Private Law* 59–69.
36 See Chapter 1, p 13.
37 See, eg, T Wilhelmsson, E Paunio and A Pohjolainen (eds), *Private Law and the Many Cultures of Europe* (The Hague: Kluwer Law International, 2007).
38 S Weatherill, 'Why object to the harmonization of private law by the EC?' (2004) 12 *European Review of Private Law* 633–60, p 653.
39 Cf H Collins, 'European private law and the cultural identity of states' (1995) 3 *European Review of Private Law* 353–65.
40 K Tuori, 'EC law: an independent legal order or a post-modern Jack-in-the-box?' in LD Eriksson and S Hurri (eds), *Dialectic of Law and Reality* (Helsinki: Faculty of Law, 1999).

comprises legislation and case law. The middle level is formed by legal culture, which relates to legal methodology and techniques of adjudication. Finally, there is the deep structure of law, where the fundamental normative principles of the law can be found. In Tuori's analysis, these different levels make up a mature legal system, but he also applies this in assessing whether a legal system, such as EU law, has reached a sufficient degree of maturity. He suggests that EU law operates largely at the surface level, and that there has been no 'sedimentation' into the middle and bottom layer, leading him to conclude that an independent European legal culture has not yet developed.[41] Perhaps one way of developing such a culture is to change the way law is taught at university level, but this is still a long way off.

Lando disagrees with the suggestions that there is an insufficiently developed European legal culture. He argues that 'contract law is more a question of ethics, economics and techniques that are common to all Europeans than it is question (sic!) of conserving ancient relics of a dead past',[42] which suggests that the seeds for a common European culture have not only been planted but are already germinating.

Wilhelmsson is more sceptical, adopting the view that there are, as yet, no elements of a common legal culture that could support a European codification.[43] He argues that pressing ahead now would invariably result in a return to more liberalist values at the expense of social justice, and that it would become more difficult to introduce more welfarist provisions into such a code. Moreover, the existing opportunity for piecemeal development and experimentation, particularly in the field of consumer protection, would be lost.[44] He advocates limited intervention in favour of a 'free flow of legal ideas'[45] instead.

A case for maintaining the existing diversity can be made for reasons other than cultural ones. Each Member State has its own economic and social structures that may require laws to suit, which is a further source of diversity.[46] Maintaining diversity permits the parties to a contract

---

41 This view is endorsed by T Wilhelmsson, 'Private law in the EU: harmonised or fragmentised Europeanisation?' (2002) 10 *European Review of Private Law* 77–94.
42 Lando, *op. cit.*, p 18.
43 Wilhelmsson (2002), *op. cit.*
44 *Ibid.*, p 86. Such experimentation can, of course, eventually produce a sufficient consensus for a particular area that European harmonisation becomes possible.
45 *Ibid.*, p 94.
46 H Wagner, 'Economic analysis of cross-border legal uncertainty', in Smits (ed), *op. cit.*, p 39.

to select the law that will best suit their needs, although there is the practical difficulty that the necessary information for comparing the advantages of one jurisdiction over another will be costly to acquire. Jurisdictions can learn from one another, as indeed has been the case for a long time. The work of comparative lawyers is to identify, compare and evaluate different approaches to a particular problem, and armed with the fruits of this labour, national legislatures and courts have the opportunity of improving their domestic laws. Although one might observe that there has been enough time for competition and that the time has come for synthesising the best rules and to harmonise contract law accordingly, that view would be based on the fallacy that there could never be new problems for which there may be competing solutions.[47]

6.2.2.3 Different views of social justice

Concerns over the role of welfarism or social justice have already been mentioned.[48] These reflect the fact that contract law is not value-neutral, and that attempts at Europeanisation cannot ignore the fact that a political dimension applies in determining the substance of particular model rules. Kennedy has demonstrated that substantive contract law doctrines and rules can be characterised as fitting somewhere on a spectrum ranging from individualism (each party to look after its own interests) to altruism (co-operation between contracting parties).[49] Quite where each particular doctrine can be placed on this spectrum will vary between jurisdictions, as some are more individualistic, whereas others tend to emphasise altruism. The overall point, however, is that it is misleading to reduce contract law to a question of technicalities, and that the compromise between individualist and altruist rules needs to be discussed explicitly. That, of course, is also the concern of the Study Group on Social Justice, which criticises the lack of debate over social justice in the process of drafting the CFR.[50]

---

47 G Wagner, 'The virtues of diversity in European private law', in Smits (ed), *op. cit.*, p 10.
48 Wilhelmsson (2002), *op. cit.*; also the Social Justice Manifesto, discussed in Chapter 5 at p 165.
49 D Kennedy, 'The political stakes in "merely technical" issues of contract law' (2001) 9 *European Review of Private Law* 7–28.
50 Chapter 5, p 165.

6.2.3 A political vision

For some, the idea of creating a European contract code (or a wider civil code) also has elements of seeking to foster a common identity, just as the civil codes of the 19th century helped to create the strong national identities of countries such as Germany and France.[51] Consequently, the adoption of Europe-wide private law would promote a shared identity between the various Member States. Such a view, however, is opposed to what is the prevailing European identity,[52] which is one that encourages plurality of languages and cultures.

6.3 EUROPEANISATION – CONCLUSIONS

The Europeanisation of contract law is a complex topic, and in order to understand it fully, one requires a firm grasp of national contract law, EU law and comparative law. Where EU legislation has been adopted, the corresponding area of contract law is characterised by an interaction of national and EU law, with general principles of EU law affecting the operation of national law.

The development to date has focused primarily – but by no means exclusively – on consumer law, where the greatest density of EU legislation can be found. But in respect of both consumer and non-consumer law, the intervention by the EU has dealt with specific problems which (arguably) affected the operation of the internal market. Dealing with discrete issues in separate measures has had the side-effect of producing legislation which lacks coherence and consistency with related measures, particularly with regard to definitions of key concepts. In addition, EU measures are based on assumptions about the substance of national law, but these are often not made explicit, which causes further confusion, evidenced by some of the cases that have reached the ECJ under the preliminary reference procedure. In this respect, the CFR could assist greatly in improving transparency.

From the perspective of English law, the requirement to give effect to EU directives has on the whole been largely unproblematic, resulting largely in the introduction of free-standing measures. In contrast, the civil law jurisdictions with a fully codified system of private law have occasionally struggled in dealing with the random interference of EU

---

51 Cf the discussion in Chapter 1.
52 Wilhelmsson (2002), *op. cit.*, p 90.

law with the internal system of their civil codes. It is therefore not surprising that the drive for greater coherence has come from the civil law jurisdictions, because concern over maintaining a complete system are greater there than in the common law jurisdictions, or the Nordic countries. Indeed, the intense focus on law as the means of furthering market integration may be motivated by the significance attached to law in the code-based jurisdictions, and the insufficient attention given to non-legal factors that affect commercial – and consumer – contracting in the internal market is worrying. Collins seems right in observing:

> It is a conceit of lawyers that the law of contract and other types of regulation of markets can significantly improve trust, thereby encouraging individuals and businesses to take the risk of entering contracts with strangers.[53]

The CFR will be a product of legal scholars, with the perfunctory involvement of selected business stakeholders, but that is unlikely to be sufficient either to provide a set of legal rules that will really be good for business or consumers, or to promote significantly further market integration.

The beneficial purpose of the CFR – and the review of the consumer *acquis* – is to improve the quality of European law-making. However, even here, the uncertainties over the exact purpose of the CFR and the talk of an optional instrument do raise suspicions, and perhaps even fears, over more widespread EU intervention in contract law, without the necessity for this having been established.

As seen both in this and the previous chapter, detailed European intervention raises difficult issues about the fundamental values inherent in such legislation. This applies both to a more limited intervention, as may occur in the field of consumer law, and a broad approach towards contract law generally. The European level has, so far, failed to engage fully with the wider political implications of deeper Europeanisation. Eventually, however, such a debate cannot be avoided – at the latest at the point when the European institutions are debating legislative proposals that would result in measures of wider reach than is the case at present. Any action beyond remedying existing and widely recognised defects in the *acquis* is likely to prove controversial.

---

53 Collins (2002) in S Grundmann and J Stuyck, *op. cit.*, p 274.

Where next, then, for the Europeanisation of contract law? The only concrete action likely to bear fruit in the foreseeable future is the review of the consumer *acquis*, probably by utilising the CFR in some way. If nothing else happens, at least there should be a more coherent consumer law in the EU (albeit in the form of a framework directive).[54]

It would be deeply regrettable, however, if the only concrete outcome of this lengthy process were an improvement to the directives on consumer protection. For a start, reliance on a directive will hardly do away with many of the problems which have beset the process of Europeanisation to date. Thus, there will still be a need for individual Member States to implement directives, which brings with it the risk of incorrect implementation, or the occasional failure to implement aspects of a directive at all. Whilst the availability of the CFR might make it easier for the Member States to identify the presumptions about national laws on which a directive is built (for example, with regard to neighbouring areas of law not covered by the directive, but with which the implementing legislation has to interact to work effectively), the extent to which national law has to be amended with reference to the CFR above and beyond those aspects immediately required by a directive is far from clear. Indeed, it is not even apparent just how much use will be made of the CFR in drafting the framework directive on consumer law.

Hopefully, the adoption of a framework directive on consumer law will only be an interim step, reflecting the desire to achieve agreement on specific legislation before the current Commission's term of office expires in 2009. This would leave the post-2009 period for seriously considering the advantages of an optional instrument on contract law – whether limited to consumer transactions, or applicable to both consumer and commercial contracts. Pursuing the idea of an optional instrument in earnest would entail a significant change of direction – away from harmonisation, and towards more complex EU legislation, which would be superimposed on all the national laws. That would have the advantage of giving sufficient room for national laws to be developed in accordance with domestic needs, with the optional instrument as the legal framework for cross-border contracts. Of course, this would also mean that EU legislation on contract law would shift its focus to cross-border contracts rather than on all contracts (which has been the practice to date). Some might object to the

54 See Commission Communication *A Single Market for 21st Century Europe* (COM (2007) 724 final), p 6, and the Legislative and Work Programme 2008 (COM (640) final), which promise legislative proposals for late 2008.

existence of parallel regimes for domestic and cross-border trans-actions, and the potential for confusion this creates. Such concerns should not be dismissed outright, but also not be determinative in con-sidering the real benefits an optional instrument might provide for the internal market. So the story of the Europeanisation of Contract Law will continue – with a major twist in the plotline on the horizon.

Bibliography

Acquis Group, *Principles of the Existing EC Contract Law – Contract I*. Munich: Sellier, 2007.

Ajani, G and Ebers, M (eds), *Uniform Terminology for European Contract Law*. Baden-Baden: Nomos, 2005.

Amstutz, M, 'In-between worlds: *Marleasing* and the emergence of interlegality in legal reasoning' (2005) 11 *European Law Journal* 766–84.

Baasch-Andersen, C, 'Defining uniformity in law' (2007) 12 *Uniform Law Review* 5–56.

Bamforth, N, 'The limits of European Union consumer contract law' (1999) 24 *European Law Review* 410–18.

Basedow, J, 'The case for a European Contract Act', in S Grundmann and J Stuyck (eds), *An Academic Green Paper on European Contract Law*. The Hague: Kluwer Law International, 2002.

Beale, H, 'Legislative control of fairness: the Directive on Unfair Terms in consumer contracts', in J Beatson and D Friedman (eds), *Good Faith and Fault In Contract Law*. Oxford: Clarendon Press, 1995.

——, 'The "Europeanisation" of contract law', in R Halson, *Exploring the Boundaries of Contract*. Aldershot: Dartmouth, 1996.

——, 'Finding the remaining traps instead of unifying contract law', in S Grundmann and J Stuyck (eds), *An Academic Green Paper on European Contract Law*. The Hague: Kluwer Law International, 2002.

——, 'Unfair terms in contracts: proposals for reform in the UK' (2004) 27 *Journal of Consumer Policy* 289–316.

——, 'What has been done, what is going on, what is to be expected: Common Frame of Reference, optional instrument and . . .?', paper presented at a seminar held in Sheffield in November 2004 (unpublished; on file with author).

——, 'The European Civil Code movement and the European Union's Common Frame of Reference' (2006) 6 *Legal Information Management* 4–11.

——, 'The European Commission's Common Frame of Reference project: a progress report' (2006) 2 *European Review of Contract Law* 303–14.

—— (2007), 'The future of the Common Frame of Reference' (2007) 3 *European Review of Contract Law* 257–76.

—— and G Howells, 'EC harmonisation of consumer sales law – a missed opportunity?' (1997) 12 *Journal of Contract Law* 21–46

——, H Kötz, A Hartkamp, D Tallon (eds), *Cases, Materials and Text on Contract Law*. Oxford: Hart Publishing, 2002.

Beatson, J and Schrage, EJH (eds) *Cases, Materials and Text on Unjustified Enrichment*. Oxford: Hart Publishing, 2003.

Berger, KP, 'The principles of European contract law and the concept of the "creeping codification" of law' (1999) 7 *European Review of Private Law* 21–34.

Bernitz, U, 'The Commission's communications and Standard Contract Terms', in S Vogenauer and S Weatherill (eds), *The Harmonisation of European Contract Law*. Oxford: Hart Publishing, 2006.

Betlem, G and Hondius, E, 'European private law after the Treaty of Amsterdam' (2001) 9 *European Review of Private Law* 3–20.

Bigwood, R, 'Pre-contractual misrepresentation and the limits of the principle in *With v O'Flanagan*' (2005) *Cambridge Law Journal* 94–125.

Bonell, MJ, 'The need and possibilities of a codified European contract law' (1997) 5 *European Review of Private Law* 505–18.

Bradgate, R, 'Experience in the United Kingdom', in *The Integration of Directive 93/13/EEC Into the National Legal Systems* (European Commission, 1999).

——, Brownsword, R and Twigg-Flesner, C, *The Impact of Adopting a Duty to Trade Fairly*. London: Department of Trade and Industry, 2003 (available at http://www.dti.gov.uk/files/file32101.pdf).

—— and Twigg-Flesner, C, *Blackstone's Guide to the Sale of Consumer Goods and Associated Guarantees*. Oxford: OUP, 2003.

Brownsword, R, *Contract Law – Themes for the Twenty-First Century*. Oxford: OUP, 2006.

—— and Howells, G, 'The implementation of the EC Directive on unfair terms in consumer contracts – some unresolved questions' [1995] *Journal of Business Law* 243–63.

——, Howells, G and Wilhelmsson, T, 'Between market and welfare: some reflections on Article 3 of the EC Directive on Unfair Terms in Consumer Contracts', in C Willett (ed), *Aspects of Fairness in Contract*. London: Blackstone Press, 1996.

Bussani, M and Mattei, U (eds), *The Common Core of European Private Law*. The Hague: Kluwer Law International, 2003.

——, *Opening Up European Law*. Munich: Sellier, 2007.

Cafaggi, F. *The Institutional Framework of European Private Law*. Oxford: OUP, 2006.

Capelletti, M (ed), *New Perspectives for a Common Law of Europe*. Florence: European University Institute, 1978.

Coing, M, 'European common law: historical foundations', in M Capelletti (ed), *New Perspectives for a Common Law of Europe*. Florence: European University Institute, 1978.

Collins, H, 'Good faith in European contract law' (1994) 14 *Oxford Journal of Legal Studies* 229.

——, 'European private law and the cultural identity of states' (1995) 3 *European Review of Private Law* 353–65.

——, 'The voice of the community in private law discourse' (1997) 3 *European Law Journal* 407–21.

——, 'Formalism and efficiency: designing European commercial contract law' (2000) 8 *European Review of Private Law* 211–35.

——, 'Transaction costs and subsidiarity in European contract law', in S Grundmann and J Stuyck (eds), *An Academic Green Paper on European Contract Law*. The Hague: Kluwer Law International, 2002.

——, 'The freedom to circulate documents: regulating contracts in Europe' (2004) 10 *European Law Journal* 787–803.

——, 'The alchemy of deriving general principles of contract law from European legislation: in search of the Philosopher's Stone' (2006) 2 *European Review of Contract Law* 213–26.

Commission, *Report of the application of Article 17 of Council Directive on the co-ordination of the law of the Member States relating to self-employed Commercial Agents* (COM (96) 364 final).

——, *Green Paper on the conversion of the Rome Convention into a Community Instrument* (COM (2002) 654 final).

——, *First Annual Progress Report on European Contract Law and the Acquis Review* (COM (2005) 456 final).

——, *EU Consumer Policy Strategy 2007–2013* (COM (2007) 99 final).

——, *Second Progress Report on the Common Frame of Reference* (COM (2007) 447 final).

——, *A Europe of Results – Applying Community Law* (COM (2007) 502 final).

Dannemann, G, 'Consolidating EC contract law: an introduction to the work of the Acquis Group' in Acquis Group, *Principles of the Existing EC Contract Law – Contract I*. Munich: Sellier, 2007.

Davidson Review – *Final Report*. London: Better Regulation Executive, 2006.

Davies, G, 'Can selling arrangements be harmonised?' (2005) 30 *European Law Review* 371–85.

Davis, P, 'The significance of parliamentary procedures in control of the Executive: a case study: the passage of Part 1 of the Legislative and Regulatory Reform Act 2006' [2007] *Public Law* 677–700.

Dean, M, 'Defining unfair terms in consumer contracts – crystal ball gazing? *Director General of Fair Trading v First National Bank plc*' (2002) 65 *Modern Law Review* 773.

Department for Business, Enterprise and Regulatory Reform, *Transposition Guide: How to Implement European Directives Effectively*, September 2007.

Drobnig, U, Snijders, HJ, and Zippo, EJ (eds), *Divergences of Property Law: An Obstacle to the Internal Market?* Munich: Sellier, 2006.

Gambaro, A, 'The Plan d'Action of the European Commission – a comment' [2003] *European Review of Private Law* 768–81.

Goode, R, 'Contract and commercial law: the logic and limits of harmonisation', in FW Grosheide and E Hondius, *International Contract Law*. Antwerp: Intersentia, 2004.

Gordley, J (ed), *The Enforceability of Promises in European Contract Law*. Cambridge: Cambridge University Press, 2001.

Grundmann, S, 'The structure of European contract law' (2001) 4 *European Review of Private Law* 505–28.

——, 'The Optional European Code on the basis of the Acquis Communautaire' (2004) 10 *European Law Journal* 678–711.

——, 'European contract law(s) of what colour?' (2005) 1 *European Review of Contract Law* 184–210.

—— and M Schauer (eds), *The Architecture of European Codes and Contract Law*. The Hague: Kluwer Law International, 2006.

—— and J Stuyck (eds), *An Academic Green Paper on European Contract Law*. The Hague, Kluwer Law International, 2002.

Haage, J, 'Law, economics and uniform contract law: a sceptical view', in J Smits (ed), *The Need for a European Contract Law*. Groningen: Europa Law Publishing, 2005.

Hartkamp, A, Hesselink, M, Hondius, E, Joustra, C, Du Perron, E and Veldman, M (eds), *Towards a European Civil Code*, 3rd edn. Nijmegen: Ars Aequi, 2004.

Heiderhoff, B., *Gemeinschaftsprivatrecht*. Munich: Sellier ELP, 2005.

—— and M Kenny, 'The Commission's 2007 Green Paper on the Consumer Acquis: deliberate deliberation' (2007) 35 *European Law Review* 740–51.

Heiss, H and Downes, N, 'Non-optional elements in an optional European contract law' (2005) 13 *European Review of Private Law* 693–712.

Hellwege, P, 'Consumer protection in Britain in need of reform' (2004) 63 *Cambridge Law Journal* 712–41.

Hesselink, M, 'The concept of good faith', in A Hartkamp *et al.* (eds), *Towards a European Civil Code*, 3rd edn. Nijmegen: Ars Aequi, 2004.

——, 'Non-mandatory rules in European contract law' (2005) 1 *European Review of Contract Law* 44–86.

—— (ed), *The Politics of a European Civil Code*. The Hague: Kluwer, 2006.

——, 'European contract law: a matter of consumer protection, citizenship, or justice?' [2007] *European Review of Private Law* 323–48.

House of Commons European Scrutiny Committee, *Article 308 of the EC Treaty*. London: TSO, 2007.

House of Lords, *European Contract Law – The Way Forward?* (HL Paper 95, 2005).

Howells, G, 'European consumer law – the minimal and maximal harmonisation debate and pro independent consumer law competence', in S Grundmann and J Stuyck (eds), *An Academic Green Paper on European Contract Law*. The Hague: Kluwer Law International, 2002.

——, 'The right of withdrawal in European consumer law', in H Schulte-Nölke and R Schulze (eds) *European Contract Law in Community Law*. Cologne: Bundesanzeiger, 2002.

——, 'The potential and limits of consumer empowerment by information' (2005) 32 *Journal of Law and Society* 349–70.

——, 'The rise of European consumer law – whither national consumer law?' (2006) 28 *Sydney Law Review* 63–88.

—— and Wilhelmsson, T, *EC Consumer Law*. Aldershot: Ashgate, 1997.

——, Micklitz, HW and Wilhelmsson, T, *European Fair Trading Law – The Unfair Commercial Practices Directive*. Aldershot: Ashgate, 2006.

Joerges, C, 'Europeanization as process: thoughts on the Europeanization of private law' (2005) 11 *European Public Law* 63–84.

Johnston, A and Unberath, H, 'Law at, to or from the centre?', in F Cafaggi, *The Institutional Framework of European Private Law*. Oxford: OUP, 2006.

Kanning, AJ, 'The emergence of a European private law: lessons from 19th century Germany' (2007) 27 *Oxford Journal of Legal Studies* 193–208.

Karsten, J, 'Passengers, consumers and travellers: the rise of passenger rights in EC transport law and its repercussions for Community consumer law and policy' (2007) 30 *Journal of Consumer Policy* 117–36.

Kasirer, N, 'The common core of European private law in boxes and bundles' (2002) 10 *European Review of Private Law* 417–37.

Kennedy, D, 'The political stakes in "merely technical" issues of contract law' (2001) 9 *European Review of Private Law* 7–28.

——, 'Thoughts on coherence, social values and national tradition in private law', in M Hesselink (ed), *The Politics of a European Civil Code*. The Hague: Kluwer, 2006.

Kenny, M, 'Globalization, interlegality and Europeanized contract law' (2003) 21 *Penn State International Law Review* 569–620.

——, 'The 2003 Action Plan on European contract law: is the Commission running wild?' (2003) 28 *European Law Review* 538–50.

——, 'The 2004 Communication on European contract law: those magnificent men in their unifying machines' (2005) 30 *European Law Review* 724–42.

——, 'Constructing a European Civil Code: quis custodiet ipsos custodes?' (2006) 12 *Columbia Journal of European Law* 775–808.

Kötz, H, 'A common private law for Europe: perspectives for the reform of European legal education', in B de Witte and C Forder (eds), *The Common Law of Europe and the Future of Legal Education*. Maastricht: Metro, 1992.

—— and A Flessner, *European Contract Law*. Oxford: Clarendon Press, 1997.

Lando, O, 'Optional or mandatory Europeanisation of contract law' (2000) 8 *European Review of Private Law* 59–69.

——, 'Why does Europe need a Civil Code', in S Grundmann and J Stuyck (eds), *An Academic Green Paper on European Contract Law*. The Hague: Kluwer Law International, 2002.

——, 'Liberal, social and "ethical" justice in European contract law' (2006) 43 *Common Market Law Review* 817–33.

——, 'Culture and contract laws' (2007) 3 *European Review of Contract Law* 1–20.

—— and H Beale, *Principles of European Contract Law Parts I and II*. The Hague: Kluwer Law International, 2000.

——, E Clive, A Prüm and R Zimmermann, *Principles of European Contract Law Part III*. The Hague: Kluwer Law International, 2003.

Larouche, P, 'Ius commune casebooks for the common law of Europe: presentation, progress, rationale' (2000) 1 *European Review of Private Law* 101–09.

Law Commission, *Unfair Terms in Contracts – Report 292*. London: TSO, 2005.

Legrand, P, 'European legal systems are not converging' (1996) 45 *International and Comparative Law Quarterly* 52–81.

——, 'Against a European Civil Code' (1997) 60 *Modern Law Review* 44–63.

——, 'Antivonbar' (2005) 1 *Journal of Comparative Law* 13–40.

Loos, M, 'The Influence of European Consumer Law on General Contract Law' (2007) 15 *European Review of Private Law* 515–31.

Lurger, B 'The future of European contract law between freedom of contract, social justice and market rationality' (2005) 1 *European Review of Contract Law* 442–68.

McClean, D and Beevers, K, *Morris – The Conflict of Laws*, 6th edn. London: Sweet & Maxwell, 2005.

McGregor, H, *Contract Code Drawn up on Behalf of the English Law Commission*. Milan: Giuffre Editore, 1993.

McKendrick, E, *The Creation of a European Law of Contracts – The Role of Standard Form Contracts and Principles of Interpretation*. The Hague: Kluwer, 2004.

Mance, J, 'Is Europe aiming to civilise the common law?' [2007] *European Business Law Review* 77–99.

Mattei, U, 'Basics first please! A critique of some recent priorities shown by the Commission's Action Plan', in A Hartkamp *et al.*, *Towards a European Civil Code*, 3rd edn. Nijmegen: Ars Aequi, 2004.

Michaels, R and Jansen, N, 'Private law beyond the state? Europeanization, globalization, privatization' (2006) 54 *American Journal of Comparative Law* 843–90.

Micklitz, HW, 'The concept of competitive contract law' (2005) 23 *Penn State International Law Review* 549–85.

——, 'Minimum/maximum harmonisation and the internal market clause', in G Howells, H Micklitz and T Wilhelmsson, *European Fair Trading Law*. Aldershot: Ashgate, 2006.

——, Reich, N and Weatherill, S, 'EU Treaty revision and consumer protection' (2004) 27 *Journal of Consumer Policy* 367–99.

——, Stuyck, J and Terryn, E (eds), *Cases, Materials and Text on Consumer Law*. Oxford: Hart Publishing, 2008.

Miller, L, 'The Common Frame of Reference and the feasibility of a common contract law in Europe' [2007] *Journal of Business Law*, 378–411.

Mitchell, C, *Interpretation of Contracts*. London: Routledge-Cavendish, 2007.

Monti, G, 'The revision of the consumer *acquis* from a competition law perspective' (2007) 3 *European Review of Contract Law* 295–314.

Müller-Graff, PC, 'EC Directives as a means of private law unification', in A Hartkamp *et al.*, *Towards a European Civil Code*, 3rd edn. Nijmegen: Ars Aequi, 2004.

Muir-Watt, H, 'The conflict of laws as a regulatory tool', in F Cafaggi, *The Institutional Framework of European Private Law*. Oxford: OUP, 2006.

Nebbia, P, *Unfair Contract Terms in European Law*. Oxford: Hart, 2007.

Neuner, J, 'Protection against discrimination in European contract law' (2006) 2 *European Review of Contract Law* 35–50.

Niglia, L, 'The non-Europeanisation of private law' (2001) 4 *European Review of Private Law* 575–99.

Nottage, L, 'Convergence, divergence and the middle way in unifying or harmonizing private law' (2004) 1 *Annual of German and European Law* 166–245.

Oughton, D and Willett, C, 'Liability for incorrect installation and other services associated with consumer goods', in G Howells, A Nordhausen, D Parry and C Twigg-Flesner, *Yearbook of Consumer Law 2007*. Ashgate: Aldershot, 2007.

Pozzo, P, 'Harmonisation of European contract law and the need for creating a common terminology' (2003) 11 *European Review of Private Law* 754–67.

—— and Jacometti, V, *Multilingualism and the Harmonisation of European Private Law*. The Hague: Kluwer, 2006.

Ramsay, I, *Consumer Law and Policy*, 2nd edn. Oxford: Hart Publishing, 2007.

Reich, N, 'Critical comments on the Commission communication "On European Contract Law" ', in S Grundmann and J Stuyck (eds), *An Academic Green Paper on European Contract Law*. The Hague: Kluwer Law International, 2002.

——, 'A European contract law, or an EU contract law regulation for consumers?' (2005) 28 *Journal of Consumer Policy* 383–407.

Rekaiti, P and van den Bergh, R, 'Cooling-off periods in the consumer laws of the EC Member States. A comparative law and economics approach' (2000) 23 *Journal of Consumer Policy* 371–407.

Riedl, K, *Vereinheitlichung des Privatrechts in Europa*. Baden-Baden: Nomos, 2004.

Riesenhuber, K, *System und Prinzipien des Europäischen Vertragsrechts*. Berlin: De Gruyter, 2003.

——, 'System and principles of EC contract law' (2005) 1 *European Review of Contract Law* 297–322.

Rösler, H, *Europäisches Konsumentenvertragsrecht*. München: Beck, 2004.

Roth, WH, 'Transposing "Pointilist" EC guidelines into systematic national codes – problems and consequences' (2002) 6 *European Review of Private Law* 761–76.

Röttinger, M, 'Towards a European Code Napoléon/AGBG/BGB? Recent EC activities for a European contract law' (2006) 12 *European Law Journal* 807–27.

Rott, P, 'Minimum harmonisation for the completion of the Internal Market? The example of consumer sales law' (2003) 40 *Common Market Law Review* 1107–35.

——, 'What is the role of the ECJ in private law?' [2005] 1 *Hanse Law Review* 6.

——, 'Harmonising different rights of withdrawal' (2006) 7 *German Law Journal* 1109–46.

——, 'Linked contracts and doorstep selling', in G Howells, A Nordhausen, D Parry and C Twigg-Flesner, *Yearbook of Consumer Law 2007*. Ashgate: Aldershot, 2007.

Rutgers, J, 'An optional instrument and social dumping' (2006) 2 *European Review of Contract Law* 199–212.

Sacco, R, 'Formation of contracts', in A Hartkamp *et al.*, *Towards a European Civil Code*, 3rd edn. Nijmegen: Ars Aequi, 2004.

Saintier, S, 'A remarkable understanding and application of the protective stance of the agency regulations by the English courts' [2001] JBL 540–53.

——, 'The principles behind the assessment of the compensation option under the agency regulations: clarity at last?' [2007] *Journal of Business Law* 90–98.

Schulte-Braucks, R and Ongena, S, 'The Late Payment Directive – a step towards an emerging European private law?' (2003) 11 *European Review of Private Law* 519–44.

Schulte-Nölke, H, 'The Commission's Action Plan on European Contract Law and the research of the Acquis Group' [2003] *ERA Forum* 142–45.

——, 'EC law on the formation of contract – from the Common Frame of Reference to the "Blue Button" ' (2007) *European Review of Contract Law* 332–49.

——, Twigg-Flesner, C and Ebers, M, *EC Consumer Law Compendium*. Munich: Sellier, 2008.

Schulze, R, 'European private law and existing EC law' (2005) 13 *European Review of Private Law* 3–19.

——, *Common Frame of Reference and Existing EC Contract Law*. Munich: Sellier, 2008.

Sefton-Green, R (ed), *Mistake, Fraud and Duties to Inform in European Contract Law*. Cambridge: Cambridge University Press, 2005.

Smits, J, 'Diversity of contract law and the European internal market', in J Smits (ed), *The Need for a European Contract Law*. Groningen: Europa Law Publishing, 2005.

Staudenmeyer, D, 'The Directive on the Sale of Consumer Goods and Associated Guarantees – a milestone in the European consumer and private law' (2000) 4 *European Review of Private Law* 547–64.

——, 'The way forward in European contract law' [2005] *European Review of Private Law* 95–104.

Steiner, J, Woods, L and Twigg-Flesner, C, *EU Law*, 9th edn. Oxford: Oxford University Press, 2006.

Steiner, P, 'The *Ius Commune* and its demise' (2004) 25 *Journal of Legal History* 161–67.

Storme, M, 'Freedom of contract: mandatory and non-mandatory rules in European contract law' (2007) 15 *European Review of Private Law* 233–50.

Study Group on a European Civil Code/Research Group on the Existing EC Private Law (Acquis Group) (eds), *Principles, Definitions and Model Rules on*

European Private Law – Draft Common Frame of Reference. Munich: Sellier, 2008.

Study Group on Social Justice in European Private Law, 'Social justice in European contract law: a manifesto' (2004) 10 *European Law Journal* 653–74.

Stuyck, J, 'European consumer law after the Treaty of Amsterdam: consumer policy in or beyond the Internal Market' (2000) 37 *Common Market Law Review* 367–400.

——, Terryn, E and van Dyck, T, 'Confidence through fairness? The new directive on unfair business-to-consumer commercial practices in the internal market' (2006) 43 *Common Market Law Review* 107–52.

Tettenborn, A, 'From chaos to cosmos – or is it confusion?' [2002] *Web Journal of Current Legal Issues* (http://webjcli.ncl.ac.uk/2002/issue2/tettenborn2.html).

Teubner, G, 'Legal irritants: good faith in British law or how unifying law ends up in new divergences' (1998) 61 *Modern Law Review* 11–32.

Treitel, GH, *The Law of Contract*, 11th edn. London: Sweet & Maxwell, 2003.

Tuori, K, 'EC law: an independent legal order or a post-modern Jack-in-the-box?' in LD Eriksson and S Hurri (eds), *Dialectic of Law and Reality.* Helsinki: Faculty of Law, 1999.

Twigg-Flesner, C, *Consumer Product Guarantees.* Aldershot: Ashgate, 2003.

——, 'Information disclosure about the quality of goods – duty or encouragement?', in G Howells, A Janssen, and R Schulze (eds), *Information Rights and Obligations.* Aldershot: Ashgate, 2005.

——, 'Recent developments in EU consumer law' (2007) 3 *European Review of Contract Law* 198–213.

——, 'Standard terms in international commercial law – the example of documentary credits', in R Schulze, *New Features of Contract Law.* Munich: Sellier, 2007.

——, Parry, D, Howells, G and Nordhausen, A, *An Analysis of the Application and Scope of the Unfair Commercial Practices Directive.* London: DTI, 2005, pp 49–61 (available at http://www.berr.gov.uk/files/file32095.pdf).

Urban, N, 'One legal language *and* the maintenance of cultural and linguistic diversity?' (2000) 8 *European Review of Private Law* 51–57.

van Caenegem, RC, *European Law in the Past and the Future.* Cambridge: CUP, 2002.

van den Berg, PAJ, *The Politics of European Codification.* Groningen: European Law Publishing, 2007.

van den Bergh, R, 'Forced harmonisation of contract law in Europe: not to be continued' in S Grundmann and J Stuyck (eds), *An Academic Green Paper on European Contract Law.* The Hague, Kluwer Law International, 2002.

van Erp, JHM, 'The pre-contractual stage', in A Hartkamp *et al.* (eds), *Towards a European Civil Code*, 3rd edn. Nijmegen: Ars Aequi, 2004.

Van Erp, S (ed) *Cases, Materials and Text on National, Supranational and International Property Law.* Oxford: Hart Publishing, 2008.

van Gerven, W, 'The ECJ case-law as a means of unification of private law?', in

A Hartkamp *et al.* (eds), *Towards a European Civil Code*, 3rd edn. Nijmegen: Ars Aequi, 2004.

——, 'Bringing (private) laws closer at the European level', in F Cafaggi, *The Institutional Framework of European Private Law*. Oxford: OUP, 2006.

——, Lever, J, Larouche, P, von Bar, C and Viney, G (eds), *Cases, Materials and Text on National, Supranational and International Tort Law – Scope of Protection*. Oxford: Hart Publishing, 1998.

Varney, E and Varney, M, 'Grounded? Air passenger rights in the European Union', in C Twigg-Flesner, D Parry, G Howells and A Nordhausen, *The Yearbook of Consumer Law 2008*. Aldershot: Ashgate, 2007.

Vogenauer, S and Weatherill, S (eds), *The Harmonisation of European Contract Law*. Oxford: Hart Publishing, 2006.

——, 'The EC's competence to pursue the harmonisation of contract law – an empirical contribution to the debate', in S Vogenauer and S Weatherill (eds), *Harmonisation of European Contract Law* (2006).

von Bar, C, 'Coverage and structure of the academic Common Frame of Reference' (2007) 3 *European Review of Contract Law* 350–61.

—— and Schulte-Nölke, H, 'Zum Stand der Arbeiten an einem Gemeinsamen Referenzrahmen für europäisches Schuld- und Sachenrecht' (2005) *Zeitschrift für Rechtspolitik* 165–68.

Wagner, G, 'The virtues of diversity in European private law', in Smits, J (ed), *The Need for a European Contract Law*. Groningen: Europa Law Publishing, 2005.

Wagner, H, 'Economic analysis of cross-border legal uncertainty', in Smits, J (ed), *The Need for a European Contract Law*. Groningen: Europa Law Publishing, 2005.

Weatherill, S, 'Pre-emption, harmonisation and the distribution of competence to regulate the internal market', in Barnard, C and Scott, J, *The Law of the Single European Market – Unpacking the Premises*. Oxford: Hart Publishing, 2002.

——, 'Can there be a common interpretation of European private law?' (2002) 31 *Georgia Journal of International and Comparative Law* 139–66, pp 163–64.

——, 'Why object to the harmonization of private law by the EC?' (2004) 12 *European Review of Private Law* 633–60.

——, 'Reflections on the EC's competence to develop a European contract law' (2005) 13 *European Review of Private Law* 405–18.

——, 'Minimum harmonisation as oxymoron?' in H Micklitz, *Verbraucherrecht in Deutschland*. Baden-Baden: Nomos, 2005.

——, 'European private law and the constitutional dimension', in F Cafaggi, *The Institutional Framework of European Private Law*. Oxford: OUP, 2006.

——, *EU Consumer Law and Policy*, 2nd edn. Cheltenham: Edward Elgar, 2006.

Whittaker, S, 'Unfair contract terms, public service and the construction of a European conception of contract' (2000) 116 *Law Quarterly Review* 95–120.

——, 'The terminology of civil protection: rights, remedies and procedures', in

B Pozzo and V Jacometti, *Multilingualism and the Harmonisation of European Private Law*. The Hague: Kluwer, 2006.

——, 'On the development of European standard contract terms' (2006) 2 *European Review of Contract Law* 51.

——, 'The relationship of the Unfair Commercial Practices Directive to European and national contract laws', in S Weatherill and U Bernitz, *The Regulation of Unfair Commercial Practices under EC Directive 2005/29*. Oxford: Hart, 2007.

——, 'The language or languages of consumer contracts' (2007) 8 *Cambridge Yearbook of European Legal Studies* 229–57.

——, 'Form and substance in the reception of EC Directives into English contract law' (2007) 3 *European Review of Contract Law* 381–409.

Wilhelmsson, T, 'Jack-in-the-box theory of European Community law', in LD Eriksson and S Hurri (eds), *Dialectic of Law and Reality*. Helsinki: Faculty of Law, 1999.

——, 'Private law in the EU: harmonised or fragmented Europeanisation' (2002) 10 *European Review of Private Law* 77–94.

——, 'The legal, the cultural and the political – conclusions from different perspectives on harmonisation of European contract law' [2002] *European Business Law Review* 541–55.

——, 'The abuse of the "confident consumer" as a justification for EC consumer law' (2004) 27 *Journal of Consumer Policy* 317–37.

——, 'The ethical pluralism of late modern Europe and codification of European contract law' in J Smits (ed), *The Need for a European Contract Law*. Groningen: Europa Law Publishing, 2005.

——, Paunio, E and Pohjolainen, A (eds), *Private Law and the Many Cultures of Europe*. The Hague: Kluwer Law International, 2007.

—— and Twigg-Flesner, C, 'Pre-contractual information duties in the *acquis communautaire*' (2006) 2 *European Review of Contract Law* 441–70.

Woods, L, *Free Movement of Goods and Services*. Aldershot: Ashgate, 2004.

Ziller, J, 'The legitimacy of codification of contract law in view of the allocation of competences between the European Union and its Member States', in M Hesselink (ed), *The Politics of a European Civil Code*. The Hague: Kluwer, 2006.

Zimmermann, R, 'Roman law and the harmonisation of private law in Europe', in A Hartkamp *et al.*, *Towards a European Civil Code*, 3rd edn. Nijmegen: Ars Aequi, 2004.

—— and Whittaker, S (eds), *Good Faith in European Contract Law*. Cambridge: Cambridge University Press, 2000.

Index

Accademia dei Giusprivatisti (Pavia Group) Code 15–16
acquis communautaire 51–101; areas excluded 52–4; background 51–2; conclusion 100–1; consumer *see* consumer *acquis* review; formation *see* formation; injunctions 99–100; key directives 54–64; non-performance *see* non-performance; performance *see* performance; pre-contractual *see* pre-contractual information duties; substance 80–9; validity 79
Acquis Group (Research Group on the Existing EC Private Law) 15, 152; and CFR 152, 153–5
agency, commercial 61, 79
approximation 9
autonomous interpretation 109–10, 128–9

Beale, H 184
Bussani, M 16

caveat emptor 134
CFR *see* Common Frame of Reference
civil law: and common law 185–7; systems 3, 4
Collins, H 183–4
commercial agency 61, 79; implementation in UK 124–30; performance/remuneration 92–4; termination payments 98–9
commercial debts, late payment 62, 87–8

Commission *see* European Commission (EC)
Common Core Project (Trento project) 16–17
Common Frame of Reference (CFR) 139, 144–59, 190–2; and arbitration 151; conception 144–5; and consumer law 147–8; critiques 144–6, 191; definitions 145–6; and ECJ 151; and EU contracts 151; functions 148–51; and implementation 149–50; model rules 146–7, 148–9, 154; as national guidance 150; and social justice *Manifesto* 165–6; terminology 145, *see also* Draft Common Frame of Reference (DCFR)
common/civil law divide 185–7
compensation and indemnity 124–30
competence 25–7, 34, 166–72; background 166–7; judicial co-operation in civil matters 167–9; legal basis 171–2, 176; open method of co-ordination (OMC) 172; residual 169–71
competition law 52
conferred competence 26
connected lender liability 98
consumer *acquis* review 54–5, 172–9; current *acquis* 54–61; evaluation 178–9; good faith/fair dealing 177; information duties 177; legal basis 176; minimum to maximum harmonisation 175–6; remedies 178; right of withdrawal 178; vertical to horizontal 173–4

see maximum harmonisation;
minimum *see* minimum
harmonisation
horizontal approach 173
horizontal direct effect 112

implementation 36–9, 103–8;
ambiguities 107–8; background
103–4; general issues 104–8;
minimum harmonisation 41–2,
105–6; regulatory options 106;
resolution by member states 106–7,
see also post-implementation
implementation, in UK 113–19; and
courts *see* national courts;
evaluation 119; framework 113–15;
minimum harmonisation 115–16;
open issues 116–18, *see also*
post-implementation
indemnity 124–30
indirect effect 112
information duties 177; post-
information 78; pre-contractual *see*
pre-contractual information duties
injunctions 99–100
insurance mediation 62, 67, 69
intelligible language 85–6
internal market 25–6, 28–30; and
consumer contract law 30–3;
protectorate 51; role of law
184–5
ius commune 3; casebook project
18–19

Kenny, M 152, 179

Lando Commission 13–14, 15, 151
Lando, O 186, 187, 188
late payment of commercial debts 62,
87–8
legal bases 27–34, 171–2, 176
legal culture 187–9
legal education, and Europeanisation
17–19
Legrand, P 186
life assurance 62, 67, 70, 77

McGregor contract code 16
Mance, J 152
Mattei, U 16

maximum harmonisation 40–1; and
minimum harmonisation 175–6
mediation, insurance 62, 67, 69
minimum harmonisation 41–2, 105–6,
115–16; and DCFR 154;
implementation 41–2, 105–6; and
maximum harmonisation 175–6; in
UK 115–16
misrepresentation 134–5

national courts: challenges 110–13;
and commercial agency 124–30;
interpretation/application 119–21;
preliminary reference to ECJ 43–8,
130–3; and unfair contract terms
121–4
national rules, and free movement
21–5
non-conforming goods 95–8;
inconvenience 97; price-reduction
98; reasonableness test 96–7;
repair/replacement 95–6;
rescission 98
non-discrimination law 53
non-performance 95–9; commercial
agency *see* commercial agency;
connected lender liability 98;
damages 95; non-conforming
goods *see* non-conforming goods,
see also performance

OMC (open method of
co-ordination) 172
open method of co-ordination
(OMC) 172
optional instrument (OI) 159–64;
background 159–60; and CFR 163,
164–5; optionality 160–2, 163–4;
scope 162–3; and social justice
Manifesto 165–6

package travel 58–9, 65, 69, 90,
95
Pavia Group Code 15–16
payment services 63, 68, 70;
information/performance 94
PCIDs *see* pre-contractual
information duties
PECL *see* *Principles of European
Contract Law*